THE 15 MINUTE DAILY ACTORS WORKOUT

**SIX MONTHS
VOLUME TWO**

_____
_____
_____

Copyright © [2024] #1209505
by [Victor Zinck Jr] First Edition
Printed in [Canada]

All rights reserved. No part of this publication may be reproduced, distributed, or transmitted in any form or by any means, including photocopying, recording, or other electronic or mechanical methods, without the prior written permission of the publisher, except in the case of brief quotations embodied in critical reviews and certain other noncommercial uses permitted by copyright law.

LEGAL DISCLAIMER

This book is intended as a resource for actors and provides exercises and techniques related to emotional development, imagination, script analysis, character observation, animal work, physical and vocal warmups, and other aspects of actor training. The content within is for informational and educational purposes only. The exercises and techniques described in this book are based on the author's experience and knowledge in the field of acting and theatre education. They are provided with the intent to assist actors in their personal and professional development. However, they are not a substitute for professional training or advice. Readers are advised to use their own judgment and should consider their physical, emotional, and mental capabilities before undertaking any of the exercises or techniques described in this book. It is recommended to consult with a professional in the field of acting and theatre education if you have any concerns or doubts about the suitability of any exercise or technique.

The author and publisher make no representations or warranties with respect to the accuracy, applicability, fitness, or completeness of the contents of this book. They shall not be liable for any damages or injury arising out of or in connection with the use of, or reliance on, any content contained in this book.

The exercises and techniques in this book are diverse and may involve physical activity. Therefore, readers are advised to approach them with caution and be aware of their own physical limitations. The author and publisher are not responsible for any injuries or damages that may occur as a result of practicing these exercises.

INDEX

CHECKLIST..18,19

WHY THIS BOOK WAS WRITTEN 5,6
WHAT THIS BOOK WILL CONSIST OF...7
TIPS FOR SUCCESS 8-17

PERFORMANCE STRATEGY........... 21, 51, 81, 111, 141, 171, 201, 231, 261, 291, 321, 351 381

ALL-AROUND ACTORS WORKOUT............. 23, 53, 83, 113, 143, 173, 203, 233, 263, 293 323, 353

SCRIPT ANALYSIS - RELATIONSHIPS & SPECIFICITY.... 25, 55, 85, 115, 145, 175, 205 235, 265, 295 325, 355

IMAGINATION - WORLD BUILDING MEDITATION.... 27, 57, 87, 117, 147, 177, 207, 237 267, 297, 327 357

OBSERVATION - CHARACTER STUDY............ 29, 59, 89, 119, 149, 179, 209, 239, 269 299, 329, 359

VOICE & DICTION..31,61, 91, 121, 151, 181, 211, 241, 271 301, 331, 361

SUBTEXT...33,63, 93, 123, 153, 183, 213, 243, 273 303, 333, 363

EMOTION..35, 65, 95, 125, 155, 185, 215, 245, 275 305, 335, 365

WRITE A LETTER IN CHARACTER............................37,67, 97, 127, 157, 187, 217, 247, 277 307, 337, 367

VERBAL IMPROVISATION IN CHARACTER.....39, 69, 99, 129, 159, 189, 219, 249, 279 309, 339 369

SELF AWARENESS DISCOVERY............................. 41, 71, 101, 131, 161, 191, 221, 251, 281 311, 341, 371

IMPROVISED STORYTELLING & WORLD EXPLORATION....43, 73, 103, 133, 163, 193 223, 253 283, 313, 343, 373

COLOUR & MUSIC FOR ANCHORING YOUR CHARACTER....45, 75, 105, 135, 165, 195 225, 285 315 345, 375

HISTORICAL EVENT/PERSON RESEARCH.......... 47, 77, 107, 137, 167, 197, 227, 257, 287 317, 347, 377

BELIEF..49, 79, 109, 139, 169, 199, 229, 259, 289 319, 349, 379

GOING FORWARD...382
RECOMMENDED BOOKS & RESOURCES..383

WHY THIS BOOK WAS WRITTEN

This is not revolutionary in any way; it's very basic. As actors, we don't have a daily practice in our craft. In almost all jobs, you undergo some form of training, and then when you're finished, you practice your skills every single day at work. That day-to-day practice is invaluable in becoming highly proficient and successful. So, as an actor, unless you're in full-time school, auditioning every day, or working on set every day, we have so much downtime without practicing our craft consistently. We're waiting... No more waiting.

No matter how long you've been in the industry, one of the biggest challenges is there's almost no structure in this lifestyle. No consistency and no set schedule, even when you're working. Everything is always changing, which we've all embraced, but how do you get better every day? How do you keep growing and evolving as an actor so that when the time comes and your phone rings, you're not shaking off the dust, but you are so prepared that you can deliver something great?

You can tell the difference between someone who doesn't exercise and someone who does. Someone who works out twice a week and someone who works out five. Do you think they have more time than you? The answer is almost always no. The difference is they have made a specific choice that exercising *that* much, is a must in their life. Not a "should", "try to", or find every excuse in the book to say why they can't. If it's THAT important to you, you will make it a must.

It's the exact same with actors. But there's no gym for the actor. No workout routine for emotions, creativity, physicality, script analysis, voice, imagination. So, I created one. A daily exercise routine, focusing on some of the most important skills any great actor needs and I could tell a difference immediately—not just in my auditions, but in my creativity, my excitement, and especially in my focus.

Your tools as an actor are either getting sharper or becoming dull. It's one or the other. A professional athlete trains every day. A doctor goes to school for almost a decade and then practices their craft while they work. They consistently train their skills and improve their methods, day in, day out. Success in any high-level career hinges on one crucial habit: consistent practice.

That is our aim with these workouts.

WHY THIS BOOK WAS WRITTEN

This book is for those of you who know how great you can be and want to become masterful at your craft. For those of you who want to be ready when that opportunity comes, so that one day when they say how lucky you are, you know the truth...

"Luck is what happens when preparation meets opportunity." Seneca

And remember, have patience with yourself as you're growing.

"You don't yell at a bud because it's not a flower yet." Larry Moss

WHAT THIS BOOK WILL CONSIST OF

There are 14 different exercises with 125 variants, outlining a 15-minute workout for you to follow every day for six months.

THE 14 EXERCISES

1: ALL AROUND ACTORS WORKOUT
2: SCRIPT ANALYSIS - RELATIONSHIPS & SPECIFICITY
3: IMAGINATION - WORLD BUILDING MEDITATION
4: OBSERVATION - CHARACTER STUDY
5: VOICE & DICTION
6: SUBTEXT
7: EMOTION
8: WRITE A LETTER IN CHARACTER
9: VERBAL IMPROVISATION IN CHARACTER
10: SELF AWARENESS DISCOVERY
11: IMPROVISED STORYTELLING & WORLD EXPLORATION
12: COLOUR AND MUSIC FOR ANCHORING YOUR CHARACTER
13: HISTORICAL EVENT or PERSON RESEARCH
14: BELIEF - YOUR BELIEF ON A SUBJECT & EMBODYING SOMEONE ELSE'S

PERFORMANCE STRATEGY & REVIEW

After every 14 days/exercises, there is a structured performance strategy and review that will go over your ongoing goals, your why, strengths, weaknesses and action plan. This helps us stay focused and train like a professional.

CHECKLIST

A DAILY, WEEKLY & MONTHLY CHECKLIST for those who like to have a specific goal and check off accomplishments as you go on this journey.

TIPS FOR SUCCESS
HOW TO MAKE THIS BOOK AS EFFECTIVE AS POSSIBLE

CONSISTENCY IS KEY: We are our habits. Change your habits and you change who you are.

Dedicate just 15 minutes a day and <u>commit</u> to regular practice. Train with the dedication of a professional.

Darren Hardy has an incredible book called "The Compound Effect" (New York: Success Books, 2010), he says initially, a train requires significant energy to start moving. Much like the initial stages of pursuing a goal or creating a new habit, it demands considerable effort with minimal visible results. However, as the train gains speed, it moves more effortlessly becoming almost unstoppable.

When people say "Oh, that's just who they are"; is an example of a seemingly unstoppable train, but all it takes is a new habit to change who we are. It will start slow but soon you will become unstoppable in this new version of yourself.

SPECIFICITY: The more specific you are with the exercises, your imagination and your goals; the more powerful and effective you will be as an actor and the faster you will grow. This will be better explained with examples soon.

JOURNAL YOUR PROGRESS: *Write it down!* Writing has a powerful effect on our clarity, focus and understanding. It's almost like etching into stone. I've given space to write for each exercise but it is limited. **Get yourself a journal** or write it in your notes on your device. When you look back on what you've accomplished, you'll see your journey and how much you've grown. The more you journal <u>your</u> thoughts and ideas on a subject, the closer you will get to knowing who you are and what kind of artist you are.

ENJOY THE JOURNEY: Acting is as much about the journey as it is about the destination. Celebrate small victories, learn from challenges, and enjoy every moment of the process. "Happiness is not a destination, it's a way of travel." - Ralph Waldo Emerson.

REMEMBER: Take these exercises and tweak them to *your style*. Decide what works for you and discard what doesn't. Be open to trying everything and through the process of elimination, you will begin to discover yourself as an artist.

TIPS FOR SUCCESS
HOW TO MAKE THIS BOOK AS EFFECTIVE AS POSSIBLE

FINDING A GOOD SPACE: This is more important than you think. Depending on our space, we can feel uncomfortable being too loud, "weird", making others uncomfortable or embarrassing ourselves while we rehearse. These worries or insecurities hold us back from our creativity and success. Find a place where you can be completely present, comfortable and creatively free. A space to explore what works and especially what doesn't.

If you don't have a space like that or you are on the go while you're using this book, then make do with what you have. Stay quiet or get comfortable being explorative around people. **Tip:** Headphones are perfect. People just think you're talking to someone on the phone.

MENTAL REHEARSAL: Actual practice has been proven to have the best results in our performance but mental rehearsal was surprisingly close.

There was a study by psychologist Alan Richardson referred to as mental rehearsal or mental practice that has been tested in the field of psychology and sports science.

In Richardson's study, participants were divided into three groups:

- Group A *physically practiced* free throws in basketball every day for 20 days.
- Group B only *mentally rehearsed* and visualized themselves successfully making free throws every day for 20 days.
- Group C, the control group, *did not practice* or engage in any mental rehearsal.

The results of the study showed that Group A, which *physically practiced*, improved their free throw shooting skills as expected. Surprisingly, Group B, the group that only engaged in *mental rehearsal*, also showed significant improvement, *although not as much as Group A*. Group C, the control group, showed no improvement.

"I visualize about a month or so in advance of what could happen, what I want to happen and what I don't want to happen. So, I was prepared for it all. In 2008, in the 200m fly, my goggles fell off in the first 25m, so I swam blind for 175m. I reverted back to what I did in training and counted my strokes. I know how many strokes I take in the first, second, third and fourth 50m of all my best 200m flies. I was ready for that because I mentally prepared for it." - Michael Phelps (Most decorated Olympian of All-time)

TIPS FOR SUCCESS
HOW TO MAKE THIS BOOK AS EFFECTIVE AS POSSIBLE

MENTAL REHEARSAL: It's like creating a detailed movie in your mind. Close your eyes and vividly imagine yourself performing a specific skill, task or *audition*. *Practice this no matter what*, but remember in those times you don't have a good space to rehearse properly, *mental rehearsal* is the perfect solution.

This technique will also strengthen your imagination which I think, is the most powerful skill we can have as an actor.

COURAGE: "A great actor stays around 6 years old." Christopher Walken

The reason why children are so fascinating and magical to watch is because they are so playful and imaginative. Still so malleable, but as you age, life teaches you to "be quiet", to "grow up" or be "cool". Children don't need courage to be creative because that is our natural state. You can get back to that. You just have to have *the courage* to break the habit of not wanting to look "silly" or whatever "it" is for you.

If you become so focused on being a great actor, you won't have any time to think about your insecurities.

Also, you are an *actor*. You're playing dress up for a living. You have to have the courage to be free. Free to be ugly and weird and magical. As soon as you embrace *this*, your imagination will ignite and you as an artist starts to emerge. It can be embarrassing and uncomfortable at first, but fairly quickly you will understand how powerful this change is.

"Have the courage to do whatever you need to do, to get where you want to go."

WORKOUTS
Following this 15-minute daily structure is a great starting point to help get you in *the habit of practice*, but remember: Take control. Spend more time on one exercise than the other, make the workouts longer and begin forming *your* own specific practice routine.

EXAMPLE
15-MINUTE WORKOUT

MY WHY: (You write your own here) Example: "I want to make comedies to make the world laugh! Laughter is the cure to so many things."
GOAL:[Be as specific as you can] Example: "I want all my characters to have a powerfully vibrant way of looking at the world. An intense point of view. And I want to not mumble. A very clear and resonant voice." Book a supporting role.

PHYSICAL WARMUP - 1 minute [Set Timer]
Freeform Dance: Put on some music and engage in freeform dancing. Allow your body to move spontaneously and without inhibition. This can help you tap into your creative instincts and develop physical expressiveness. **Tip:** Try music you've never listened to.

VOCAL WORK - 3 minutes [Set timer]
Lip Trills: Close your lips together lightly, like you're going to blow a raspberry. Then, blow air through your closed lips while making sounds. You should feel a tickling sensation.

EMOTIONAL RECALL - 5 minutes - [Set Timer]
Romantic Nostalgia:
Select a personal memory from your own life that evokes feelings of romantic nostalgia. Vividly recreate the chosen memory. Imagine the setting, the people involved, and the details of the situation. Use all your senses to immerse yourself in the memory. **Tip:** Trust your body. Allow the emotions to wash over you and let your body react and move in whatever way it wants to and speak any dialogue or words associated with the memory out loud as if you were speaking to the person in the memory. Now close your eyes and take a few deep breaths to relax— Focus and begin your recall.

ANIMAL WORK -
Research - 2 minutes [Set Timer] Exercise - 3 minutes [Set Timer]

FLAMINGO
Research - 2 minutes - Go to Google or YouTube etc and search flamingo. If you don't have internet access, take this time to recall when you've seen a flamingo either in person, images, tv. You don't have to be exact.

Animal Exercise - 3 minutes - Morph your body into this creature as much as possible. Walk, make their sounds, and imagine how they see the world. Beauty, Danger etc. Let your imagination take you. Once you believe yourself— slowly evolve yourself into human form but DON'T lose the slight, almost imperceptible characteristics of your animal. Now walk and talk like a regular human and see how embodying this animal affects everything. Your voice, movement, the way you look at the world. **Tip:** This is your playground. Have the courage to have fun!

Discovery Journal - 1 minute [Set Timer]
3 Main Characteristics: Pink, quick movements, mate for life. (Whatever stands out to YOU to embody their essence)
[Journal what you took from today's workout. What you want to remember. What you want to work on, expand on]

WORKOUT COMPLETED

EXAMPLE
15-MINUTE WORKOUT SCRIPT ANALYSIS

RELATIONSHIP and SPECIFICITY

Title: The Unspoken
INT. OLD CHURCH HALLWAY - DAY
The hallway is dimly lit, filled with hushed tones and somber faces. LUCAS (mid-30s, stoic and introspective) stands alone, looking at a family photo. ELLA (early 30s, resilient but visibly emotional) approaches hesitantly.

ELLA
Lucas?

Lucas turns, surprised. A moment of recognition, then a guarded expression settles in.

LUCAS
(after a moment)
Ella?

Ella nods, the weight of the moment heavy on her.

ELLA
I know... I didn't expect my first meeting with my brother to be—

LUCAS
At our parents' funeral...

Ella steps closer, a mix of hope and uncertainty.

ELLA
Yeah. That.
(Long beat)
Did you know?

LUCAS
Did I know what?

ELLA
About me. That I existed?

Off of her surprise, Lucas hugs her tight.

LUCAS
Of course not. I don't know why they kept it—You, from me either.

ELLA
I do.

Clearly, it's not a happy story. Lucas can see Ella has been through so much. After a tense moment.

ELLA (cont'd)
But.. Maybe today isn't the best—

LUCAS
No. It's okay. I want to hear it. If... You want to tell me.

Ella has never trusted someone so quickly... She doesn't say anything just nods and they walk down the long path through the cemetery... A lifetime to talk about.

WORKOUT COMPLETED [✓]

INT. OLD CHURCH: Same church I was baptized. Same musty smell too. I used to like this place... Not today.

DAY: Feels like the longest day in the world. I just want it to be night so I can go to sleep.

Dimly Lit: Matches the way I feel... People just look like "shadows."

Hushed tones and somber faces: People crying. Holding each other. Looking at me and talking about me.

Family photo: This is all I'm looking at though. I remember that day at the zoo. On my dad's shoulders. My mom biting my foot pretending to be a lion because I was so sad the enclosure was closed. She made me laugh so much... I loved this day.

ELLA: I was told about her yesterday by my aunt. My dad had a child before I was born with another woman. My mom knew, apparently too and they never told me. WHY wouldn't they tell me...

Surprised: This woman is just staring at me... Wait.. My aunt showed me a picture of Ella and...

Recognition: That's her. She has my dad's nose.

Guarded expression: It hurts to see my dad in you. I don't know what to say or how to do this. Especially today.

First meeting: Overwhelmed with so many emotions and thoughts.

My brother: I always wanted a sibling. To hear someone say "my brother" means a lot. When my parents died I thought it was only me now, but there's *you*.

Parent's funeral: The worst day of my life. They died in a car crash. Died on impact apparently. On the way back from their favourite vacation spot. I'm really grateful they were together... Closed Caskett because the bodies were too mangled.

That I existed: Of course I didn't. I would have found you.

I do: Woah... I can tell this isn't good. I'm scared to hear it.

I want to hear it: I don't care how scared I am. I'm your big brother. You're my little sister and I want you in my life. That feeling beats my fear.

Nods: Relief and Joy on the darkest day. She wants to be family.

OBJECTIVE: Get through this day as fast as possible. **WIN or LOSE:** Lose, but for a wonderful reason. I get to get to know my sister. **WHO** is in the scene: I am Lucas. Ella, extended family, a bunch of people I don't know, my parents, Sarah and Neal, in their closed casket.

WHAT is happening: My parents have died suddenly in a brutal car crash and my sister who I didn't even know about till yesterday, showed up at the funeral. **WHERE:** Back in my home town I haven't been to in 10 years. The Church I was baptized in. **WHEN:** Present day. 1 pm in the afternoon. Time has never moved so slowly. **EXTRA:** My secret is I don't know why I hate my parents at this moment... For leaving me alone? For lying to me for my whole life that I have a sister?

TIPS FOR SUCCESS
HOW TO MAKE THIS BOOK AS EFFECTIVE AS POSSIBLE

COMMITMENT TO THIS DAILY WORKOUT: Professional athletes spend on average, 20-40 hours <u>a week</u> training. Youth athletes spend 5-10 hours.

It looks like an intimidating number, but it's the truth. Now ask yourself and be honest: *"How many hours a week do I practice?"* and *"How good do I want to be?"*

These are 15-minute workouts. Seven days a week adds up to a total of 1.75 hours per week. That's it. But, after one year you'll have an extra 91 hours of training.

Our training as actors include classes, workshops, audition prep, auditions, working on set or stage, even watching TV/film/documentaries intentionally, etc This career can be extremely difficult to train *that* many hours, especially on our own. So, what do we do? We have to create a structure for ourselves. Allow this book to help.

Simply **having a goal** and **following a checklist** can have a powerful effect on our success. Goals give us direction and purpose. They can act as a compass, guiding your actions and decisions towards a defined endpoint. Without goals, efforts can become scattered and unproductive, but with them, every step you take is a step closer to your dream. The checklist provided gives us measurable progress and accomplishment. Even if it's only a small checkmark every day.

Just like the train metaphor, it will start slow but you will gain momentum if you continue to move forward every day. Success is also a habit. Start small—Only a simple checkmark and watch how the momentum of "every day" affects your career.

TIP: THERE WAS A STUDY AND THEORY BY DR. EDWIN LOCKE AND DR. GARY LATHAM THAT <u>SETTING HIGH, CHALLENGING GOALS</u> (SOMETIMES PERCEIVED AS UNATTAINABLE) ENCOURAGES GREATER EFFORT, FOCUS, PERSISTENCE, AND MOTIVATION, LEADING TO BETTER PERFORMANCE OUTCOMES. **THESE TYPES OF GOALS CAN PUSH INDIVIDUALS OUT OF THEIR COMFORT ZONES, FORCING THEM TO INNOVATE AND THINK CREATIVELY.**

TIPS FOR SUCCESS
HOW TO MAKE THIS BOOK AS EFFECTIVE AS POSSIBLE

DREAM BIG: Don't be afraid to make an audacious goal. **REMEMBER:** If you don't achieve it, take a step back and *look at what you did achieve*. If your goal was audacious and almost certainly unattainable, you'll most likely have accomplished a lot more than you would have if your goal was "realistic". *Sometimes,* you'll even surprise yourself and achieve that "unattainable" goal and you will realize the purpose of a goal and the power of a dream.

"Combine your GOAL with your WHY and you have a recipe for motivation and success."

YOUR "WHY": One of the most effective and important tools is finding your WHY and reminding yourself of it every day. Especially the days that get tough. When your WHY is clear and specific, it has the most profound effect on your focus and drive. "He who has a why to live can bear almost any how" - Friedrich Nietzsche

GENERAL VS SPECIFIC: My 'why' is I want to be a movie star and win an Oscar. *OR*: I want to give people what movies gave me. Hope, love, fantasy and escape. I want someone to walk up to me, shake my hand and say, "Thank you for helping me." When I win my Oscar, I see my wife, kids and mom sitting in the front row."

Be as specific as you can.
Write it out fully then simplify it into a few words or a sentence.
Change it as it evolves.

MY WHY

_____
_____
_____
_____
_____
_____
_____
_____
_____
_____

TIPS FOR SUCCESS
HOW TO MAKE THIS BOOK AS EFFECTIVE AS POSSIBLE

GOALS: Goals help us focus. *They are lighthouses.* There are so many ways to reach the lighthouse and every journey will change, but you will always know where you are headed if you have a goal. Without it, you can become a ship lost at sea. The more specific you become with your goals, the journey becomes simple. Not easy; nothing worth it is, but *simple*. It's like putting on horse blinders. **The more specific your goal, that's all you can see.**

GOAL EXAMPLES: > Work on my memory > Strengthen my emotions > New headshots
ACTION STEP(s) are how and what you will do to achieve this goal.
 > Buy memory book Moonwalking with Einstein > Set daily alarm to do an emotional exercise > Call Ashleyross Studios and set up an appointment

In order of Importance
MY GOALS

1.

   Action Step(s):

2.

   Action Step(s):

3.

   Action Step(s):

4.

   Action Step(s):

TIPS FOR SUCCESS
HOW TO MAKE THIS BOOK AS EFFECTIVE AS POSSIBLE

PERFORMANCE STRATEGY 14-DAY REVIEW
Every 14 workouts/days there will be a *Performance Strategy and Review*. You will fill it out before the first workout in order to help with focus and your awareness of yourself as an artist.

I found that most self-help, educational books I've read, give you a wonderful idea and a powerful transformation tool, but rarely give you the practical application to apply their concept to your day-to-day life and create a new habit.

Anders Ericsson has a brilliant book called PEAK (Ericsson, K. Anders, and Robert Pool. 2016. Peak: Secrets from the New Science of Expertise) where he talks about "deliberate practice." It's about pushing beyond one's comfort zone, receiving immediate feedback, and <u>continuously refining one's technique.</u> It's not just repetition but a mindful and systematic approach to skill improvement.

This **Checklist, Daily Discovery Journal and 14-Day Strategy Review** will help with that style of skill improvement with an ongoing evaluation of *where you are now, where you are going and how you will get there*. It will also help you develop the new habit of *"sharpening your tools".*

I love that story of the two men chopping wood. One worked non-stop all day, not even a break for lunch. The other chopped steadily but took a brief break every hour. The first man thought to himself, he would surely chop more. However, at the end of the day, the second man had chopped significantly more wood. Confused, he asked, "How!? You were taking breaks and I worked so much harder and longer!" The second man replied, "I wasn't just taking breaks. *I was sharpening my axe."*

Taking the time to maintain your tools/skills can lead to greater efficiency and better results. It's not always the quantity of work but the quality and effectiveness of that work that matters most.

TIPS FOR SUCCESS
HOW TO MAKE THIS BOOK AS EFFECTIVE AS POSSIBLE

CREATING A NEW HABIT: They say a habit takes 21 days to form and 66 days to become automatic. Turn this quick workout into a daily habit and make it a part of your lifestyle. You may have a strategy that works best for you but here is a great starting point to add to your daily routine.

- [ ] After you find your **WHY** and have your specific **GOALS, write them again on a separate piece of paper** and **make sure you can see them every day.** "Out of sight, out of mind." Simple but powerful.

- [ ] **Set a daily alarm** on your phone, *reminding* you to workout.

- [ ] **Use the CHECKLIST** on the next page as you go through these workouts. This visual representation can be a powerful motivator when you see your accomplishments build over time.

- [ ] **Use the PERFORMANCE STRATEGY 14-DAY REVIEW** diligently. Like a map to your ultimate goal and be as specific as you can. Clarity will make your path simple; Again, not easy, but simple, if you know where you are and where you want to go.

Eventually, this will become automatic.
Success is also a habit.

TIP: USE THIS STRATEGY IN ALL ASPECTS OF YOUR CAREER, ESPECIALLY FOR YOUR TEACHERS / COACHES / DIRECTORS. TALK TO THEM BEFORE AND BE AWARE AND VULNERABLE ENOUGH TO LET THEM KNOW EXACTLY WHO YOU ARE AND WHAT YOU ARE WORKING ON RIGHT NOW AS AN ACTOR. IT WILL HELP YOU BE DELIBERATE IN YOUR WORK AND ALLOW THEM TO DO THEIR JOB THE BEST THEY CAN. **REMEMBER**: YOU ARE A BEAUTIFULLY IMPERFECT INSTRUMENT. KNOW YOUR INSTRUMENT AS BEST YOU CAN SO YOU CAN CREATE SYMPHONY BETWEEN YOU AND YOUR TEAM.

Now get after it!! It's going to take work but go get your dreams.

CHECKLIST

GOAL
WORKOUTS PER WEEK: ☐

MONTH SEVEN
- ☐ WEEK 1
- ☐ WEEK 2
- ☐ WEEK 3
- ☐ WEEK 4

MONTHLY GOAL
ALL 4 WEEKS ☐

MONTH EIGHT
- ☐ WEEK 1
- ☐ WEEK 2
- ☐ WEEK 3
- ☐ WEEK 4

MONTHLY GOAL
ALL 4 WEEKS ☐

MONTH NINE
- ☐ WEEK 1
- ☐ WEEK 2
- ☐ WEEK 3
- ☐ WEEK 4

MONTHLY GOAL
ALL 4 WEEKS ☐

MONTH TEN
- ☐ WEEK 1
- ☐ WEEK 2
- ☐ WEEK 3
- ☐ WEEK 4

MONTHLY GOAL
ALL 4 WEEKS ☐

MONTH ELEVEN
- ☐ WEEK 1
- ☐ WEEK 2
- ☐ WEEK 3
- ☐ WEEK 4

MONTHLY GOAL
ALL 4 WEEKS ☐

MONTH TWELVE
- ☐ WEEK 1
- ☐ WEEK 2
- ☐ WEEK 3
- ☐ WEEK 4

MONTHLY GOAL
ALL 4 WEEKS ☐

BECOME SO FOCUSED ON YOUR DREAM YOU HAVE NO ROOM FOR INSECURITY & DOUBT

FOCUS IS A MUSCLE

PERFORMANCE STRATEGY

DAY ONE VOLUME TWO
CHECK IN

TAKE A MOMENT OF REFLECTION AND BREAKDOWN WHERE YOU ARE RIGHT NOW IN YOUR CAREER AND AS AN ACTOR.
THE MORE SPECIFIC YOU ARE THE MORE CLEAR YOU CAN SEE WHERE YOU ARE NOW SO YOU CAN GET TO WHERE YOU WANT TO GO FASTER

★ ★ ★ ★ ★

Kathryn Joosten: Started her acting career in her 40s and won two Emmy Awards for her role in "Desperate Housewives."

DATE:

BREAKDOWN WHERE YOU ARE RIGHT NOW AS AN ACTOR - WHAT YOU ARE GREAT AT, WHAT YOU ARE WORKING ON NOW OR NEED TO WORK ON ETC.

STRENGTHS:

WEAKNESSES:

IMPROVEMENT STRATEGY
HOW CAN YOU IMPROVE ON THESE AREAS FOR THE NEXT 14 DAYS:

GOAL FOR THE NEXT 14 EXERCISES
THE MORE SPECIFIC YOU ARE THE GREATER THE RESULT

Action Step(s):

You've achieved success in your field when you don't know whether what you're doing is work or play.
Warren Beatty

MY WHY:

GOAL(s):

PHYSICAL WARMUP - LIGHT PLAY - 1 minute [Set Timer]
Dancing in the Dark: Move in a dimly lit space, focusing on the sensation of movement rather than the visual aspect. **Tip:** Close your eyes occasionally to heighten your other senses.

VOCAL WORK - 3 minutes [Set Timer]
Sighing Glissandos: Inhale deeply and then release a sigh, sliding from the top of your register down to the bottom on an "ah" sound. **Tip:** Imagine letting go of all your stress with each sigh.

EMOTIONAL RECALL - 5 minutes [Set Timer]
Panic and Desperation:
Bring to mind a moment of desperation, where panic took over. Let your breath and heartbeat mimic that frantic state. **Tip:** Let the urgency of the moment be reflected in quick, sporadic movements.

ANIMAL WORK - BAT
Research - 2 minutes [Set Timer]
Consider the bat's nocturnal life and echolocation.

Animal Exercise - 3 minutes [Set Timer]
Flap your 'wings' gently and navigate with your ears, imagining the echoes in the dark. **Tip:** The unseen is your canvas.

Discovery Journal - 1 Minute [Set Timer]

3 Main Characteristics: (Whatever stands out to YOU to embody the essence)

_____
_____
_____
_____
_____
_____
_____

WORKOUT COMPLETED [ ]

The hardest thing to do is work out what you want and stick to it.
Rosamund Pike

SCRIPT ANALYSIS for **RELATIONSHIPS & SPECIFICITY** - 15 minutes [Set Timer]
Choose your character, circle everything in this script you have a relationship with. Including people, places, things, smells, time of day etc. **Write what your relationship with those items are and be specific.** The more specific and fun you have with your relationships, the more interesting your characters will be and the more fun the audience has. **Tip:** Everything isn't in the scene. Use your imagination to create details, only if it's contextually appropriate. **Extra:** Write your > **Objective, win or lose? Consequence of failing?** The *Who What Where When Why.*

Title: **A Deal to Die For**
INT. QUAINT ITALIAN RESTAURANT - EVENING
A cozy yet outdated Italian restaurant. A secluded table, FREDDY (slightly neurotic small-time crook) and GINA (deadpan, sharp-witted criminal) sit with plates of untouched spaghetti.

FREDDY
I hear you got a job for me. Something... unconventional.
GINA
Unconventional is one word for it. I need someone to fake their own death.
FREDDY
Fake their own death? That's... (chuckles) that's creative.
GINA
Insurance scam. Big payout.
FREDDY
And let me guess, I'm the lucky corpse?
GINA
You've got no ties, Freddy. No one will miss you.
FREDDY
Ouch. I mean, it's true, but still stings.
GINA
We stage a dramatic exit for you, collect the insurance, and you lie low in Fiji or somewhere sipping a margarita.
FREDDY
Fiji, huh? Always wanted to go there. (beat) Can I trust you?
GINA
Those were just rumours. It's foolproof. Can't really screw up being dead.
FREDDY
Well, when you put it like that...
GINA
We split the insurance money. You get a new life, I get my cut.
FREDDY
And if I say no?
GINA
Then you miss out on the easiest job you'll ever have.
FREDDY
Never liked Italian food anyway. When do we start?
GINA
Tomorrow. Start saying your goodbyes. To yourself.

Freddy takes a bite of his spaghetti as Gina sips her wine, a smirk hidden behind her glass.

WORKOUT COMPLETED [ ]

I'm curious about people. That's the essence of my acting.
Greg Kinnear

IMAGINATION

We have a lot of tools in our arsenal as actors but **I believe imagination is the most powerful.** "If you hook into the character's belief system and you believe it 100%, there is no way the audience won't." - Meryl Streep "Imagination is more important than knowledge for knowledge is limited. - Einstein. Everyone has an Imagination but it must be worked out to get stronger. Think of your imagination as a limitless playground. In this space, you can be anyone, go anywhere, and do anything. **Have the courage to allow yourself to play!**

Solo Imaginary World Exploration - 6 Minutes [Set Timer]

Find a quiet space to relax and focus. **Close your eyes** and **let your imagination run wild. Tip:** Engage all your senses to explore this environment. Touch, taste, smell etc. Allow your emotions to guide you. **Extra:** After you establish this world in your imagination, you could introduce characters and have a dialogue with them. Are they friends or foes?

IMAGINARY WORLD: Cloud Kingdom: Explore cities floating on clouds, traversing the skies in airships.

JOURNAL YOUR EXPERIENCE - 2 Minutes [Set Timer]

_____
_____
_____
_____
_____
_____

Your Characters Filter - 5 Minutes [Set Timer]

Everyone including the characters you play see the world through their own specific perspective/filter. I like to use the word filter because you can take out a filter, clean it, change its style, colour, an optimist or a pessimist, comedian or a nihilist, etc. **Find a quiet space** to focus. **Close your eyes and let go of your personal thoughts and emotions** to make space for your characters. **Open your eyes, and allow the filter provided to effect everything around you. Tip**: Explore wherever you are and interact with the objects. **Extra:** How does *this* character walk and move in their world?

FILTER: Gritty Detective: Always on the lookout for clues and hidden truths

JOURNAL YOUR EXPERIENCE - 2 Minutes [Set Timer]

_____
_____
_____
_____
_____
_____

WORKOUT COMPLETED [ ]

I never said, 'I want to be alone.' I only said, 'I want to be left alone.' There is all the difference.
Greta Garbo

CHARACTER STUDY "PEOPLE WATCHING"

Actors are required to portray characters that are believable and relatable. You don't have to agree with them but you have to understand them. Walk like them, talk like them, see the world like them. So, in order to fill our toolbox, we have to **go out into the world and study**. Then practice them over and over so we can "walk in their shoes', comfortably and confidently. Study their movements, mannerisms, the "vibe" they give off, the clothes they wear etc. **Fill your toolbox with the rhythms and idiosyncrasies of human behaviour.**

OBSERVATION CHARACTER STUDY - 15 Minutes [Set Timer]

Find a busy place where you can **sit and observe.** Choose anyone you find interesting. **Write down what stands out about them.** *The way they sit, drink their coffee, walk, talk, interact with others etc.* **Tip: Mirror them immediately.** This will help memorize the feeling of that character so whenever you come back to these characters you're discovering, your body will remember. **Extra**: Before you go to sleep, read over the characters from today and reenact their movements.

COLOURS: We as humans respond to colours like frequencies. If you pay attention closely, you can see everyone has their own 'colour' that defines their core. An essence that informs how they operate and move through the world.

WHAT COLOUR ARE THEY:

WORKOUT COMPLETED [ ]

The more you do, the more you can do.
William Hazlitt

VOICE & DICTION

I wish I had learned this at the beginning of my career. The confidence to communicate clearly and powerfully is a game-changer for you as an actor. **Think of your voice as a musical instrument that needs regular tuning. This workout is your daily tuning session,** ensuring that your instrument is always ready. "The word 'theatre' comes from the Greeks. It means the seeing place. It is the place people come to see the truth about life and the social situation." - Stella Adler. Embrace this workout as a key to unlocking and portraying *that* truth by letting your voice be the vehicle that transports your audience into the heart of your story.

READ PASSAGE - 30 Seconds [Set Timer]
Speak the passage and take note of its quality. **Tip**: Record Audio to compare afterward.

> "The festival bursts with colour and sound. Music fills the air, people dance in the streets, and the atmosphere buzzes with joy and laughter. Lights adorn every corner, turning the night into a canvas of celebration."

RELAXATION - 1 Minute [Set Timer]
Deep Breathing: Sit and Inhale deeply through your nose, filling your lungs, then exhale slowly through your mouth. Imagine stress leaving your body with each breath.

Nay Nay Nay - 1 Minute [Set Timer]
Pick a song and sing the word "Nay" repeatedly. Start with a comfortable pitch and gradually move the sound from your nose to your chest, ensuring each "Nay" is clear and resonant. Stretch your range as best you can to strengthen.

Sustained 'S' - 2 Minutes [Set Timer]
Inhale deeply and then exhale slowly, making a continuous 's' sound. Keep the sound as even and steady as you can. Always push a little longer than you think you can.

Vowel Pronunciation Drill - 2 Minutes [Set Timer]
Slowly go through each vowel sound **(A, E, I, O, U)**, **holding and exaggerating each sound. Combine them with consonants** (e.g., ba, be, bi, bo, bu). Pay attention to the clarity and sharpness of each sound. Repeat a few times before moving to the next.

Lip Trills - 3 minutes - [Set timer]
Close your lips together lightly, like you're going to blow a raspberry. Then, blow air through your closed lips while making sounds. You should feel a tickling sensation. Pick a song and Lip Trill the whole along with it. **Tip**: Stretch your range as much as you can and pick a song you've never listened to.

The Cork Exercise - 4 Minutes [Set Timer]
Place a cork between your teeth and try to read a passage aloud. This forces your articulation muscles to work harder. If you don't have a cork, bite down gently on your thumb. You can use the following text for this exercise:

READ PASSAGE AGAIN - 30 Seconds [Set Timer]
Speak the passage and take note of its quality. **Tip**: Record Audio to compare.

Discovery Journal - 1 Minute [Set Timer]

WORKOUT COMPLETED [ ]

A champion is defined not by their wins but by how they can recover when they fall.
Serena Williams

SUBTEXT

Subtext is what lies beneath the surface of our words. It's the hidden layer of meaning, driven by the character's internal thoughts, emotions, desires, and motivations. Subtext is one of my favourite things as an actor because so much can be said with one simple line of dialogue. The power of "Hello" can be exciting if you told that person years ago "If I ever see you again, I'll kill you. Maybe it's the most beautiful person you've ever seen. Now, say "hello". *Subtext* shows the audience what your relationship with the characters/places/situations are, without having to explain it. We experience it every day and it is our job to create characters that interact as we do.

VOCAL WORK - 3 minutes - [Set Timer]
Lip Trills: Close your lips together lightly, like you're going to blow a raspberry. Then, blow air through your closed lips while making sounds. You should feel a tickling sensation. Pick a song and Lip Trill along with it. **Tip**: Stretch your range as much as you can and pick a song you've never listened to.

SUBTEXT PRACTICE
Use the line of dialogue provided and practice each of these subtexts **out loud.** Move on to the next, only when you believe yourself. Trust that you will know when *that* is. Before you begin, **pick a spot to look at and imagine** in detail, **who you are speaking with**. **Tip**: *Sometimes* we mean exactly what we are saying. Look for that too. **Extra**: Substitute someone you have a strong relationship with in real life, good or bad, and see it's affect.

Initial Line: "Guess who's back in town? Jenna, from our high school art class."
Your Response Line: "Jenna? Wow, that's unexpected. She was always so... Remember the mural she painted that she got caught doing? It's still there I think. Think I should reach out?"

SUBTEXTS - 6 Minutes [Set Timer]
[ ] Intrigued: You're curious about Jenna's journey since high school.
[ ] Indifferent: You barely remember her and feel no particular way.
[ ] Reflective: Jenna's return makes you think about your own path since school.
[ ] Surprised: You never thought you'd hear about her again.
[ ] Admiring: You always looked up to her talent and daring spirit.
[ ] Your Own Subtext

RELATIONSHIP SUBTEXTS - 6 Minutes [Set Timer]
[ ] The Old Friend who shared a close bond with Jenna.
[ ] The person you don't like who you know, only wants her for one thing...
[ ] Your big brother who always grills you to take more chances / go after what you want!
[ ] Your mom who wants you to find a person yesterday and have babies.
[ ] The Former Bully at a bar who just spilled a drink on you.
[ ] Your Own Subtext

Discovery Journal

_____
_____
_____

WORKOUT COMPLETED [ ]

If you're going to live, leave a legacy. Make a mark on the world that can't be erased.
Maya Angelou

EMOTIONS

The 'moment before', **the emotional preparation, is the most important key to a great scene.** If you start any scene *without* an emotional preparation it feels like trying to drive a car in neutral. The preparation is the uphill climb of every rollercoaster; Once you grind all the way to the top, the chains let go and the rest of the ride takes care of itself. "No one wants to see a play or a movie and look at technical proficiency. You want to be moved, you want a human experience, you want to feel less alone" - Viola Davis. **Practice your emotions over and over** so when it's time, you aren't worried "Will I get there?" **You're imagination and emotions should be a tinderbox, so easy to light up. All it take is half a spark.**

EULOGY - 12 Minutes [Set Timer]

Find a quiet comfortable space. Choose someone in your life who is alive and important to you. Create an imaginary reason for why they have died. Now start from the point of the phone call— Imagine who calls, what they say and what you say. Eventually find yourself at the funeral, about to begin the eulogy. See the casket, is it open or closed?? What is that person wearing and any other details for yourself. Before you begin to speak, look into the audience and see who is there- Family, friends etc **Then begin the eulogy. Tip:** Be as specific as you can with everything. **Inside of specificity is where you will find the triggers to your heart.** Let your imagination take you wherever you want in this exercise. **Example:** Placing her favourite sheep stuffed animal in the casket, tucked under her arm like she always held it, then kissing her goodbye one last time.

DISCOVERY JOURNAL - 3 Minutes [Set Timer]

Make sure to **include the specific triggers** you experience because you can use these **TRIGGER MOMENTS** in the future instead of repeating the *entire* exercise.

_____
_____
_____
_____
_____
_____
_____
_____
_____
_____
_____
_____
_____
_____
_____
_____
_____
_____

WORKOUT COMPLETED [ ]

You pray for rain, you gotta deal with the mud too. That's a part of it.
Denzel Washington

THE CORK EXERCISE - 4 Minutes [Set Timer]
Place a cork between your teeth and read a passage aloud. This forces your articulation muscles to work harder. If you don't have a cork, bite down gently on your thumb. You can use the following text for this exercise:

> "On a quiet farm, the rooster's crow heralds the break of day. Fields stretch far and wide, dotted with bales of hay. The scent of fresh soil and growing crops fills the air, a tribute to the earth's bounty."

WRITE A LETTER - 10 Minutes [Set Timer]
Get a piece of paper or write this in your device. **Take a moment** to let this situation and relationship sink in. Then let your imagination run wild and **write them a letter.**

Your Character: Grace, a small business owner who has put everything into building her dream café.
Other Character: Alex, a former friend and business partner who embezzled funds from the café, leading to financial strain and nearly causing the business to fail.

Relationship: Grace and Alex's friendship spanned years, and starting the café together was a shared dream. The betrayal of trust not only jeopardized the café but deeply wounded Grace, who had always believed in and trusted Alex unconditionally.

Context of the Letter: With the café's future hanging in the balance and after confronting the legal and emotional fallout of Alex's actions, Grace decides to write a letter to Alex. This letter is Grace's way of expressing her sense of betrayal, disappointment, and anger. It's also an attempt to understand why Alex, someone she considered a close friend, would commit such a hurtful act, and a way to find closure and move forward from this painful chapter.

Discovery Journal - 1 minute [Set Timer]

_____
_____
_____
_____
_____
_____

WORKOUT COMPLETED [ ]

The fight is won or lost far away from witnesses – behind the lines, in the gym, and out there on the road, long before I dance under those lights.
Muhammad Ali

VOCAL WORK - 3 minutes [Set timer]

Lip Trills: Close your lips together lightly, like you're going to blow a raspberry. Then, blow air through your closed lips while making sounds. You should feel a tickling sensation. Pick a song and Lip Trill along with it. **Tip**: Stretch your range as much as you can and pick a song you've never listened to.

VERBAL IMPROV - 10 Minutes [Set Timer]

Find a space where you are comfortable and free to express yourself. Take a moment to **let this situation, character and prompt, sink in**. Then let your imagination run wild: **Picture who you are talking to** then **begin with the prompt** and **continue to verbalize everything** this character would say. **Tip**: This is exploration! There is no "getting it right". BE BRAVE to explore and discover.

Character: Sam, known for their strong sense of justice and commitment to fairness, recently learned that their coworker and friend, Morgan, who has always been ambitious yet secretive, has been manipulating office politics to sabotage another colleague's career. This behaviour is particularly distressing to Sam, who values integrity above all in the workplace.

Prompt: "Morgan, I've uncovered what you've been doing to undermine our colleague. It's time we talked about your actions and the consequences."

Who are you talking to:

Describe them in two specific words:

Discovery Journal - 2 minutes [Set Timer]

_____
_____
_____
_____
_____
_____
_____
_____

WORKOUT COMPLETED [ ]

Acting should be bigger than life.
Scripts should be bigger than life.
It should all be bigger than life.
Bette Davis

SELF AWARENESS

The more you understand yourself, the more you are able to understand and develop your characters. Like you, your characters have thoughts, beliefs, traumas, passions etc. When you become aware of your own and start to see how those experiences and beliefs have shaped your life, how you operate and view the world, then you can develop your characters that are much more rich and vivid.

PHYSICAL WARMUP - 2 minutes [Set Timer]
Freeform Dance: Put on some music and engage in freeform dancing. Allow your body to move spontaneously and without inhibition. This can help you tap into your creative instincts and develop physical expressiveness. **Tip**: Try music you've never listened to.

CURRENT EMOTIONAL INVENTORY - 3 Minutes [Set Timer]
Write down and **record your current emotions**. Identify what you're feeling at this moment and why. **Tip**: Be as specific as you can, **don't disregard anything.** You can also **scan your body** to see how and where your current emotion is affecting you. Your posture, the way you walk, bouncing foot, sore neck etc

CURRENT EMOTIONAL STATE:

SELF DISCOVERY QUESTIONS - 10 Minutes [Set Timer]
I suggest a journal or writing it in your phone's notes so you don't run out of space here.

What experiences have shaped my view of relationships and love?

What advice would you give to someone through these experiences?

WORKOUT COMPLETED [ ]

Talent is an accident of genes -
and a responsibility.
Alan Rickman

IMAGINATION

We have a lot of tools in our arsenal as actors but I believe imagination is the most powerful. "If you hook into the character's belief system and you believe it 100%, there is no way the audience won't." - Meryl Streep. Everyone has an Imagination but it must be worked out to get stronger. Think of your imagination as a limitless playground. In this space, you can be anyone, go anywhere, and do anything. **Have the courage to allow yourself to play!**

VOCAL WORK - 2 Minutes - [Set timer]
Lip Trills: Close your lips together lightly, like you're going to blow a raspberry. Then, blow air through your closed lips while making sounds. You should feel a tickling sensation. Pick a song and Lip Trill along with it. **Tip**: Stretch your range as much as you can and pick a song you've never listened to.

IMPROVISED STORYTELLING - 5 Minutes [Set Timer]
Speak out the scenario provided and continue the story! Focus on vivid details, character development and how the main character overcomes the main obstacle. **Tip**: Try not to stop speaking so you don't have time to "think". Allow your imagination to keep moving forward without interruption. **Tip**: Record these stories on your device, in case it's great but more importantly to see your progress as you go on.

STARTING POINT: You are Harper, a librarian who discovers an ancient, unmarked book in a forgotten corner of the library. Upon opening it, you find that the pages are blank, but as you touch them, the book begins to write its own stories based on your thoughts and experiences.

IMAGINARY WORLD EXPLORATION - 6 Minutes [Set Timer]

Find a quiet space to relax and focus. **Close your eyes** and let your imagination run wild. **Tip:** Engage all your senses to explore this environment. Touch, taste, smell etc and allow your emotions to guide you. **Extra:** After you explore this world with your senses, you could introduce characters and have a dialogue with them. Are they friends or foes?

IMAGINARY WORLD: THE ETHEREAL AURORA - Imagine a mystical landscape where the sky is a canvas of shifting colours, creating breathtaking auroras that dance and twirl above. In this fantastical world, you can witness the beauty of the Ethereal Aurora, each colour representing a distinct emotion.

JOURNAL YOUR EXPERIENCE - 2 Minutes [Set Timer]

_____
_____
_____
_____
_____
_____
_____

WORKOUT COMPLETED [ ]

I never said all actors are cattle; what I said was all actors should be treated like cattle.
Alfred Hitchcock

ANCHORING INTO YOUR CHARACTER COLOUR & MUSIC

Anchoring yourself into your character is vital. It's one of the most freeing feelings when you understand their *essence* because everything they do, how they do it and what their purpose is, becomes so clear to you and the audience. Every choice you make after you find your *anchor*, feels easy, because you're acting from who and what your character is at the core. You can call it an essence, an aura, vibe, energy etc. We all have it and feel it from everyone around us. There are many ways into your character but music and colour are my favourite. Music can inform the script, your character, even each scene. Colours, I think you will find, can work incredibly because we as humans respond to colours like frequencies. Colours evoke many feelings and if you pay attention closely, you can see everyone has their own 'colour' that defines their core. An essence that informs how they operate and move through the world.

THEIR COLOUR - 2 Minutes [Set Timer]
Think of **someone you know**, and **define them with a colour**. **Tip**: Trust yourself. Your initial colour is usually close. **Tip**: Start with basic colours then eventually become much more specific. **Example**: Corinna is an earthy green with rays of sunlight flowing through the green. **Extra**: Ask someone who knows *that person* as well, what they think this person's colour is and why. See how close your answers are or not.

YOUR CHARACTERS COLOUR
Read the given character description just as you would an audition, **assign a colour to that character.** Now take that colour you chose and **allow it to infuse into your entire body**, affecting your every move, your speaking, the way you see the world etc. **Take any book** you have, flip to a random page and **read the text as this Colour/Character**. **Tip**: Be specific, choose a colour that excites you and don't be afraid to get creative.

CHARACTER DESCRIPTION: [GREER] Greer is a seasoned archaeologist, dedicated to uncovering ancient civilizations and their secrets. Dressed in practical field gear, with a weathered hat and a trusty satchel, Greer's attire reflects a life spent on digs and in excavation sites. Their office is a trove of artifacts, maps, and dusty tomes, evidencing a lifetime of exploration and discovery. Greer possesses a wealth of knowledge about the past, but also harbours a sense of melancholy for civilizations lost to time. Their character blends a profound respect for history with a touch of adventure.

CHOOSE THEIR COLOUR - 4 Minutes [Set Timer]
THEIR COLOUR:

CHOOSE THEIR SONG - 4 Minutes [Set Timer]
THEIR SONG:

READ PASSAGE FROM BOOK - 2 Minutes [Set Timer]

FREEFORM DANCE - 2 minutes - [Set Timer]
Put on the selected music and **engage in freeform dancing, anchored in your colour/ character,** Allow your body to move spontaneously and without inhibition. This can help you tap into your creative instincts and develop physical expressiveness *while staying in character.* **Tip**: Journal about the differences as opposed to how you normally dance.

JOURNAL YOUR EXPERIENCE - 1 Minute [Set Timer]

WORKOUT COMPLETED [ ]

To be an actor you have to have a certain
amount of madness in you.
Nicole Kidman

HISTORICAL RESEARCH

We are in the information era and have access to the world and its rich history at our fingertips. This exploration is not about 'learning facts'; it's a journey to the heart of human experience. The empathy and the understanding, especially on the things you disagree with, are incredibly valuable. If you look closely, you'll find the way people think, at different times in history, their attitudes, choices, and the way they move their bodies can teach you so much about us, right now. Fill your toolbox so it's overflowing with information and ideas to pull from so your imagination has so much to play with.

PHYSICAL WARMUP - 2 minutes - [Set Timer]
Freeform Dance: Put on some music and engage in freeform dancing. Allow your body to move spontaneously and without inhibition. This can help you tap into your creative instincts and develop physical expressiveness. **Tip**: Try music you've never listened to.

RESEARCH - 13 Minutes [Set Timer]
YouTube, streaming platforms, the internet or books, **research the given era/person/moment in time,** journal or make notes on your device, so when you want to find this information, it's organized and readily accessible. As you go, **write anything and everything *you* find fascinating. Tip:** If the topic doesn't interest you, choose your own, or take a chance and still research it, but from a different perspective. Physicalities, voice, ideals, etc. Trust your body that when you see something interesting, you'll know. **Extra**: Speak it out and copy their movements. Our memory recall is massively affected by our bodies. Be specific and when you re-read your notes, you'll be amazed by how much your mind and body remember.

TOPIC:
Hedy Lamarr (1914-2000): An Austrian-American actress and inventor, Lamarr was once dubbed the "Most Beautiful Woman in the World" and had a successful film career in Hollywood. However, she was also a talented inventor; her most significant contribution was the development of a radio guidance system for Allied torpedoes during World War II, which used spread spectrum and frequency hopping technology. This technology later became a basis for modern Wi-Fi and Bluetooth.

WORKOUT COMPLETED [ ]

Even miracles take a little time.
Fairy Godmother, Cinderella

BELIEF

Beliefs are the convictions that something exists or is true, especially without proof. That is also the definition of what we do as actors. We play make-believe. Our beliefs shape our world, especially our beliefs about ourselves and it works for the characters you play. Understand your beliefs and how they influence your mind, body and spirit, then you will be able to better understand others, so you can embody them. Allow the beliefs of your character to colour your perception of your world and your interaction with everything in it. "Acting is the best magic trick in the world. We applaud performances not because it's real, but because you made us believe."

VOCAL WORK - 2 Minutes - [Set timer]

Lip Trills: Close your lips together lightly, like you're going to blow a raspberry. Then, blow air through your closed lips while making sounds. You should feel a tickling sensation. Pick a song and Lip Trill along with it. **Tip**: Stretch your range as much as you can and pick a song you've never listened to.

BELIEF WORKOUT

Get your journal or write in here. **Define your personal belief/view** on the given subject. **Grab any book you own,** flip to a random page and **read it out loud,** colouring the words and intention with your belief system. **Tip**: Write trigger words you can hook into in the future: **Optimism-** Always smiling, grateful, opportunity, sunshine yellow.

YOUR PERSONAL BELIEF

Trust- 7 Minutes [Set Timer]

_____
_____
_____
_____

READ WITH BELIEF - 2 Minutes [Set Timer]

CHARACTERS BELIEF

Trust

Trust is not freely given but earned. It's a fortress built brick by brick with proof. I'm not swayed by words. I've been hurt too many times. There is so much bullshit in the world. I only trust only when evidence outweighs doubt.

READ WITH CHARACTERS BELIEF - 2 Minutes [Set Timer]

Forget your personal view and **fully embrace the character's belief**. **Read out loud again.**

JOURNAL YOUR EXPERIENCE - 2 Minutes [Set Timer]

_____
_____
_____

WORKOUT COMPLETED [ ]

PERFORMANCE STRATEGY
14 DAY REVIEW

TAKE A MOMENT OF REFLECTION AND BREAKDOWN WHERE YOU ARE RIGHT NOW IN YOUR CAREER AND AS AN ACTOR. THE MORE SPECIFIC YOU ARE THE MORE CLEAR YOU CAN SEE WHERE YOU ARE NOW SO YOU CAN GET TO WHERE YOU WANT TO GO FASTER

★ ★ ★ ★ ★

Ludwig van Beethoven: Despite beginning to lose his hearing in his late 20s and eventually becoming completely deaf, Beethoven composed some of the most celebrated and influential music in classical history.

DATE:

MY WHY
WHY ARE YOU DOING WHAT YOU ARE DOING
BE SPECIFIC

MY MAIN GOALS
IN-ORDER OF IMPORTANCE

1.

   Action Step(s):

2.

   Action Step(s):

3.

   Action Step(s):

FROM THE LAST 14 DAYS ☆☆☆☆☆
5 STAR RATING

YOUR KEY POINTS AND TAKEAWAYS - WHY THAT AMOUNT OF STAR RATING, LIKES, DISLIKES, THE BIGGEST LESSON YOU LEARNED, GOOD OR BAD:

STRENGTHS:

WEAKNESSES:

IMPROVEMENT STRATEGY
HOW CAN YOU IMPROVE ON THESE AREAS FOR THE NEXT 14 DAYS:

GOAL FROM LAST :
DID YOU ACHIEVE IT?

WHY OR WHY NOT?

GOAL FOR THE NEXT 14 EXERCISES
THE MORE SPECIFIC YOU ARE THE GREATER THE RESULT

   Action Step(s):

It's about how much you can take and keep moving forward. That's how winning is done.
Rocky Balboa, Rocky Balboa

MY WHY:

GOAL(s):

PHYSICAL WARMUP - AROMA RHYTHM - 1 minute [Set Timer]
Scented Steps: Pick an aroma and let the quality of the scent inspire your dance - spicy, sweet, fresh, or earthy. **Tip:** Imagine the scent filling the room and influencing your energy.

VOCAL WORK - 3 minutes [Set timer]
Lip Trills: Close your lips together lightly, like you're going to blow a raspberry. Then, blow air through your closed lips while making sounds. You should feel a tickling sensation.

EMOTIONAL RECALL - 5 minutes [Set Timer]
Excruciating Embarrassment: Recall a moment of extreme embarrassment. Feel the heat rise in your cheeks and the impulse to cover or hide. **Tip:** Re-live the moment with the perspective of self-compassion.

ANIMAL WORK - MANTIS
Research - 2 minutes [Set Timer]
Explore the praying mantis's precise and sudden movements.

Animal Exercise - 3 minutes [Set Timer]
Stand still, then strike with quick precision, mimicking the mantis's hunting technique. **Tip:** Focus brings success; be ready to pounce.

Discovery Journal - 1 Minute [Set Timer]
3 Main Characteristics: (Whatever stands out to YOU to embody the essence)

_____
_____
_____
_____
_____
_____
_____

WORKOUT COMPLETED [ ]

You can be the ripest, juiciest peach in the world, and there's still going to be somebody who hates peaches.
Dita Von Teese, Burlesque

SCRIPT ANALYSIS for **RELATIONSHIPS & SPECIFICITY** - 15 minutes [Set Timer]
Choose your character, circle everything in this script you have a relationship with. Including people, places, things, smells, time of day etc. **Write what your relationship with those items are and be specific.** The more specific and fun you have with your relationships, the more interesting your characters will be and the more fun the audience has. **Tip:** Everything isn't in the scene. Use your imagination to create details, only if it's contextually appropriate. **Extra:** Write your > **Objective, win or lose? Consequence of failing?** The **Who What Where When Why.**

Title: **The Price of Ambition**
INT. LUXURY APARTMENT - NIGHT

A lavish, high-rise apartment overlooking the city. The room is stylish but cold. RAY (a polished-ruthless mob boss) sits at a sleek table. Across from him, JULIA (late 20s, ambitious and cunning).

RAY
You've made quite a name for yourself.
JULIA
I learn from the best.
RAY
And now you want a piece of it.
JULIA
Not a piece, Ray. A partnership.
RAY
Partnership... You're bold, I'll give you that.
JULIA
Bold moves have gotten me this far.
RAY
This world isn't kind to the bold. It eats them alive.
JULIA
Only if they're not smart about it.
RAY
You think you're smarter than the rest?
JULIA
I don't think. I know.
RAY
Confidence is good. Arrogance is deadly.
JULIA
I'm still here, aren't I?
RAY
Which tells me you're either very skilled or very lucky.
JULIA
Why can't it be both?
RAY
In this game, luck runs out. Skill doesn't.
JULIA
Then it's a good thing I'm skilled.
RAY
If you cross me, your children's children will know my name. Clear?
JULIA
Crystal.

Julia stands, looking out at the city skyline. Ray watches her, his thoughts unreadable. Friends or Foes...

WORKOUT COMPLETED [ ]

The best love is the kind that awakens the
soul and makes us reach for more.
Noah, The Notebook

IMAGINATION

We have a lot of tools in our arsenal as actors but **I believe imagination is the most powerful.** "If you hook into the character's belief system and you believe it 100%, there is no way the audience won't." - Meryl Streep "Imagination is more important than knowledge for knowledge is limited. - Einstein. Everyone has an Imagination but it must be worked out to get stronger. Think of your imagination as a limitless playground. In this space, you can be anyone, go anywhere, and do anything. **Have the courage to allow yourself to play!**

Solo Imaginary World Exploration - 6 Minutes [Set Timer]

Find a quiet space to relax and focus. **Close your eyes** and **let your imagination run wild. Tip:** Engage all your senses to explore this environment. Touch, taste, smell etc. Allow your emotions to guide you. **Extra:** After you establish this world in your imagination, you could introduce characters and have a dialogue with them. Are they friends or foes?

IMAGINARY WORLD: Subterranean Crystal Caverns: Journey through caves lit by glowing crystals, holding Earth's ancient secrets.

JOURNAL YOUR EXPERIENCE - 2 Minutes [Set Timer]

_____
_____
_____
_____
_____
_____
_____

Your Characters Filter - 5 Minutes [Set Timer]

Everyone including the characters you play see the world through their own specific perspective/filter. I like to use the word filter because you can take out a filter, clean it, change its style, colour, an optimist or a pessimist, comedian or a nihilist, etc. **Find a quiet space** to focus. **Close your eyes and let go of your personal thoughts and emotions** to make space for your characters. **Open your eyes, and allow the filter provided to effect everything around you. Tip**: Explore wherever you are and interact with the objects. **Extra:** How does *this* character walk and move in their world?

FILTER: Romantic Dreamer: Views the world through a lens of love and idealism.

JOURNAL YOUR EXPERIENCE - 2 Minutes [Set Timer]

_____
_____
_____
_____
_____
_____
_____

WORKOUT COMPLETED [ ]

The crucial thing to remember as an actor is that the actor is not on stage to have an experience to expose himself to the audience, but to help tell a story.
A practical handbook for the actor

CHARACTER STUDY "PEOPLE WATCHING"

Actors are required to portray characters that are believable and relatable. You don't have to agree with them but you have to understand them. Walk like them, talk like them, see the world like them. So, in order to fill our toolbox, we have to **go out into the world and study**. Then practice them over and over so we can "walk in their shoes', comfortably and confidently. Study their movements, mannerisms, the "vibe" they give off, the clothes they wear etc. **Fill your toolbox with the rhythms and idiosyncrasies of human behaviour.**

OBSERVATION CHARACTER STUDY - 15 Minutes [Set Timer]

Find a busy place where you can **sit and observe.** Choose anyone you find interesting. **Write down what stands out about them.** *The way they sit, drink their coffee, walk, talk, interact with others etc.* **Tip**: **Mirror them immediately**. This will help memorize the feeling of that character so whenever you come back to these characters you're discovering, your body will remember. **Extra**: Before you go to sleep, read over the characters from today and reenact their movements.

_____
_____
_____
_____
_____
_____
_____
_____
_____
_____
_____
_____
_____
_____
_____
_____
_____
_____
_____
_____
_____
_____

COLOURS: We as humans respond to colours like frequencies. If you pay attention closely, you can see everyone has their own 'colour' that defines their core. An essence that informs how they operate and move through the world.

WHAT COLOUR ARE THEY:

WORKOUT COMPLETED [ ]

I'm scared of everything. I'm scared of what I saw, I'm scared of what I did, of who I am, and most of all I'm scared of walking out of this room and never feeling the rest of my whole life the way I feel when I'm with you.
Baby, Dirty Dancing

VOICE & DICTION

I wish I had learned this at the beginning of my career. The confidence to communicate clearly and powerfully is a game-changer for you as an actor. **Think of your voice as a musical instrument that needs regular tuning. This workout is your daily tuning session,** ensuring that your instrument is always ready. "The word 'theatre' comes from the Greeks. It means the seeing place. It is the place people come to see the truth about life and the social situation." - Stella Adler. Embrace this workout as a key to unlocking and portraying *that* truth by letting your voice be the vehicle that transports your audience into the heart of your story.

READ PASSAGE - 30 Seconds [Set Timer]
Speak the passage and take note of its quality. **Tip**: Record Audio to compare afterward.

> "In the tranquil garden, nature's harmony is at play. Bees buzz among flowers, water trickles in the fountain, and the air is fragrant with blooms. The beauty of growth and life is evident in every petal and leaf."

RELAXATION - 1 Minute [Set Timer]
Deep Breathing: Sit and Inhale deeply through your nose, filling your lungs, then exhale slowly through your mouth. Imagine stress leaving your body with each breath.

Nay Nay Nay - 1 Minute [Set Timer]
Pick a song and sing the word "Nay" repeatedly. Start with a comfortable pitch and gradually move the sound from your nose to your chest, ensuring each "Nay" is clear and resonant. Stretch your range as best you can to strengthen.

Sustained 'S' - 2 Minutes [Set Timer]
Inhale deeply and then exhale slowly, making a continuous 's' sound. Keep the sound as even and steady as you can. Always push a little longer than you think you can.

Vowel Pronunciation Drill - 2 Minutes [Set Timer]
Slowly go through each vowel sound **(A, E, I, O, U), holding and exaggerating each sound. Combine them with consonants** (e.g., ba, be, bi, bo, bu). Pay attention to the clarity and sharpness of each sound. Repeat a few times before moving to the next.

Lip Trills - 3 minutes - [Set timer]
Close your lips together lightly, like you're going to blow a raspberry. Then, blow air through your closed lips while making sounds. You should feel a tickling sensation. Pick a song and Lip Trill the whole along with it. **Tip**: Stretch your range as much as you can and pick a song you've never listened to.

The Cork Exercise - 4 Minutes [Set Timer]
Place a cork between your teeth and try to read a passage aloud. This forces your articulation muscles to work harder. If you don't have a cork, bite down gently on your thumb. You can use the following text for this exercise:

READ PASSAGE AGAIN - 30 Seconds [Set Timer]
Speak the passage and take note of its quality. **Tip**: Record Audio to compare.

Discovery Journal - 1 Minute [Set Timer]

WORKOUT COMPLETED [ ]

If the actor gives himself something physically doable that he has personal investment in for every scene, he will always have something more important to put his attention on than the success or failure of his own performance.
A practical handbook for the actor

SUBTEXT

Subtext is what lies beneath the surface of our words. It's the hidden layer of meaning, driven by the character's internal thoughts, emotions, desires, and motivations. Subtext is one of my favourite things as an actor because so much can be said with one simple line of dialogue. The power of "Hello" can be exciting if you told that person years ago "If I ever see you again, I'll kill you. Maybe it's the most beautiful person you've ever seen. Now, say "hello". *Subtext* shows the audience what your relationship with the characters/places/situations are, without having to explain it. We experience it every day and it is our job to create characters that interact as we do.

VOCAL WORK - 3 minutes - [Set Timer]
Lip Trills: Close your lips together lightly, like you're going to blow a raspberry. Then, blow air through your closed lips while making sounds. You should feel a tickling sensation. Pick a song and Lip Trill along with it. **Tip**: Stretch your range as much as you can and pick a song you've never listened to.

SUBTEXT PRACTICE
Use the line of dialogue provided and practice each of these subtexts **out loud.** Move on to the next, only when you believe yourself. Trust that you will know when *that* is. Before you begin, **pick a spot to look at and imagine** in detail, **who you are speaking with**. **Tip**: *Sometimes* we mean exactly what we are saying. Look for that too. **Extra**: Substitute someone you have a strong relationship with in real life, good or bad, and see it's affect.

Initial Line: "'Midnight Eclipse' announced a surprise concert in town!"
Your Response Line: "No way, 'Midnight Eclipse'? Wild. The memories... Their music was the soundtrack to our childhood. This is going to be more than just a concert. Are you thinking what I'm thinking?"

SUBTEXTS - 6 Minutes [Set Timer]
[ ] Ecstatic: You're a die-hard fan and this is a dream come true.
[ ] Bitter: You associate the band with a painful breakup.
[ ] Disbelieving: You find it hard to believe they're as good as they used to be.
[ ] Wistful: Their music reminds you of lost youth and unfulfilled dreams.
[ ] Energized: You're ready to relive and recreate those wild days.
[ ] Your Own Subtext

RELATIONSHIP SUBTEXTS - 6 Minutes [Set Timer]
[ ] The Old Gang Member: Planning to reunite the crew for one more wild night.
[ ] The Ex who shared your love for the band, stirring up mixed emotions.
[ ] The Newer Friend who doesn't understand your obsession with the band.
[ ] The Sibling you lost touch with but always went to concerts with.
[ ] The Co-worker who always argued about the band's legacy.
[ ] Your Own Subtext

Discovery Journal

___

WORKOUT COMPLETED [ ]

The thrill of acting is making a character real. Acting is a form of confession.
Tallulah Bankhead

EMOTIONS

The 'moment before', **the emotional preparation, is the most important key to a great scene.** If you start any scene <u>without</u> an emotional preparation it feels like trying to drive a car in neutral. The preparation is the uphill climb of every rollercoaster; Once you grind all the way to the top, the chains let go and the rest of the ride takes care of itself. "No one wants to see a play or a movie and look at technical proficiency. You want to be moved, you want a human experience, you want to feel less alone" - Viola Davis. **Practice your emotions over and over** so when it's time, you aren't worried "Will I get there?" **You're imagination and emotions should be a tinderbox, so easy to light up. All it take is half a spark.**

EULOGY - 12 Minutes [Set Timer]

Find a quiet comfortable space. Choose someone in your life who is alive and important to you. Create an imaginary reason for why they have died. Now start from the point of the phone call— Imagine who calls, what they say and what you say. Eventually find yourself at the funeral, about to begin the eulogy. See the casket, is it open or closed?? What is that person wearing and any other details for yourself. Before you begin to speak, look into the audience and see who is there- Family, friends etc **Then begin the eulogy. Tip:** <u>Be as specific as you can with everything</u>. **Inside of specificity is where you will find the triggers to your heart.** Let your imagination take you wherever you want in this exercise. **Example:** Placing her favourite sheep stuffed animal in the casket, tucked under her arm like she always held it, then kissing her goodbye one last time.

DISCOVERY JOURNAL - 3 Minutes [Set Timer]

Make sure to **include the specific triggers** you experience because you can use these **TRIGGER MOMENTS** in the future instead of repeating the *entire* exercise.

___
___
___
___
___
___
___
___
___
___
___
___
___
___
___
___
___
___
___

WORKOUT COMPLETED [ ]

Stay hungry for knowledge and always seek to expand your skills. The more you learn, the more versatile you become.
Mahershala Ali

THE CORK EXERCISE - 4 Minutes [Set Timer]
Place a cork between your teeth and read a passage aloud. This forces your articulation muscles to work harder. If you don't have a cork, bite down gently on your thumb. You can use the following text for this exercise:

> "In the bustling train station, travellers rush by, each on their own journey. The echo of announcements fills the air, alongside the rhythmic clatter of trains arriving and departing, a testament to the constant motion of life."

WRITE A LETTER - 10 Minutes [Set Timer]
Get a piece of paper or write this in your device. **Take a moment** to let this situation and relationship sink in. Then let your imagination run wild and **write them a letter.**

Your Character: Michael, a dedicated firefighter who has always put his job first.
Other Character: Sarah, Michael's estranged wife, left after years of struggling with the dangers and uncertainties of Michael's profession.

Relationship: Michael and Sarah's marriage was once filled with love and mutual support, but the constant stress and fear brought on by Michael's job began to erode their relationship. Sarah's decision to leave was a wake-up call for Michael, bringing to light the personal sacrifices he had made for his career.

Context of the Letter: Faced with the reality of losing Sarah and reflecting on the toll his career has taken on their life together, Michael writes a letter to Sarah. This letter is an emotional blend of regret, understanding, and a plea for reconciliation. It's Michael's attempt to express his love for Sarah, acknowledge the pain his career has caused, and express his willingness to find a balance between his duty and their relationship.

Discovery Journal - 1 minute [Set Timer]

_____
_____
_____
_____
_____
_____
_____

WORKOUT COMPLETED [ ]

Acting is standing up naked and turning around very slowly.
Rosalind Russell

VOCAL WORK - 3 minutes [Set timer]

Lip Trills: Close your lips together lightly, like you're going to blow a raspberry. Then, blow air through your closed lips while making sounds. You should feel a tickling sensation. Pick a song and Lip Trill along with it. **Tip**: Stretch your range as much as you can and pick a song you've never listened to.

VERBAL IMPROV - 10 Minutes [Set Timer]

Find a space where you are comfortable and free to express yourself. Take a moment to **let this situation, character and prompt, sink in**. Then let your imagination run wild: **Picture who you are talking to** then **begin with *the prompt*** and **continue to verbalize everything** this character would say. **Tip**: This is exploration! There is no "getting it right". BE BRAVE to explore and discover.

Character: Jordan, a compassionate social worker, has just discovered that their roommate, Taylor, who is generally kind-hearted but impulsive, has been engaging in online scams. This revelation is deeply troubling for Jordan, especially since their own family was financially devastated by a similar scam in the past.

Prompt: "Taylor, I found out about the online scams you're involved in. We need to discuss this immediately."

Who are you talking to:

Describe them in two specific words:

Discovery Journal - 2 minutes [Set Timer]

_____
_____
_____
_____
_____
_____
_____
_____

WORKOUT COMPLETED [ ]

Acting is really about having the courage to fail in front of people.
Adam Driver

SELF AWARENESS

The more you understand yourself, the more you are able to understand and develop your characters. Like you, your characters have thoughts, beliefs, traumas, passions etc. When you become aware of your own and start to see how those experiences and beliefs have shaped your life, how you operate and view the world, then you can develop your characters that are much more rich and vivid.

PHYSICAL WARMUP - 2 minutes [Set Timer]

Freeform Dance: Put on some music and engage in freeform dancing. Allow your body to move spontaneously and without inhibition. This can help you tap into your creative instincts and develop physical expressiveness. **Tip**: Try music you've never listened to.

CURRENT EMOTIONAL INVENTORY - 3 Minutes [Set Timer]

Write down and **record your current emotions**. Identify what you're feeling at this moment and why. **Tip**: Be as specific as you can, **don't disregard anything.** You can also **scan your body** to see how and where your current emotion is affecting you. Your posture, the way you walk, bouncing foot, sore neck etc

CURRENT EMOTIONAL STATE:

SELF DISCOVERY QUESTIONS - 10 Minutes [Set Timer]

I suggest a journal or writing it in your phone's notes so you don't run out of space here.

What are my thoughts on spirituality or religion?

When someone has a strong, opposing view, what happens?

WORKOUT COMPLETED [ ]

The vision of a champion is bent over, drenched in sweat, at the point of exhaustion, when nobody else is looking.
Mia Hamm

IMAGINATION

We have a lot of tools in our arsenal as actors but I believe imagination is the most powerful. "If you hook into the character's belief system and you believe it 100%, there is no way the audience won't." - Meryl Streep. Everyone has an Imagination but it must be worked out to get stronger. Think of your imagination as a limitless playground. In this space, you can be anyone, go anywhere, and do anything. **Have the courage to allow yourself to play!**

VOCAL WORK - 2 Minutes - [Set timer]
Lip Trills: Close your lips together lightly, like you're going to blow a raspberry. Then, blow air through your closed lips while making sounds. You should feel a tickling sensation. Pick a song and Lip Trill along with it. **Tip**: Stretch your range as much as you can and pick a song you've never listened to.

IMPROVISED STORYTELLING - 5 Minutes [Set Timer]
Speak out the scenario provided and continue the story! Focus on vivid details, character development and how the main character overcomes the main obstacle. **Tip**: Try not to stop speaking so you don't have time to "think". Allow your imagination to keep moving forward without interruption. **Tip:** Record these stories on your device, in case it's great but more importantly to see your progress as you go on.

STARTING POINT: You are Riley, a conservator at a local museum, who uncovers a hidden compartment in a centuries-old painting during restoration. Inside, you find a mysterious locket containing—

IMAGINARY WORLD EXPLORATION - 6 Minutes [Set Timer]

Find a quiet space to relax and focus. **Close your eyes** and let your imagination run wild. **Tip:** Engage all your senses to explore this environment. Touch, taste, smell etc and allow your emotions to guide you. **Extra:** After you explore this world with your senses, you could introduce characters and have a dialogue with them. Are they friends or foes?

IMAGINARY WORLD: WHISPERING SAND DUNES - A desert of endless sand dunes where the gentle whispers of the wind seem to carry ancient secrets. The vast, untouched landscape invokes a sense of solitude and wonder.

JOURNAL YOUR EXPERIENCE - 2 Minutes [Set Timer]
_____
_____
_____
_____
_____
_____
_____
_____

WORKOUT COMPLETED [ ]

The gratification comes in the doing,
not in the results.
James Dean

ANCHORING INTO YOUR CHARACTER COLOUR & MUSIC

Anchoring yourself into your character is vital. It's one of the most freeing feelings when you understand their *essence* because everything they do, how they do it and what their purpose is, becomes so clear to you and the audience. Every choice you make after you find your *anchor*, feels easy, because you're acting from who and what your character is at the core. You can call it an essence, an aura, vibe, energy etc. We all have it and feel it from everyone around us. There are many ways into your character but music and colour are my favourite. Music can inform the script, your character, even each scene. Colours, I think you will find, can work incredibly because we as humans respond to colours like frequencies. Colours evoke many feelings and if you pay attention closely, you can see everyone has their own 'colour' that defines their core. An essence that informs how they operate and move through the world.

THEIR COLOUR - 2 Minutes [Set Timer]
Think of **someone you know**, and **define them with a colour**. **Tip**: Trust yourself. Your initial colour is usually close. **Tip**: Start with basic colours then eventually become much more specific. **Example**: Corinna is an earthy green with rays of sunlight flowing through the green. **Extra**: Ask someone who knows *that person* as well, what they think this person's colour is and why. See how close your answers are or not.

YOUR CHARACTERS COLOUR
Read the given character description just as you would an audition, **assign a colour to that character.** Now take that colour you chose and **allow it to infuse into your entire body**, affecting your every move, your speaking, the way you see the world etc. **Take any book** you have, flip to a random page and **read the text as this Colour/Character**. **Tip**: Be specific, choose a colour that excites you and don't be afraid to get creative.

CHARACTER DESCRIPTION: [CAMERON] Cameron is an enigmatic cybersecurity expert, working in a high-tech, secure office filled with multiple monitors and state-of-the-art equipment. They dress in smart casual attire, often with a hint of tech wear, like a smartwatch or augmented reality glasses. Cameron's job involves protecting sensitive data from cyber threats, requiring a blend of technical genius, strategic thinking, and a constant awareness of evolving digital dangers. Despite their expertise in the digital realm, Cameron is reserved and enigmatic, preferring to let their work speak for itself. Their character is a juxtaposition of a reserved personality and a high-stakes drive.

CHOOSE THEIR COLOUR - 4 Minutes [Set Timer]
THEIR COLOUR:

CHOOSE THEIR SONG - 4 Minutes [Set Timer]
THEIR SONG:

READ PASSAGE FROM BOOK - 2 Minutes [Set Timer]

FREEFORM DANCE - 2 minutes - [Set Timer]
Put on the selected music and **engage in freeform dancing, anchored in your colour/character,** Allow your body to move spontaneously and without inhibition. This can help you tap into your creative instincts and develop physical expressiveness *while staying in character.* **Tip**: Journal about the differences as opposed to how you normally dance.

JOURNAL YOUR EXPERIENCE - 1 Minute [Set Timer]

WORKOUT COMPLETED [ ]

Preparing to do the thing isn't doing the thing. Scheduling time to do the thing isn't doing the thing. Making a to-do list for the thing isn't doing the thing. Telling people you're going to do the thing isn't doing the thing. Messaging friends who may or may not be doing the thing isn't doing the thing. Writing a banger tweet about how you're going to do the thing isn't doing the thing. Hating on yourself for not doing the thing isn't doing the thing. Hating on other people who have done the thing isn't doing the thing. Hating on the obstacles in the way of doing the thing isn't doing the thing. Fantasizing about all of the adoration you'll receive once you do the thing isn't doing the thing. Reading about how to do the thing isn't doing the thing. Reading about how other people did the thing isn't doing the thing. Reading this essay isn't doing the thing. The only thing that is doing the thing is doing the thing.

StrangestLoop.io

RESEARCH

We are in the information era and have access to the world and its rich history at our fingertips. This exploration is not about 'learning facts'; it's a journey to the heart of human experience. The empathy and the understanding, especially on the things you disagree with, are incredibly valuable. If you look closely, you'll find the way people think, at different times in history, their attitudes, choices, and the way they move their bodies can teach you so much about us, right now. Fill your toolbox so it's overflowing with information and ideas to pull from so your imagination has so much to play with.

PHYSICAL WARMUP - 2 minutes - [Set Timer]
Freeform Dance: Put on some music and engage in freeform dancing. Allow your body to move spontaneously and without inhibition. This can help you tap into your creative instincts and develop physical expressiveness. **Tip**: Try music you've never listened to.

RESEARCH - 13 Minutes [Set Timer]
YouTube, streaming platforms, the internet or books, **research the given era/person/moment in time,** journal or make notes on your device, so when you want to find this information, it's organized and readily accessible. As you go, **write anything and everything _you_ find fascinating. Tip:** If the topic doesn't interest you, choose your own, or take a chance and still research it, but from a different perspective. Physicalities, voice, ideals, etc. Trust your body that when you see something interesting, you'll know. **Extra**: Speak it out and copy their movements. Our memory recall is massively affected by our bodies. Be specific and when you re-read your notes, you'll be amazed by how much your mind and body remember.

TOPIC:
Vaslav Nijinsky (1889-1950): A Russian ballet dancer and choreographer of Polish descent, Nijinsky was one of the most gifted male dancers in history, known for his virtuosity and the intensity of his characterizations. He could perform seemingly impossible leaps, and his ability to portray complex characters on stage was unparalleled. Unfortunately, his career was cut short by early-onset schizophrenia. While there is limited film footage of Nijinsky, photographs and written accounts from contemporaries provide a glimpse into his extraordinary talent and the eccentricity that marked both his performances and personal life.

WORKOUT COMPLETED [ ]

Creating a character is about what they think, not what they look like.
Viola Davis

BELIEF

Beliefs are the convictions that something exists or is true, especially without proof. That is also the definition of what we do as actors. We play make-believe. Our beliefs shape our world, especially our beliefs about ourselves and it works for the characters you play. Understand your beliefs and how they influence your mind, body and spirit, then you will be able to better understand others, so you can embody them. Allow the beliefs of your character to colour your perception of your world and your interaction with everything in it. "Acting is the best magic trick in the world. We applaud performances not because it's real, but because you made us believe."

VOCAL WORK - 2 Minutes - [Set timer]

Lip Trills: Close your lips together lightly, like you're going to blow a raspberry. Then, blow air through your closed lips while making sounds. You should feel a tickling sensation. Pick a song and Lip Trill along with it. **Tip:** Stretch your range as much as you can and pick a song you've never listened to.

BELIEF WORKOUT

Get your journal or write in here. **Define your personal belief/view** on the given subject. **Grab any book you own,** flip to a random page and **read it out loud,** colouring the words and intention with your belief system. **Tip:** Write trigger words you can hook into in the future: **Optimism-** Always smiling, grateful, opportunity, sunshine yellow.

YOUR PERSONAL BELIEF

Clothing & Style- 7 Minutes [Set Timer]

_____
_____
_____
_____

READ WITH BELIEF - 2 Minutes [Set Timer]

CHARACTERS BELIEF

Clothing & Style

Clothing is a second skin. It's how the world takes you in and is the first thing people see before they get to know you. Have some respect for who you are and take pride in discovering "your style"

READ WITH CHARACTERS BELIEF - 2 Minutes [Set Timer]
Forget your personal view and **fully embrace the character's belief. Read out loud again.**

JOURNAL YOUR EXPERIENCE - 2 Minutes [Set Timer]

_____
_____
_____
_____

WORKOUT COMPLETED [ ]

PERFORMANCE STRATEGY
14 DAY REVIEW

TAKE A MOMENT OF REFLECTION AND BREAKDOWN WHERE YOU ARE RIGHT NOW IN YOUR CAREER AND AS AN ACTOR. THE MORE SPECIFIC YOU ARE THE MORE CLEAR YOU CAN SEE WHERE YOU ARE NOW SO YOU CAN GET TO WHERE YOU WANT TO GO FASTER

★ ★ ★ ★ ★

J.K. Simmons: Known for years as a character actor, Simmons achieved mainstream success relatively late in his career, winning an Oscar for "Whiplash."

DATE:

MY WHY
WHY ARE YOU DOING WHAT YOU ARE DOING
BE SPECIFIC

MY MAIN GOALS
IN-ORDER OF IMPORTANCE

1.

   Action Step(s):

2.

   Action Step(s):

3.

   Action Step(s):

FROM THE LAST 14 DAYS
5 STAR RATING

☆☆☆☆☆

YOUR KEY POINTS AND TAKEAWAYS - WHY THAT AMOUNT OF STAR RATING, LIKES, DISLIKES, THE BIGGEST LESSON YOU LEARNED, GOOD OR BAD:

STRENGTHS:

WEAKNESSES:

IMPROVEMENT STRATEGY
HOW CAN YOU IMPROVE ON THESE AREAS FOR THE NEXT 14 DAYS:

GOAL FROM LAST :
DID YOU ACHIEVE IT?

WHY OR WHY NOT?

GOAL FOR THE NEXT 14 EXERCISES
THE MORE SPECIFIC YOU ARE THE GREATER THE RESULT

   Action Step(s):

Theatre is a sacred space for actors. You are responsible; you are in the driving-seat.
Greta Scacchi

MY WHY:

GOAL(s):

PHYSICAL WARMUP - 1 minute [Set Timer]
Colour Dance:
Choose a colour and dance how it makes you feel. Let the colour's energy guide your movement. **Tip:** Visualize the colour radiating from your body as you dance.

VOCAL WORK - 3 minutes [Set Timer]
Humming Slides: Start with a comfortable pitch, and hum gently, sliding up and down through your range. Feel the vibration in your chest, lips, and head. **Tip**: Keep it smooth, like a siren going up and down.

EMOTIONAL RECALL - 5 minutes [Set Timer]
Suffocating Guilt: Access a memory where guilt was overwhelming. Speak the apologies or confessions you held back. **Tip**: Feel the weight lift as you express these words now.

ANIMAL WORK - SLOTH
Research - 2 minutes [Set Timer]
Observe the sloth's leisurely pace and deliberate movements.

Animal Exercise - 3 minutes [Set Timer]
Move with extreme slowness, conserving energy and being intentional with every gesture. **Tip:** Patience is your virtue; every move is calculated.

Discovery Journal - 1 Minute [Set Timer]
3 Main Characteristics: (Whatever stands out to YOU to embody the essence)

_____
_____
_____
_____
_____
_____
_____
_____

WORKOUT COMPLETED [ ]

To be a good actor you have to be something like a criminal, to be willing to break the rules to strive for something new.
Nicolas Cage

SCRIPT ANALYSIS for **RELATIONSHIPS & SPECIFICITY** - 15 minutes [Set Timer]
Choose your character, circle everything in this script you have a relationship with. Including people, places, things, smells, time of day etc. **Write what your relationship with those items are** and **be specific**. The more specific and fun you have with your relationships, the more interesting your characters will be and the more fun the audience has. **Tip:** Everything isn't in the scene. Use your imagination to create details, only if it's contextually appropriate. **Extra:** Write your > ***Objective, win or lose? Consequence of failing?*** The ***Who What Where When Why.***

Title: **Crossroads of Destiny**
INT. ABANDONED WAREHOUSE - NIGHT
An expansive, derelict warehouse, dimly lit, flickering lights. EDDIE and SARAH stand amidst crates and shadows. The air is thick with tension.

EDDIE
What are we doing here, Sarah?
SARAH
We have to talk. About—
EDDIE
No. We don't.
SARAH
I can't sleep. I can't eat. I need to talk—
Eddie grabs her by the arms and gets face to face.
EDDIE
Have you told anyone? Have you?!
SARAH
No.
EDDIE
Good. Because...Well, you know what will happen if you do.
SARAH
Jake, knows.
EDDIE
What!? How? Did you tell him?
SARAH
No! He was there. He saw it all.
Eddie lets her go and realizes...
SARAH(cont'd)
What do we do? I can't go to jail, Eddie... I can't!
EDDIE
Shut up. Obviously you're useless, so I will take care of it. Don't talk to anyone. Do you understand? Do. You. Understand?
SARAH
Yes... Thank you, Eddie.
EDDIE
This was your idea.
SARAH
I know, I didn't think...
Eddie doesn't give a shit and walks out, leaving Sarah in her regret.
SARAH
I'm sorry.

WORKOUT COMPLETED [ ]

The actor is the athlete of the heart.
Antonin Artaud

IMAGINATION

We have a lot of tools in our arsenal as actors but **I believe imagination is the most powerful.** "If you hook into the character's belief system and you believe it 100%, there is no way the audience won't." - Meryl Streep "Imagination is more important than knowledge for knowledge is limited. - Einstein. Everyone has an Imagination but it must be worked out to get stronger. Think of your imagination as a limitless playground. In this space, you can be anyone, go anywhere, and do anything. **Have the courage to allow yourself to play!**

Solo Imaginary World Exploration - 6 Minutes [Set Timer]

Find a quiet space to relax and focus. **Close your eyes** and **let your imagination run wild. Tip:** Engage all your senses to explore this environment. Touch, taste, smell etc. Allow your emotions to guide you. **Extra:** After you establish this world in your imagination, you could introduce characters and have a dialogue with them. Are they friends or foes?

IMAGINARY WORLD: Ancient Tree City: Discover a hidden civilization within a colossal tree's branches.

JOURNAL YOUR EXPERIENCE - 2 Minutes [Set Timer]

_____
_____
_____
_____
_____
_____

Your Characters Filter - 5 Minutes [Set Timer]

Everyone including the characters you play see the world through their own specific perspective/filter. I like to use the word filter because you can take out a filter, clean it, change its style, colour, an optimist or a pessimist, comedian or a nihilist, etc. **Find a quiet space** to focus. **Close your eyes and let go of your personal thoughts and emotions** to make space for your characters. **Open your eyes, and allow the filter provided to effect everything around you. Tip:** Explore wherever you are and interact with the objects. **Extra:** How does *this* character walk and move in their world?

FILTER: Jaded Nihilist: Believes in the ultimate meaninglessness of life.

JOURNAL YOUR EXPERIENCE - 2 Minutes [Set Timer]

_____
_____
_____
_____
_____
_____
_____

WORKOUT COMPLETED [ ]

I'll tell you where big dreams go to die. They go to the planning place. Getting ready place. Preparing myself. It's the biggest con-job we work on ourselves.
There's always a set of reasons to wait. Make your move before youre ready.
Price Pritchett

CHARACTER STUDY "PEOPLE WATCHING"

Actors are required to portray characters that are believable and relatable. You don't have to agree with them but you have to understand them. Walk like them, talk like them, see the world like them. So, in order to fill our toolbox, we have to **go out into the world and study**. Then practice them over and over so we can "walk in their shoes', comfortably and confidently. Study their movements, mannerisms, the "vibe" they give off, the clothes they wear etc. **Fill your toolbox with the rhythms and idiosyncrasies of human behaviour.**

OBSERVATION CHARACTER STUDY - 15 Minutes [Set Timer]

Find a busy place where you can **sit and observe.** Choose anyone you find interesting. **Write down what stands out about them.** *The way they sit, drink their coffee, walk, talk, interact with others etc.* **Tip**: **Mirror them immediately.** This will help memorize the feeling of that character so whenever you come back to these characters you're discovering, your body will remember. **Extra**: Before you go to sleep, read over the characters from today and reenact their movements.

_____
_____
_____
_____
_____
_____
_____
_____
_____
_____
_____
_____
_____
_____
_____
_____
_____
_____
_____

COLOURS: We as humans respond to colours like frequencies. If you pay attention closely, you can see everyone has their own 'colour' that defines their core. An essence that informs how they operate and move through the world.

WHAT COLOUR ARE THEY:

WORKOUT COMPLETED [ ]

The stage is not merely the meeting place of all the arts, but is also the return of art to life.
Oscar Wilde

VOICE & DICTION

I wish I had learned this at the beginning of my career. The confidence to communicate clearly and powerfully is a game-changer for you as an actor. **Think of your voice as a musical instrument that needs regular tuning. This workout is your daily tuning session,** ensuring that your instrument is always ready. "The word 'theatre' comes from the Greeks. It means the seeing place. It is the place people come to see the truth about life and the social situation." - Stella Adler. Embrace this workout as a key to unlocking and portraying *that* truth by letting your voice be the vehicle that transports your audience into the heart of your story.

READ PASSAGE - 30 Seconds [Set Timer]
Speak the passage and take note of it's quality. **Tip**: Record Audio to compare afterward.

> "A mystical forest shrouded in mystery. Ancient trees stand tall, their leaves whispering secrets of old, and the moss-covered ground tells tales of mystical creatures that roam in the moonlight."

RELAXATION - 1 Minute [Set Timer]
Deep Breathing: Sit and Inhale deeply through your nose, filling your lungs, then exhale slowly through your mouth. Imagine stress leaving your body with each breath.

Nay Nay Nay - 1 Minute [Set Timer]
Pick a song and sing the word "Nay" repeatedly. Start with a comfortable pitch and gradually move the sound from your nose to your chest, ensuring each "Nay" is clear and resonant. Stretch your range as best you can to strengthen.

Sustained 'S' - 2 Minutes [Set Timer]
Inhale deeply and then exhale slowly, making a continuous 's' sound. Keep the sound as even and steady as you can. Always push a little longer than you think you can.

Vowel Pronunciation Drill - 2 Minutes [Set Timer]
Slowly go through each vowel sound **(A, E, I, O, U), holding and exaggerating each sound. Combine them with consonants** (e.g., ba, be, bi, bo, bu). Pay attention to the clarity and sharpness of each sound. Repeat a few times before moving to the next.

Lip Trills - 3 minutes - [Set timer]
Close your lips together lightly, like you're going to blow a raspberry. Then, blow air through your closed lips while making sounds. You should feel a tickling sensation. Pick a song and Lip Trill the whole along with it. **Tip**: Stretch your range as much as you can and pick a song you've never listened to.

The Cork Exercise - 4 Minutes [Set Timer]
Place a cork between your teeth and try to read a passage aloud. This forces your articulation muscles to work harder. If you don't have a cork, bite down gently on your thumb. You can use the following text for this exercise:

READ PASSAGE AGAIN - 30 Seconds [Set Timer]
Speak the passage and take note of its quality. **Tip**: Record Audio to compare.

Discovery Journal - 1 Minute [Set Timer]

WORKOUT COMPLETED [ ]

Acting is all about honesty. When I'm not being honest, I'm just acting.
George Burns

SUBTEXT

Subtext is what lies beneath the surface of our words. It's the hidden layer of meaning, driven by the character's internal thoughts, emotions, desires, and motivations. Subtext is one of my favourite things as an actor because so much can be said with one simple line of dialogue. The power of "Hello" can be exciting if you told that person years ago "If I ever see you again, I'll kill you. Maybe it's the most beautiful person you've ever seen. Now, say "hello". *Subtext* shows the audience what your relationship with the characters/places/situations are, without having to explain it. We experience it every day and it is our job to create characters that interact as we do.

VOCAL WORK - 3 minutes - [Set Timer]
Lip Trills: Close your lips together lightly, like you're going to blow a raspberry. Then, blow air through your closed lips while making sounds. You should feel a tickling sensation. Pick a song and Lip Trill along with it. **Tip**: Stretch your range as much as you can and pick a song you've never listened to.

SUBTEXT PRACTICE
Use the line of dialogue provided and practice each of these subtexts **out loud.** Move on to the next, only when you believe yourself. Trust that you will know when *that* is. Before you begin, **pick a spot to look at and imagine** in detail, **who you are speaking with. Tip**: *Sometimes* we mean exactly what we are saying. Look for that too. **Extra**: Substitute someone you have a strong relationship with in real life, good or bad, and see it's affect.

Initial Line: "How are you?"
Your Response Line: "Good. It's been a rollercoaster lately. Same old, same old. How about you? What's new on your end?"

SUBTEXTS - 6 Minutes [Set Timer]
[ ] Overwhelmed: You're juggling too much and feel like you're barely keeping up.
[ ] Reflective: You're in a period of introspection and personal growth.
[ ] Secret: You've won the lottery and you don't want anyone to know.
[ ] Hopeful: Despite challenges, you're optimistic about what's ahead.
[ ] Discontent: You're dissatisfied with how things are going in your life.
[ ] Your Own Subtext

RELATIONSHIP SUBTEXTS - 6 Minutes [Set Timer]
[ ] The Old Friend: You've shared everything but now feel distant.
[ ] The Concerned Family Member: They always worry and hover more than you'd like.
[ ] The Ex-Partner: There's unresolved tension and unspoken words between you.
[ ] The New Colleague: Trying to make a good impression while being authentic.
[ ] The Neighbor You Secretly Admire: You're trying to seem okay when you're not.
[ ] Your Own Subtext

Discovery Journal

_____
_____
_____
_____

WORKOUT COMPLETED [ ]

Movies will make you famous;
Television will make you rich; But
theatre will make you good.
Terrence Mann

EMOTIONS

The 'moment before', **the emotional preparation, is the most important key to a great scene.** If you start any scene *without* an emotional preparation it feels like trying to drive a car in neutral. The preparation is the uphill climb of every rollercoaster; Once you grind all the way to the top, the chains let go and the rest of the ride takes care of itself. "No one wants to see a play or a movie and look at technical proficiency. You want to be moved, you want a human experience, you want to feel less alone" - Viola Davis. **Practice your emotions over and over** so when it's time, you aren't worried "Will I get there?" **You're imagination and emotions should be a tinderbox, so easy to light up. All it take is half a spark.**

EULOGY - 12 Minutes [Set Timer]

Find a quiet comfortable space. Choose someone in your life who is alive and important to you. Create an imaginary reason for why they have died. Now start from the point of the phone call— Imagine who calls, what they say and what you say. Eventually find yourself at the funeral, about to begin the eulogy. See the casket, is it open or closed?? What is that person wearing and any other details for yourself. Before you begin to speak, look into the audience and see who is there- Family, friends etc **Then begin the eulogy. Tip:** Be as specific as you can with everything. **Inside of specificity is where you will find the triggers to your heart.** Let your imagination take you wherever you want in this exercise. **Example**: Placing her favourite sheep stuffed animal in the casket, tucked under her arm like she always held it, then kissing her goodbye one last time.

DISCOVERY JOURNAL - 3 Minutes [Set Timer]

Make sure to **include the specific triggers** you experience because you can use these **TRIGGER MOMENTS** in the future instead of repeating the *entire* exercise.

WORKOUT COMPLETED [ ]

I steal from every movie ever made.
Quentin Tarantino

THE CORK EXERCISE - 4 Minutes [Set Timer]
Place a cork between your teeth and read a passage aloud. This forces your articulation muscles to work harder. If you don't have a cork, bite down gently on your thumb. You can use the following text for this exercise:

> "As the sun sets, the beach is bathed in a warm, amber glow. Waves gently kiss the shore, leaving patterns on the sand. Families pack up their picnics, and children's laughter fades into the twilight."

WRITE A LETTER - 10 Minutes [Set Timer]
Get a piece of paper or write this in your device. **Take a moment** to let this situation and relationship sink in. Then let your imagination run wild and **write them a letter.**

Your Character: Emily, a successful gallery owner with a passion for art and a keen eye for talent.
Other Character: Ryan, Emily's former partner and acclaimed artist, betrayed Emily by having an affair with a mutual friend, leading to a public scandal.

Relationship: Emily and Ryan's relationship was not just romantic; it was a creative partnership that blended love with a shared dedication to the art world. Emily played a crucial role in Ryan's rise to fame, and their bond seemed unbreakable until Ryan's infidelity turned their personal and professional lives upside down.

Context of the Letter: In the aftermath of the scandal and the end of their relationship, Emily is left to deal with both the emotional heartbreak and the professional repercussions. She writes a letter to Ryan as a way to confront the betrayal, express her profound sense of loss and disillusionment, and seek understanding of why Ryan destroyed the beautiful life and partnership they had built together.

Discovery Journal - 1 minute [Set Timer]

_____
_____
_____
_____
_____
_____

WORKOUT COMPLETED [ ]

The actor should be able to create
the universe in the palm of his hand.
Laurence Olivier

VOCAL WORK - 3 minutes [Set timer]
Lip Trills: Close your lips together lightly, like you're going to blow a raspberry. Then, blow air through your closed lips while making sounds. You should feel a tickling sensation. Pick a song and Lip Trill along with it. **Tip**: Stretch your range as much as you can and pick a song you've never listened to.

VERBAL IMPROV - 10 Minutes [Set Timer]

Find a space where you are comfortable and free to express yourself. Take a moment to **let this situation, character and prompt, sink in**. Then let your imagination run wild: **Picture who you are talking to** then **begin with *the prompt*** and **continue to verbalize everything** this character would say. **Tip**: This is exploration! There is no "getting it right". BE BRAVE to explore and discover.

Character: Chris, known for their level-headedness and empathy, has recently found out that their longtime neighbour and friend, Alex, has been involved in a hit-and-run accident. This news is particularly distressing as Chris's family member was once a victim of a similar incident.

Prompt: "Alex, I can't ignore what I've heard about the accident. We need to talk about it right away."

Who are you talking to:

Describe them in two specific words:

Discovery Journal - 2 minutes [Set Timer]

_____
_____
_____
_____
_____
_____
_____
_____
_____
_____

WORKOUT COMPLETED [ ]

An actor must never be afraid to make
a fool of himself.
Harvey Cocks

SELF AWARENESS

The more you understand yourself, the more you are able to understand and develop your characters. Like you, your characters have thoughts, beliefs, traumas, passions etc. When you become aware of your own and start to see how those experiences and beliefs have shaped your life, how you operate and view the world, then you can develop your characters that are much more rich and vivid.

PHYSICAL WARMUP - 2 minutes [Set Timer]
Freeform Dance: Put on some music and engage in freeform dancing. Allow your body to move spontaneously and without inhibition. This can help you tap into your creative instincts and develop physical expressiveness. **Tip**: Try music you've never listened to.

CURRENT EMOTIONAL INVENTORY - 3 Minutes [Set Timer]
Write down and **record your current emotions**. Identify what you're feeling at this moment and why. **Tip**: Be as specific as you can, **don't disregard anything.** You can also **scan your body** to see how and where your current emotion is affecting you. Your posture, the way you walk, bouncing foot, sore neck etc

CURRENT EMOTIONAL STATE:

SELF DISCOVERY QUESTIONS - 10 Minutes [Set Timer]
I suggest a journal or writing it in your phone's notes so you don't run out of space here.

What makes me feel fulfilled or satisfied? (Extra: Relive that feeling and how does it affect your body)

How do I handle change or uncertainty? (Extra: Write down an example of when this happened, what you did and how it made you feel)

WORKOUT COMPLETED [ ]

The best actors instinctively feel out what the other actors need, and they just accommodate it.
Christopher Nolan

IMAGINATION

We have a lot of tools in our arsenal as actors but I believe imagination is the most powerful. "If you hook into the character's belief system and you believe it 100%, there is no way the audience won't." - Meryl Streep. Everyone has an Imagination but it must be worked out to get stronger. Think of your imagination as a limitless playground. In this space, you can be anyone, go anywhere, and do anything. **Have the courage to allow yourself to play!**

VOCAL WORK - 2 Minutes - [Set timer]
Lip Trills: Close your lips together lightly, like you're going to blow a raspberry. Then, blow air through your closed lips while making sounds. You should feel a tickling sensation. Pick a song and Lip Trill along with it. **Tip**: Stretch your range as much as you can and pick a song you've never listened to.

IMPROVISED STORYTELLING - 5 Minutes [Set Timer]
Speak out the scenario provided and continue the story! Focus on vivid details, character development and how the main character overcomes the main obstacle. **Tip**: Try not to stop speaking so you don't have time to "think". Allow your imagination to keep moving forward without interruption. **Tip:** Record these stories on your device, in case it's great but more importantly to see your progress as you go on.

STARTING POINT: You are Charlie, a seasoned lighthouse keeper, who discovers an old, sealed bottle washed up on the shore near the lighthouse. Inside the bottle is a letter, but — It's being written in real-time. The person is apparently trapped and explaining how to get where they are. You begin your journey to rescue them!

IMAGINARY WORLD EXPLORATION - 6 Minutes [Set Timer]

Find a quiet space to relax and focus. **Close your eyes** and let your imagination run wild. **Tip:** Engage all your senses to explore this environment. Touch, taste, smell etc and allow your emotions to guide you. **Extra:** After you explore this world with your senses, you could introduce characters and have a dialogue with them. Are they friends or foes?

IMAGINARY WORLD: FIREFLY GROVE - A magical grove where fireflies illuminate the night with their soft, golden glow. The forest floor is carpeted with luminescent mushrooms, creating a fairy-tale ambiance.

JOURNAL YOUR EXPERIENCE - 2 Minutes [Set Timer]

_____
_____
_____
_____
_____
_____
_____

WORKOUT COMPLETED [ ]

Acting is magical. Change your look and your attitude, and you can be anyone.
Alicia Witt

ANCHORING INTO YOUR CHARACTER COLOUR & MUSIC

Anchoring yourself into your character is vital. It's one of the most freeing feelings when you understand their *essence* because everything they do, how they do it and what their purpose is, becomes so clear to you and the audience. Every choice you make after you find your *anchor*, feels easy, because you're acting from who and what your character is at the core. You can call it an essence, an aura, vibe, energy etc. We all have it and feel it from everyone around us. There are many ways into your character but music and colour are my favourite. Music can inform the script, your character, even each scene. Colours, I think you will find, can work incredibly because we as humans respond to colours like frequencies. Colours evoke many feelings and if you pay attention closely, you can see everyone has their own 'colour' that defines their core. An essence that informs how they operate and move through the world.

THEIR COLOUR - 2 Minutes [Set Timer]
Think of **someone you know**, and **define them with a colour**. **Tip**: Trust yourself. Your initial colour is usually close. **Tip**: Start with basic colours then eventually become much more specific. **Example**: Corinna is an earthy green with rays of sunlight flowing through the green. **Extra**: Ask someone who knows *that person* as well, what they think this person's colour is and why. See how close your answers are or not.

YOUR CHARACTERS COLOUR
Read the given character description just as you would an audition, **assign a colour to that character.** Now take that colour you chose and **allow it to infuse into your entire body**, affecting your every move, your speaking, the way you see the world etc. **Take any book** you have, flip to a random page and **read the text as this Colour/Character**. **Tip**: Be specific, choose a colour that excites you and don't be afraid to get creative.

CHARACTER DESCRIPTION: [DEVON] Devon is a skilled barista and coffee enthusiast, running a quaint, eclectic coffee shop in the heart of the city. Their attire is casual yet trendy, often sporting a signature apron adorned with coffee-related pins and patches. The coffee shop, filled with the aroma of freshly ground coffee, reflects Devon's passion for the craft, featuring an array of artisanal brews and a cozy, welcoming ambiance. They are an artist in their own right, known for intricate latte art and a deep knowledge of coffee varieties and brewing techniques. Devon's character combines a warm, sociable demeanour with meticulous attention to detail.

CHOOSE THEIR COLOUR - 4 Minutes [Set Timer]
THEIR COLOUR:

CHOOSE THEIR SONG - 4 Minutes [Set Timer]
THEIR SONG:

READ PASSAGE FROM BOOK - 2 Minutes [Set Timer]

FREEFORM DANCE - 2 minutes - [Set Timer]
Put on the selected music and **engage in freeform dancing, anchored in your colour/character,** Allow your body to move spontaneously and without inhibition. This can help you tap into your creative instincts and develop physical expressiveness *while staying in character.* **Tip**: Journal about the differences as opposed to how you normally dance.

JOURNAL YOUR EXPERIENCE - 1 Minute [Set Timer]

WORKOUT COMPLETED [ ]

The only thing that will stop you from
fulfilling your dreams is you.
Tom Bradley

HISTORICAL RESEARCH

We are in the information era and have access to the world and its rich history at our fingertips. This exploration is not about 'learning facts'; it's a journey to the heart of human experience. The empathy and the understanding, especially on the things you disagree with, are incredibly valuable. If you look closely, you'll find the way people think, at different times in history, their attitudes, choices, and the way they move their bodies can teach you so much about us, right now. Fill your toolbox so it's overflowing with information and ideas to pull from so your imagination has so much to play with.

PHYSICAL WARMUP - 2 minutes - [Set Timer]
Freeform Dance: Put on some music and engage in freeform dancing. Allow your body to move spontaneously and without inhibition. This can help you tap into your creative instincts and develop physical expressiveness. **Tip**: Try music you've never listened to.

RESEARCH - 13 Minutes [Set Timer]
YouTube, streaming platforms, the internet or books, **research the given era/person/moment in time,** journal or make notes on your device, so when you want to find this information, it's organized and readily accessible. As you go, **write anything and everything _you_ find fascinating. Tip:** If the topic doesn't interest you, choose your own, or take a chance and still research it, but from a different perspective. Physicalities, voice, ideals, etc. Trust your body that when you see something interesting, you'll know. **Extra**: Speak it out and copy their movements. Our memory recall is massively affected by our bodies. Be specific and when you re-read your notes, you'll be amazed by how much your mind and body remember.

TOPIC:
Amelia Earhart (1897-1937): A pioneering American aviator who became the first female pilot to fly solo across the Atlantic Ocean. Her public appearances, newsreel footage, and interviews provide a window into her adventurous spirit, determination, and the challenges she faced as a woman in a male-dominated field. Earhart's mysterious disappearance during her attempt to circumnavigate the globe remains a subject of fascination.

_____
_____
_____
_____
_____
_____
_____
_____
_____
_____
_____
_____
_____
_____
_____

WORKOUT COMPLETED [ ]

The actor's job is to reveal the soul of a character.
Forest Whitaker

BELIEF

Beliefs are the convictions that something exists or is true, especially without proof. That is also the definition of what we do as actors. We play make-believe. Our beliefs shape our world, especially our beliefs about ourselves and it works for the characters you play. Understand your beliefs and how they influence your mind, body and spirit, then you will be able to better understand others, so you can embody them. Allow the beliefs of your character to colour your perception of your world and your interaction with everything in it. "Acting is the best magic trick in the world. We applaud performances not because it's real, but because you made us believe."

VOCAL WORK - 2 Minutes - [Set timer]
Lip Trills: Close your lips together lightly, like you're going to blow a raspberry. Then, blow air through your closed lips while making sounds. You should feel a tickling sensation. Pick a song and Lip Trill along with it. **Tip**: Stretch your range as much as you can and pick a song you've never listened to.

BELIEF WORKOUT
Get your journal or write in here. **Define your personal belief/view** on the given subject. **Grab any book you own,** flip to a random page and **read it out loud,** colouring the words and intention with your belief system. **Tip**: Write trigger words you can hook into in the future: **Optimism-** Always smiling, grateful, opportunity, sunshine yellow.

YOUR PERSONAL BELIEF
Survival of the Fittest- 7 Minutes [Set Timer]

_____
_____
_____
_____

READ WITH BELIEF - 2 Minutes [Set Timer]

CHARACTERS BELIEF
Survival of the Fittest
Life is a relentless battle for dominance and survival. Like a predator in the wild, I believe in using my strengths to outmaneuver and overpower the competition. Compassion is a luxury in the face of nature's harsh realities. _Only the strongest and most ruthless thrive._

READ WITH CHARACTERS BELIEF - 2 Minutes [Set Timer]
Forget your personal view and **fully embrace the character's belief**. Read out loud again.

JOURNAL YOUR EXPERIENCE - 2 Minutes [Set Timer]

_____
_____
_____
_____

WORKOUT COMPLETED [ ]

PERFORMANCE STRATEGY

14 DAY REVIEW

TAKE A MOMENT OF REFLECTION AND BREAKDOWN WHERE YOU ARE RIGHT NOW IN YOUR CAREER AND AS AN ACTOR. THE MORE SPECIFIC YOU ARE THE MORE CLEAR YOU CAN SEE WHERE YOU ARE NOW SO YOU CAN GET TO WHERE YOU WANT TO GO FASTER

★ ★ ★ ★ ★

Jack Ma: Rejected from dozens of jobs, including KFC, he went on to found Alibaba, one of the largest e-commerce platforms in the world.

DATE:

MY WHY
WHY ARE YOU DOING WHAT YOU ARE DOING
BE SPECIFIC

MY MAIN GOALS
IN-ORDER OF IMPORTANCE

1.

   Action Step(s):

2.

   Action Step(s):

3.

   Action Step(s):

FROM THE LAST 14 DAYS ☆☆☆☆☆
5 STAR RATING

YOUR KEY POINTS AND TAKEAWAYS - WHY THAT AMOUNT OF STAR RATING, LIKES, DISLIKES, THE BIGGEST LESSON YOU LEARNED, GOOD OR BAD:

STRENGTHS:

WEAKNESSES:

IMPROVEMENT STRATEGY
HOW CAN YOU IMPROVE ON THESE AREAS FOR THE NEXT 14 DAYS:

GOAL FROM LAST :
DID YOU ACHIEVE IT?

WHY OR WHY NOT?

GOAL FOR THE NEXT 14 EXERCISES
THE MORE SPECIFIC YOU ARE THE GREATER THE RESULT

   Action Step(s):

A dream doesn't become reality through magic; it takes sweat, determination, and hard work.
Colin Powell

MY WHY:

GOAL(s):

PHYSICAL WARMUP - 1 minute [Set Timer]
Freeform Dance: Put on some music and engage in freeform dancing. Allow your body to move spontaneously and without inhibition. This can help you tap into your creative instincts and develop physical expressiveness. **Tip:** Try music you've never listened to.

VOCAL WORK - 3 minutes [Set Timer]
Fricative 'V' Sounds: Sustain a 'v' sound, feeling the buzz on your teeth and lips. Vary the pitch up and down while keeping the fricative constant. **Tip:** Keep the airflow steady for consistent vibration.

EMOTIONAL RECALL - 5 minutes [Set Timer]
Deep-seated Envy: Reflect on a time you envied someone's success or happiness. Embrace the complexity of admiring and coveting simultaneously. **Tip:** Focus on the push-pull nature of envy and aspiration.

ANIMAL WORK - BUTTERFLY
Research - 2 minutes [Set Timer]
Contemplate the butterfly's delicate flight and transformation from a caterpillar.

Animal Exercise - 3 minutes [Set Timer]
Flutter gracefully and land lightly, then carry the butterfly's elegance and beauty. **Tip:** What colours are you?

Discovery Journal - 1 Minute [Set Timer]
3 Main Characteristics: (Whatever stands out to YOU to embody the essence)

_____
_____
_____
_____
_____
_____
_____
_____

WORKOUT COMPLETED [ ]

An actor must interpret life, and in order to do so must be willing to accept all the experiences life has to offer.
James Dean

SCRIPT ANALYSIS for RELATIONSHIPS & SPECIFICITY - 15 minutes [Set Timer]
Choose your character, circle everything in this script you have a relationship with. Including people, places, things, smells, time of day etc. **Write what your relationship with those items are** and **be specific.** The more specific and fun you have with your relationships, the more interesting your characters will be and the more fun the audience has. **Tip:** Everything isn't in the scene. Use your imagination to create details, <u>only if</u> it's contextually appropriate. **Extra:** Write your > **Objective, win or lose? Consequence of failing?** The **Who What Where When Why.**

Title: Ring of Regret
INT. RUN-DOWN GYM The gym is old, dim light filters through dusty windows. VINCE (50s, a once-great boxer turned coach) sits on a bench, wrapping his knuckles. DANNY (late 20s, promising)approaches him, a sense of urgency in his step.

VINCE
You're late, Danny.
DANNY
Got held up. Things are getting complicated.
VINCE
They always are in this city. What's on your mind?
DANNY
It's Joey Morelli. He's offering me a deal.
VINCE
Morelli? That's dangerous territory. What kind of deal?
DANNY
The kind that could set me up for life. But I gotta take a dive next fight.
VINCE
You know how this goes, kid. It starts with one fight...
DANNY
I know, I know. But I got debts, Vince. I need this.
VINCE
Not *this*, you don't.
DANNY
You ain't in my shoes! You don't know what it's like.
VINCE
Old story, Kid. One I've seen over and over. I just, really hoped it wouldn't be your story.
DANNY
Yeah, well I don't want to end up like you. Has-been tryin' to ride on my tail.
VINCE
There are worse things than a has-been. A cheat, for one.

Danny looks away, torn. Vince places a hand on his shoulder.
VINCE
You got a shot at greatness, kid. Don't let guys like Morelli take that from you.
DANNY
I need time to think.
VINCE
Take all the time you need. Just remember, some choices, you can't undo. This is one of those choices.

Danny nods, leaving Vince alone. Vince looks at the empty ring...

WORKOUT COMPLETED [ ]

Good acting is all about subtlety. It's about trying to make it look as much as like real life as possible.
Bill Nighy

IMAGINATION

We have a lot of tools in our arsenal as actors but **I believe imagination is the most powerful.** "If you hook into the character's belief system and you believe it 100%, there is no way the audience won't." - Meryl Streep "Imagination is more important than knowledge for knowledge is limited. - Einstein. Everyone has an Imagination but it must be worked out to get stronger. Think of your imagination as a limitless playground. In this space, you can be anyone, go anywhere, and do anything. **Have the courage to allow yourself to play!**

Solo Imaginary World Exploration - 6 Minutes [Set Timer]

Find a quiet space to relax and focus. **Close your eyes** and **let your imagination run wild. Tip:** Engage all your senses to explore this environment. Touch, taste, smell etc. Allow your emotions to guide you. **Extra:** After you establish this world in your imagination, you could introduce characters and have a dialogue with them. Are they friends or foes?

IMAGINARY WORLD: Maze of Mirrors in a Parallel Universe: Wander through a mirror maze reflecting alternate realities and life choices.

JOURNAL YOUR EXPERIENCE - 2 Minutes [Set Timer]

_____
_____
_____
_____
_____

Your Characters Filter - 5 Minutes [Set Timer]

Everyone including the characters you play see the world through their own specific perspective/filter. I like to use the word filter because you can take out a filter, clean it, change its style, colour, an optimist or a pessimist, comedian or a nihilist, etc. **Find a quiet space** to focus. **Close your eyes and let go of your personal thoughts and emotions** to make space for your characters. **Open your eyes, and allow the filter provided to effect everything around you. Tip**: Explore wherever you are and interact with the objects. **Extra:** How does *this* character walk and move in their world?

FILTER: Mystic: Perceives hidden energies and mystical signs in everything.

JOURNAL YOUR EXPERIENCE - 2 Minutes [Set Timer]

_____
_____
_____
_____
_____
_____

WORKOUT COMPLETED [ ]

You have to dream before your dreams can come true.
A.P.J. Abdul Kalam

CHARACTER STUDY "PEOPLE WATCHING"

Actors are required to portray characters that are believable and relatable. You don't have to agree with them but you have to understand them. Walk like them, talk like them, see the world like them. So, in order to fill our toolbox, we have to **go out into the world and study**. Then practice them over and over so we can "walk in their shoes', comfortably and confidently. Study their movements, mannerisms, the "vibe" they give off, the clothes they wear etc. **Fill your toolbox with the rhythms and idiosyncrasies of human behaviour.**

OBSERVATION CHARACTER STUDY - 15 Minutes [Set Timer]

Find a busy place where you can **sit and observe.** Choose anyone you find interesting. **Write down what stands out about them.** *The way they sit, drink their coffee, walk, talk, interact with others etc.* **Tip**: **Mirror them immediately.** This will help memorize the feeling of that character so whenever you come back to these characters you're discovering, your body will remember. **Extra**: Before you go to sleep, read over the characters from today and reenact their movements.

_____
_____
_____
_____
_____
_____
_____
_____
_____
_____
_____
_____
_____
_____
_____
_____
_____
_____
_____
_____
_____

COLOURS: We as humans respond to colours like frequencies. If you pay attention closely, you can see everyone has their own 'colour' that defines their core. An essence that informs how they operate and move through the world.

WHAT COLOUR ARE THEY:

WORKOUT COMPLETED [ ]

Acting is a spiritual quest to touch human beings.
Larry Moss

VOICE & DICTION

I wish I had learned this at the beginning of my career. The confidence to communicate clearly and powerfully is a game-changer for you as an actor. **Think of your voice as a musical instrument that needs regular tuning. This workout is your daily tuning session,** ensuring that your instrument is always ready. "The word 'theatre' comes from the Greeks. It means the seeing place. It is the place people come to see the truth about life and the social situation." - Stella Adler. Embrace this workout as a key to unlocking and portraying *that* truth by letting your voice be the vehicle that transports your audience into the heart of your story.

READ PASSAGE - 30 Seconds [Set Timer]
Speak the passage and take note of its quality. **Tip**: Record Audio to compare afterward.

"As the sun sets, the sky becomes a canvas of colours. Hues of orange, pink, and purple spread across the horizon, reflecting on the calm waters below. The world slows, basking in the tranquillity of the twilight hour."

RELAXATION - 1 Minute [Set Timer]
Deep Breathing: Sit and Inhale deeply through your nose, filling your lungs, then exhale slowly through your mouth. Imagine stress leaving your body with each breath.

Nay Nay Nay - 1 Minute [Set Timer]
Pick a song and sing the word "Nay" repeatedly. Start with a comfortable pitch and gradually move the sound from your nose to your chest, ensuring each "Nay" is clear and resonant. Stretch your range as best you can to strengthen.

Sustained 'S' - 2 Minutes [Set Timer]
Inhale deeply and then exhale slowly, making a continuous 's' sound. Keep the sound as even and steady as you can. Always push a little longer than you think you can.

Vowel Pronunciation Drill - 2 Minutes [Set Timer]
Slowly go through each vowel sound **(A, E, I, O, U), holding and exaggerating each sound. Combine them with consonants** (e.g., ba, be, bi, bo, bu). Pay attention to the clarity and sharpness of each sound. Repeat a few times before moving to the next.

Lip Trills - 3 minutes - [Set timer]
Close your lips together lightly, like you're going to blow a raspberry. Then, blow air through your closed lips while making sounds. You should feel a tickling sensation. Pick a song and Lip Trill the whole along with it. **Tip**: Stretch your range as much as you can and pick a song you've never listened to.

The Cork Exercise - 4 Minutes [Set Timer]
Place a cork between your teeth and try to read a passage aloud. This forces your articulation muscles to work harder. If you don't have a cork, bite down gently on your thumb. You can use the following text for this exercise:

READ PASSAGE AGAIN - 30 Seconds [Set Timer]
Speak the passage and take note of its quality. **Tip**: Record Audio to compare.

Discovery Journal - 1 Minute [Set Timer]

WORKOUT COMPLETED [ ]

Acting is a question of absorbing other people's personalities and adding some of your own experience.
Jean-Paul Sartre

SUBTEXT

Subtext is what lies beneath the surface of our words. It's the hidden layer of meaning, driven by the character's internal thoughts, emotions, desires, and motivations. Subtext is one of my favourite things as an actor because so much can be said with one simple line of dialogue. The power of "Hello" can be exciting if you told that person years ago "If I ever see you again, I'll kill you. Maybe it's the most beautiful person you've ever seen. Now, say "hello". *Subtext* shows the audience what your relationship with the characters/places/situations are, without having to explain it. We experience it every day and it is our job to create characters that interact as we do.

VOCAL WORK - 3 minutes - [Set Timer]
Lip Trills: Close your lips together lightly, like you're going to blow a raspberry. Then, blow air through your closed lips while making sounds. You should feel a tickling sensation. Pick a song and Lip Trill along with it. **Tip**: Stretch your range as much as you can and pick a song you've never listened to.

SUBTEXT PRACTICE
Use the line of dialogue provided and practice each of these subtexts **out loud.** Move on to the next, only when you believe yourself. Trust that you will know when *that* is. Before you begin, **pick a spot to look at and imagine** in detail, **who you are speaking with**. **Tip**: *Sometimes* we mean exactly what we are saying. Look for that too. **Extra**: Substitute someone you have a strong relationship with in real life, good or bad, and see it's affect.

Initial Line: "Hey, haven't seen you in a while..."
Your Response Line: "Yeah, it has been a minute. Life's been... full of surprises, let's say. Some good, some challenging. Keeps things interesting. You?"

SUBTEXTS - 6 Minutes [Set Timer]
[ ] Busy: Life's been hectic, and you're struggling to find a balance.
[ ] Adventurous: You've been trying new things and exploring new horizons.
[ ] Contemplative: Recent events have made you reassess your priorities.
[ ] Guarded: You're not ready to share the full extent of what's happening in your life.
[ ] Fear: The thing you need to tell them will most likely destroy your friendship.
[ ] Your Own Subtext

RELATIONSHIP SUBTEXTS - 6 Minutes [Set Timer]
[ ] The Former Best Friend: There's a history, but you've drifted apart.
[ ] The Ex who's trying to rekindle a connection: Mixed emotions surface.
[ ] The Neighbor with Whom You Share a Secret: Treading carefully in conversation.
[ ] The Colleague You Admire: Trying to keep things professional yet personal.
[ ] Your Grandfather: Verbally and physically abusive when you were a child.
[ ] Your Own Subtext

Discovery Journal

_____
_____
_____
_____

WORKOUT COMPLETED [ ]

What acting means is that you've got to get
out of your own skin.
Katharine Hepburn

EMOTIONS

The 'moment before', **the emotional preparation, is the most important key to a great scene.** If you start any scene <u>without</u> an emotional preparation it feels like trying to drive a car in neutral. The preparation is the uphill climb of every rollercoaster; Once you grind all the way to the top, the chains let go and the rest of the ride takes care of itself. "No one wants to see a play or a movie and look at technical proficiency. You want to be moved, you want a human experience, you want to feel less alone" - Viola Davis. **Practice your emotions over and over** so when it's time, you aren't worried "Will I get there?" **You're imagination and emotions should be a tinderbox, so easy to light up. All it take is half a spark.**

EULOGY - 12 Minutes [Set Timer]

Find a quiet comfortable space. Choose someone in your life who is alive and important to you. Create an imaginary reason for why they have died. Now start from the point of the phone call— Imagine who calls, what they say and what you say. Eventually find yourself at the funeral, about to begin the eulogy. See the casket, is it open or closed?? What is that person wearing and any other details for yourself. Before you begin to speak, look into the audience and see who is there- Family, friends etc **Then begin the eulogy. Tip:** <u>Be as specific as you can with everything</u>. **Inside of specificity is where you will find the triggers to your heart.** Let your imagination take you wherever you want in this exercise. **Example**: Placing her favourite sheep stuffed animal in the casket, tucked under her arm like she always held it, then kissing her goodbye one last time.

DISCOVERY JOURNAL - 3 Minutes [Set Timer]

Make sure to **include the specific triggers** you experience because you can use these **TRIGGER MOMENTS** in the future instead of repeating the *entire* exercise.

WORKOUT COMPLETED [ ]

You know what your problem is?
You don't realize how big you are.
You have to remind people who you are.
André Benjamin

THE CORK EXERCISE - 4 Minutes [Set Timer]
Place a cork between your teeth and read a passage aloud. This forces your articulation muscles to work harder. If you don't have a cork, bite down gently on your thumb. You can use the following text for this exercise:

"In the heart of winter, the world is a wonderland of snow. Each flake falls silently, blanketing the earth in a pristine white. Trees stand adorned in frost, and the air is filled with the crispness of the cold."

WRITE A LETTER - 10 Minutes [Set Timer]
Get a piece of paper or write this in your device. **Take a moment** to let this situation and relationship sink in. Then let your imagination run wild and **write them a letter.**

Your Character: Alex, a young architect who has always been career-focused.
Other Character: Jordan, Alex's first love from college, suddenly reappeared after disappearing without explanation years ago.

Relationship: Alex and Jordan's romance was intense and deeply passionate during their college years, seeming like a once-in-a-lifetime love. However, Jordan's abrupt disappearance left Alex heartbroken and unable to fully commit to another relationship since.

Context of the Letter: After years of no contact and unresolved feelings, Alex is shocked when Jordan returns, wanting to rekindle their relationship. Jordan's return and the revelation of the reasons for their departure upend Alex's world. Alex writes a letter to Jordan, filled with a mix of unresolved love, lingering pain, and a search for closure. The letter is a way for Alex to express all the emotions held back for years, questioning the possibilities of what could have been and what the future might still hold.

Discovery Journal - 1 minute [Set Timer]

_____
_____
_____
_____
_____
_____

WORKOUT COMPLETED [ ]

Learn the rules like a pro, so you can break them like an artist.
Picasso

VOCAL WORK - 3 minutes [Set timer]

Lip Trills: Close your lips together lightly, like you're going to blow a raspberry. Then, blow air through your closed lips while making sounds. You should feel a tickling sensation. Pick a song and Lip Trill along with it. **Tip**: Stretch your range as much as you can and pick a song you've never listened to.

VERBAL IMPROV - 10 Minutes [Set Timer]

Find a space where you are comfortable and free to express yourself. Take a moment to **let this situation, character and prompt, sink in**. Then let your imagination run wild: **Picture who you are talking to** then **begin with *the prompt*** and **continue to verbalize everything** this character would say. **Tip**: This is exploration! There is no "getting it right". BE BRAVE to explore and discover.

Character: Taylor, a dedicated nurse, has recently discovered that their colleague and close friend, Jordan, is taking prescription medication from the hospital for personal use. This revelation is especially alarming as Taylor's brother struggled with prescription drug abuse, which had profound effects on their family.

Prompt: "Jordan, I know what's been happening. We need to talk about this now."

Who are you talking to:

Describe them in two specific words:

Discovery Journal - 2 minutes [Set Timer]
_____
_____
_____
_____
_____
_____
_____
_____

WORKOUT COMPLETED [ ]

Acting is a masochistic form of
exhibitionism. It is not quite the
occupation of an adult.
Laurence Olivier

SELF AWARENESS

The more you understand yourself, the more you are able to understand and develop your characters. Like you, your characters have thoughts, beliefs, traumas, passions etc. When you become aware of your own and start to see how those experiences and beliefs have shaped your life, how you operate and view the world, then you can develop your characters that are much more rich and vivid.

PHYSICAL WARMUP - 2 minutes [Set Timer]

Freeform Dance: Put on some music and engage in freeform dancing. Allow your body to move spontaneously and without inhibition. This can help you tap into your creative instincts and develop physical expressiveness. **Tip**: Try music you've never listened to.

CURRENT EMOTIONAL INVENTORY - 3 Minutes [Set Timer]

Write down and **record your current emotions**. Identify what you're feeling at this moment and why. **Tip**: Be as specific as you can, **don't disregard anything.** You can also **scan your body** to see how and where your current emotion is affecting you. Your posture, the way you walk, bouncing foot, sore neck etc

CURRENT EMOTIONAL STATE:

SELF DISCOVERY QUESTIONS - 10 Minutes [Set Timer]

I suggest a journal or writing it in your phone's notes so you don't run out of space here.

Where am I from and how does my cultural background influence my worldview?

WORKOUT COMPLETED [ ]

An actor should always let humility
outweigh ambition.
Anna Kendrick

IMAGINATION

We have a lot of tools in our arsenal as actors but I believe imagination is the most powerful. "If you hook into the character's belief system and you believe it 100%, there is no way the audience won't." - Meryl Streep. Everyone has an Imagination but it must be worked out to get stronger. Think of your imagination as a limitless playground. In this space, you can be anyone, go anywhere, and do anything. **Have the courage to allow yourself to play!**

VOCAL WORK - 2 Minutes - [Set timer]

Lip Trills: Close your lips together lightly, like you're going to blow a raspberry. Then, blow air through your closed lips while making sounds. You should feel a tickling sensation. Pick a song and Lip Trill along with it. **Tip**: Stretch your range as much as you can and pick a song you've never listened to.

IMPROVISED STORYTELLING - 5 Minutes [Set Timer]

Speak out the scenario provided and continue the story! Focus on vivid details, character development and how the main character overcomes the main obstacle. **Tip**: Try not to stop speaking so you don't have time to "think". Allow your imagination to keep moving forward without interruption. **Tip**: Record these stories on your device, in case it's great but more importantly to see your progress as you go on.

STARTING POINT: You are Alex, a dedicated birdwatcher, who stumbles upon a rare, mythical bird during an early morning hike.

IMAGINARY WORLD EXPLORATION - 6 Minutes [Set Timer]

Find a quiet space to relax and focus. **Close your eyes** and let your imagination run wild. **Tip:** Engage all your senses to explore this environment. Touch, taste, smell etc and allow your emotions to guide you. **Extra:** After you explore this world with your senses, you could introduce characters and have a dialogue with them. Are they friends or foes?

IMAGINARY WORLD: COFFEE SHOP CONUNDRUM - A typical morning at your favourite neighbourhood coffee shop, where the barista greets you with a warm smile and the aroma of freshly brewed coffee fills the air. However, as you take your first sip, you realize that each sip. transports you to a different place. You decide to stay at one of the spots but be careful! Your coffee is now almost gone...

JOURNAL YOUR EXPERIENCE - 2 Minutes [Set Timer]

_____
_____
_____
_____
_____
_____
_____

WORKOUT COMPLETED [ ]

Everything you've ever wanted is on the
other side of fear.
George Addair

ANCHORING INTO YOUR CHARACTER COLOUR & MUSIC

Anchoring yourself into your character is vital. It's one of the most freeing feelings when you understand their *essence* because everything they do, how they do it and what their purpose is, becomes so clear to you and the audience. Every choice you make after you find your *anchor*, feels easy, because you're acting from who and what your character is at the core. You can call it an essence, an aura, vibe, energy etc. We all have it and feel it from everyone around us. There are many ways into your character but music and colour are my favourite. Music can inform the script, your character, even each scene. Colours, I think you will find, can work incredibly because we as humans respond to colours like frequencies. Colours evoke many feelings and if you pay attention closely, you can see everyone has their own 'colour' that defines their core. An essence that informs how they operate and move through the world.

THEIR COLOUR - 2 Minutes [Set Timer]
Think of **someone you know**, and **define them with a colour**. **Tip**: Trust yourself. Your initial colour is usually close. **Tip**: Start with basic colours then eventually become much more specific. **Example**: Corinna is an earthy green with rays of sunlight flowing through the green. **Extra**: Ask someone who knows *that person* as well, what they think this person's colour is and why. See how close your answers are or not.

YOUR CHARACTERS COLOUR
Read the given character description just as you would an audition, **assign a colour to that character.** Now take that colour you chose and **allow it to infuse into your entire body**, affecting your every move, your speaking, the way you see the world etc. **Take any book** you have, flip to a random page and **read the text as this Colour/Character**. **Tip**: Be specific, choose a colour that excites you and don't be afraid to get creative.

CHARACTER DESCRIPTION: [ASHTON] Ashton is a young, dedicated wildlife conservationist working in remote and rugged terrains. Their wardrobe is purely functional, with binoculars and a camera always at hand. Ashton's small tent in the wilderness serves as a base for their conservation efforts. They possess a deep, spiritual connection with nature, often putting themselves in harm's way to protect endangered species. Ashton's character is a blend of adventurous spirit, scientific curiosity, and a heartfelt commitment to preserving the natural world.

CHOOSE THEIR COLOUR - 4 Minutes [Set Timer]
THEIR COLOUR:

CHOOSE THEIR SONG - 4 Minutes [Set Timer]
THEIR SONG:

READ PASSAGE FROM BOOK - 2 Minutes [Set Timer]

FREEFORM DANCE - 2 minutes - [Set Timer]
Put on the selected music and **engage in freeform dancing, anchored in your colour/character,** Allow your body to move spontaneously and without inhibition. This can help you tap into your creative instincts and develop physical expressiveness *while staying in character.* **Tip**: Journal about the differences as opposed to how you normally dance.

JOURNAL YOUR EXPERIENCE - 1 Minute [Set Timer]

WORKOUT COMPLETED [ ]

You've gotta be original. Because if you're like someone else, what do they need you for.
Bernadette Peters

HISTORICAL RESEARCH

We are in the information era and have access to the world and its rich history at our fingertips. This exploration is not about 'learning facts'; it's a journey to the heart of human experience. The empathy and the understanding, especially on the things you disagree with, are incredibly valuable. If you look closely, you'll find the way people think, at different times in history, their attitudes, choices, and the way they move their bodies can teach you so much about us, right now. Fill your toolbox so it's overflowing with information and ideas to pull from so your imagination has so much to play with.

PHYSICAL WARMUP - 2 minutes - [Set Timer]
Freeform Dance: Put on some music and engage in freeform dancing. Allow your body to move spontaneously and without inhibition. This can help you tap into your creative instincts and develop physical expressiveness. **Tip**: Try music you've never listened to.

RESEARCH - 13 Minutes [Set Timer]
YouTube, streaming platforms, the internet or books, **research the given era/person/moment in time,** journal or make notes on your device, so when you want to find this information, it's organized and readily accessible. As you go, **write anything and everything *you* find fascinating. Tip**: If the topic doesn't interest you, choose your own, or take a chance and still research it, but from a different perspective. Physicalities, voice, ideals, etc. Trust your body that when you see something interesting, you'll know. **Extra**: Speak it out and copy their movements. Our memory recall is massively affected by our bodies. Be specific and when you re-read your notes, you'll be amazed by how much your mind and body remember.

TOPIC:
Edith Piaf (1915-1963): A French singer-songwriter, cabaret performer, and film actress noted for her distinctive voice and chanson performances. Extensive recordings of her performances and interviews showcase her emotional singing style and her dramatic life story, which includes overcoming personal tragedies and achieving fame against the odds.

WORKOUT COMPLETED [ ]

The beauty of acting is that you can convey the deepest and most complicated feelings without saying a word.
Emilia Clarke

BELIEF

Beliefs are the convictions that something exists or is true, especially without proof. That is also the definition of what we do as actors. We play make-believe. Our beliefs shape our world, especially our beliefs about ourselves and it works for the characters you play. Understand your beliefs and how they influence your mind, body and spirit, then you will be able to better understand others, so you can embody them. Allow the beliefs of your character to colour your perception of your world and your interaction with everything in it. "Acting is the best magic trick in the world. We applaud performances not because it's real, but because you made us believe."

VOCAL WORK - 2 Minutes - [Set timer]

Lip Trills: Close your lips together lightly, like you're going to blow a raspberry. Then, blow air through your closed lips while making sounds. You should feel a tickling sensation. Pick a song and Lip Trill along with it. **Tip**: Stretch your range as much as you can and pick a song you've never listened to.

BELIEF WORKOUT

Get your journal or write in here. **Define your personal belief/view** on the given subject. **Grab any book you own,** flip to a random page and **read it out loud,** colouring the words and intention with your belief system. **Tip**: Write trigger words you can hook into in the future: **Optimism-** Always smiling, grateful, opportunity, sunshine yellow.

YOUR PERSONAL BELIEF

Hierarchy- 7 Minutes [Set Timer]

_____
_____
_____
_____

READ WITH BELIEF - 2 Minutes [Set Timer]

CHARACTERS BELIEF

Hierarchy

It's just how the world works and is vital for our success as a species. If you are younger or older. A woman or a man. Boss or employee. There is a hierarchy built into everything we do. I respect it and thrive from it.

READ WITH CHARACTERS BELIEF - 2 Minutes [Set Timer]

Forget your personal view and **fully embrace the character's belief. Read out loud again.**

JOURNAL YOUR EXPERIENCE - 2 Minutes [Set Timer]

_____
_____
_____
_____

WORKOUT COMPLETED [ ]

PERFORMANCE STRATEGY

14 DAY REVIEW

TAKE A MOMENT OF REFLECTION AND BREAKDOWN WHERE YOU ARE RIGHT NOW IN YOUR CAREER AND AS AN ACTOR.
THE MORE SPECIFIC YOU ARE THE MORE CLEAR YOU CAN SEE WHERE YOU ARE NOW SO YOU CAN GET TO WHERE YOU WANT TO GO FASTER

★   ★   ★   ★   ★

Temple Grandin, diagnosed with autism as a child when little was known about the condition, went on to revolutionize livestock handling systems worldwide. A respected expert in animal behaviour and a passionate advocate for autism awareness, her life's work defied initial expectations and transformed industries.

DATE:

MY WHY
WHY ARE YOU DOING WHAT YOU ARE DOING
BE SPECIFIC

MY MAIN GOALS
IN-ORDER OF IMPORTANCE

1.

    Action Step(s):

2.

    Action Step(s):

3.

    Action Step(s):

FROM THE LAST 14 DAYS ☆☆☆☆☆
5 STAR RATING

YOUR KEY POINTS AND TAKEAWAYS - WHY THAT AMOUNT OF STAR RATING, LIKES, DISLIKES, THE BIGGEST LESSON YOU LEARNED, GOOD OR BAD:

STRENGTHS:

WEAKNESSES:

IMPROVEMENT STRATEGY
HOW CAN YOU IMPROVE ON THESE AREAS FOR THE NEXT 14 DAYS:

GOAL FROM LAST :
DID YOU ACHIEVE IT?

WHY OR WHY NOT?

GOAL FOR THE NEXT 14 EXERCISES
THE MORE SPECIFIC YOU ARE THE GREATER THE RESULT

    Action Step(s):

I think the best actors are the most generous, the kindest, the greatest people and at their worst they are vain, greedy and insecure.
Kenneth Branagh

MY WHY:

GOAL(s):

PHYSICAL WARMUP - 1 minute [Set Timer]
Character Walks: Adopt the walk of the angriest person in the world and let that evolve into dance. **Tip:** Let the character's backstory fuel the emotion of your movements.

VOCAL WORK - 3 minutes [Set Timer]
Hooty Owl Hums: Hum on an 'oo' vowel, thinking of the hoot of an owl, going up and down in pitch. Aim for a round, warm sound. **Tip:** Visualize your sound echoing through a forest to encourage openness.

EMOTIONAL RECALL - 5 minutes [Set Timer]
Burning Anger: Summon a memory where you felt profound anger. Let the heat of that emotion fuel your expressions and gestures. **Tip:** Channel the energy of anger into physicality without judgment.

ANIMAL WORK - OCTOPUS

Research - 2 minutes [Set Timer]
Observe the octopus's fluid movements, camouflage, and intelligence.

Animal Exercise - 3 minutes [Set Timer]
Embody the octopus's undulating tentacles and adaptability. Keep a sense of fluidity and cunning as you return to human behaviour. Tip: What type of personality does this octopus have?

Discovery Journal - 1 Minute [Set Timer]
3 Main Characteristics: (Whatever stands out to YOU to embody the essence)

_____
_____
_____
_____
_____
_____
_____
_____

WORKOUT COMPLETED [ ]

Do not follow where the path may lead. Go instead where there is no path and leave a trail.
Ralph Waldo Emerson

SCRIPT ANALYSIS for **RELATIONSHIPS & SPECIFICITY** - 15 minutes [Set Timer]
Choose your character, circle everything in this script you have a relationship with. Including people, places, things, smells, time of day etc. **Write what your relationship with those items are** and **be specific.** The more specific and fun you have with your relationships, the more interesting your characters will be and the more fun the audience has. **Tip:** Everything isn't in the scene. Use your imagination to create details, only if it's contextually appropriate. **Extra:** Write your > **Objective, win or lose? Consequence of failing?** The **Who What Where When Why.**

Title: **Paradox Protocol**
INT. TIME RESEARCH FACILITY - CONTINUUM CHAMBER - NIGHT
A futuristic chamber filled with pulsating lights and complex machinery. In the centre, the ORION DEVICE, a time travel machine named in memory of EVA's mentor. EVA (Brilliant and resolute scientist) is calibrating the Orion Device. MAX (determined and resourceful), her former classmate and current rival, bursts in.

MAX
Eva, we have to stop the Orion experiment now!

EVA
This is Professor Orion's life's work.

MAX
I've seen the consequences, Eva. In the future, the Orion causes a catastrophe.

EVA
Seen?

MAX
Yes, I used the prototype time vest to jump ahead.

EVA
You used the vest? And you lived... It works. It works!

MAX
Yes, not really sure if you heard me, but it destroys the world, Eva! Gone!

EVA
We can change that. The data from the Orion could unlock time travel's potential.

MAX
What if it doesn't work... You'll be destroying everything Professor Orion stood for?
Eva looks conflicted, torn between her mentor's legacy, the looming threat and Progress...

EVA
Fine... Fine. Shut it down!
Suddenly, an alarm blares. The Orion Device activates on its own, humming with energy.

EVA(cont'd)
What's happening? The shutdown sequence initiated!

MAX
It's the paradox effect! The time loop is trying to maintain itself!
As the chamber vibrates, a portal opens. Future versions of Eva and Max step out. FUTURE EVA holds an old photo of herself with Professor Orion

FUTURE EVA
You need to complete the Orion cycle! It's bigger than us!

MAX
But the temporal destruction!

FUTURE MAX
(Holding an aged, worn-out version of the time vest)
There's a reason for all of this. Trust us!

Present Eva, clutching Professor Orion's old notebook, exchanges a look with Present Max. They stand at a crossroads, their decisions echoing through time.

WORKOUT COMPLETED [ ]

In acting, I always try to go back to what would actually be the real situation, the real human behaviour in life.
Robert De Niro

IMAGINATION

We have a lot of tools in our arsenal as actors but **I believe imagination is the most powerful.** "If you hook into the character's belief system and you believe it 100%, there is no way the audience won't." - Meryl Streep "Imagination is more important than knowledge for knowledge is limited. - Einstein. Everyone has an Imagination but it must be worked out to get stronger. Think of your imagination as a limitless playground. In this space, you can be anyone, go anywhere, and do anything. **Have the courage to allow yourself to play!**

Solo Imaginary World Exploration - 6 Minutes [Set Timer]

Find a quiet space to relax and focus. **Close your eyes** and **let your imagination run wild. Tip:** Engage all your senses to explore this environment. Touch, taste, smell etc. Allow your emotions to guide you. **Extra:** After you establish this world in your imagination, you could introduce characters and have a dialogue with them. Are they friends or foes?

IMAGINARY WORLD: Time-Frozen Metropolis: Traverse a city frozen in time, with suspended people and objects.

JOURNAL YOUR EXPERIENCE - 2 Minutes [Set Timer]

_____
_____
_____
_____
_____
_____

Your Characters Filter - 5 Minutes [Set Timer]

Everyone including the characters you play see the world through their own specific perspective/filter. I like to use the word filter because you can take out a filter, clean it, change its style, colour, an optimist or a pessimist, comedian or a nihilist, etc. **Find a quiet space** to focus. **Close your eyes and let go of your personal thoughts and emotions** to make space for your characters. **Open your eyes, and allow the filter provided to effect everything around you. Tip:** Explore wherever you are and interact with the objects. **Extra:** How does _this_ character walk and move in their world?

FILTER: Noble Hero: Sees themselves as a protector and upholder of justice.

JOURNAL YOUR EXPERIENCE - 2 Minutes [Set Timer]

_____
_____
_____
_____
_____
_____

WORKOUT COMPLETED [ ]

Embrace vulnerability. Great acting comes from being willing to expose your true emotions and be open to the moment.
Tom Hanks

CHARACTER STUDY "PEOPLE WATCHING"

Actors are required to portray characters that are believable and relatable. You don't have to agree with them but you have to understand them. Walk like them, talk like them, see the world like them. So, in order to fill our toolbox, we have to **go out into the world and study**. Then practice them over and over so we can "walk in their shoes', comfortably and confidently. Study their movements, mannerisms, the "vibe" they give off, the clothes they wear etc. **Fill your toolbox with the rhythms and idiosyncrasies of human behaviour.**

OBSERVATION CHARACTER STUDY - 15 Minutes [Set Timer]

Find a busy place where you can **sit and observe.** Choose anyone you find interesting. **Write down what stands out about them.** *The way they sit, drink their coffee, walk, talk, interact with others etc.* **Tip**: **Mirror them immediately.** This will help memorize the feeling of that character so whenever you come back to these characters you're discovering, your body will remember. **Extra**: Before you go to sleep, read over the characters from today and reenact their movements.

_____
_____
_____
_____
_____
_____
_____
_____
_____
_____
_____
_____
_____
_____
_____
_____
_____
_____
_____
_____
_____

COLOURS: We as humans respond to colours like frequencies. If you pay attention closely, you can see everyone has their own 'colour' that defines their core. An essence that informs how they operate and move through the world.

WHAT COLOUR ARE THEY:

WORKOUT COMPLETED [ ]

The most exciting acting tends to happen in roles you never thought you could play.
John Lithgow

VOICE & DICTION

I wish I had learned this at the beginning of my career. The confidence to communicate clearly and powerfully is a game-changer for you as an actor. **Think of your voice as a musical instrument that needs regular tuning. This workout is your daily tuning session,** ensuring that your instrument is always ready. "The word 'theatre' comes from the Greeks. It means the seeing place. It is the place people come to see the truth about life and the social situation." - Stella Adler. Embrace this workout as a key to unlocking and portraying *that* truth by letting your voice be the vehicle that transports your audience into the heart of your story.

READ PASSAGE - 30 Seconds [Set Timer]
Speak the passage and take note of its quality. **Tip**: Record Audio to compare afterward.

"Amidst ancient ruins, whispers of history echo. Crumbling walls tell stories of empires lost, and the wind sings through arches and hallways, carrying voices of the past. The stones, weathered and worn, stand as silent witnesses to centuries gone by."

RELAXATION - 1 Minute [Set Timer]
Deep Breathing: Sit and Inhale deeply through your nose, filling your lungs, then exhale slowly through your mouth. Imagine stress leaving your body with each breath.

Nay Nay Nay - 1 Minute [Set Timer]
Pick a song and sing the word "Nay" repeatedly. Start with a comfortable pitch and gradually move the sound from your nose to your chest, ensuring each "Nay" is clear and resonant. Stretch your range as best you can to strengthen.

Sustained 'S' - 2 Minutes [Set Timer]
Inhale deeply and then exhale slowly, making a continuous 's' sound. Keep the sound as even and steady as you can. Always push a little longer than you think you can.

Vowel Pronunciation Drill - 2 Minutes [Set Timer]
Slowly go through each vowel sound **(A, E, I, O, U)**, **holding and exaggerating each sound. Combine them with consonants** (e.g., ba, be, bi, bo, bu). Pay attention to the clarity and sharpness of each sound. Repeat a few times before moving to the next.

Lip Trills - 3 minutes - [Set timer]
Close your lips together lightly, like you're going to blow a raspberry. Then, blow air through your closed lips while making sounds. You should feel a tickling sensation. Pick a song and Lip Trill the whole along with it. **Tip**: Stretch your range as much as you can and pick a song you've never listened to.

The Cork Exercise - 4 Minutes [Set Timer]
Place a cork between your teeth and try to read a passage aloud. This forces your articulation muscles to work harder. If you don't have a cork, bite down gently on your thumb. You can use the following text for this exercise:

READ PASSAGE AGAIN - 30 Seconds [Set Timer]
Speak the passage and take note of its quality. **Tip**: Record Audio to compare.

Discovery Journal - 1 Minute [Set Timer]

WORKOUT COMPLETED [ ]

Do not let what you cannot do interfere with
what you can do.
John Wooden

SUBTEXT

Subtext is what lies beneath the surface of our words. It's the hidden layer of meaning, driven by the character's internal thoughts, emotions, desires, and motivations. Subtext is one of my favourite things as an actor because so much can be said with one simple line of dialogue. The power of "Hello" can be exciting if you told that person years ago "If I ever see you again, I'll kill you. Maybe it's the most beautiful person you've ever seen. Now, say "hello". *Subtext* shows the audience what your relationship with the characters/places/situations are, without having to explain it. We experience it every day and it is our job to create characters that interact as we do.

VOCAL WORK - 3 minutes - [Set Timer]
Lip Trills: Close your lips together lightly, like you're going to blow a raspberry. Then, blow air through your closed lips while making sounds. You should feel a tickling sensation. Pick a song and Lip Trill along with it. **Tip**: Stretch your range as much as you can and pick a song you've never listened to.

SUBTEXT PRACTICE
Use the line of dialogue provided and practice each of these subtexts **out loud.** Move on to the next, only when you believe yourself. Trust that you will know when *that* is. Before you begin, **pick a spot to look at and imagine** in detail, **who you are speaking with.** **Tip**: *Sometimes* we mean exactly what we are saying. Look for that too. **Extra**: Substitute someone you have a strong relationship with in real life, good or bad, and see it's affect.

Initial Line: "I've been thinking about you lately."
Your Response Line: "Have you? Didn't expect you to say that. Life's taken some turns since... What have you been thinking about?"

SUBTEXTS - 6 Minutes [Set Timer]
[ ] Surprised: You didn't expect to still be on their mind.
[ ] Curious: You wonder what memories or events triggered their thoughts.
[ ] Cautious: You're unsure of their intentions and feel a bit guarded.
[ ] Flattered: It feels good to know you've been thought of.
[ ] Unsettled: The past between you is complicated, and this brings mixed feelings.
[ ] Your Own Subtext

RELATIONSHIP SUBTEXTS - 6 Minutes [Set Timer]
[ ] The One That Got Away: There's still a hint of 'what if' in your interactions.
[ ] The Old Flame Who Hurt You: Past wounds make this a delicate conversation.
[ ] The Friend Who Moved Away: You've missed them more than you realized.
[ ] The Sibling You've Had a Falling Out With: This could be a step towards reconciliation.
[ ] The Mentor Who Changed Your Life: Their influence still lingers in your decisions.
[ ] Your Own Subtext

Discovery Journal

___

___

___

___

___

WORKOUT COMPLETED [ ]

Your life is your canvas, and you are the masterpiece. There are a million ways to be kind, amazing, fabulous, creative, bold, and interesting.
R Kerli

EMOTIONS

The 'moment before', **the emotional preparation, is the most important key to a great scene.** If you start any scene *without* an emotional preparation it feels like trying to drive a car in neutral. The preparation is the uphill climb of every rollercoaster; Once you grind all the way to the top, the chains let go and the rest of the ride takes care of itself. "No one wants to see a play or a movie and look at technical proficiency. You want to be moved, you want a human experience, you want to feel less alone" - Viola Davis. **Practice your emotions over and over** so when it's time, you aren't worried "Will I get there?" **You're imagination and emotions should be a tinderbox, so easy to light up. All it take is half a spark.**

EULOGY - 12 Minutes [Set Timer]

Find a quiet comfortable space. Choose someone in your life who is alive and important to you. Create an imaginary reason for why they have died. Now start from the point of the phone call— Imagine who calls, what they say and what you say. Eventually find yourself at the funeral, about to begin the eulogy. See the casket, is it open or closed?? What is that person wearing and any other details for yourself. Before you begin to speak, look into the audience and see who is there- Family, friends etc **Then begin the eulogy. Tip:** Be as specific as you can with everything. **Inside of specificity is where you will find the triggers to your heart.** Let your imagination take you wherever you want in this exercise. **Example**: Placing her favourite sheep stuffed animal in the casket, tucked under her arm like she always held it, then kissing her goodbye one last time.

DISCOVERY JOURNAL - 3 Minutes [Set Timer]

Make sure to **include the specific triggers** you experience because you can use these **TRIGGER MOMENTS** in the future instead of repeating the *entire* exercise.

___
___
___
___
___
___
___
___
___
___
___
___
___
___
___
___
___
___
___
___

WORKOUT COMPLETED [ ]

To be an actor, you have to be a child.
Paul Newman

THE CORK EXERCISE - 4 Minutes [Set Timer]
Place a cork between your teeth and read a passage aloud. This forces your articulation muscles to work harder. If you don't have a cork, bite down gently on your thumb. You can use the following text for this exercise:

"Through the dense jungle, a path winds, revealing glimpses of hidden wonders. Exotic birds call to each other, and the rustle of leaves betrays unseen animals. The jungle is alive with secrets, inviting the bold to discover its mysteries."

WRITE A LETTER - 10 Minutes [Set Timer]
Get a piece of paper or write this in your device. **Take a moment** to let this situation and relationship sink in. Then let your imagination run wild and **write them a letter.**

Your Character: Ethan, a successful novelist known for his gripping thrillers.

Other Character: Vanessa, Ethan's ex-spouse and literary agent, who recently wrote a tell-all book revealing Ethan's deepest secrets and struggles, jeopardizing his career and personal life.

Relationship: Ethan and Vanessa's relationship was once a powerhouse combination of professional success and personal intimacy. However, their bitter divorce led to Vanessa using her intimate knowledge of Ethan's life to write a sensational and damaging book.

Context of the Letter: Confronted with the public exposure of his private life, Ethan writes a letter to Vanessa. The letter is an amalgamation of hurt, outrage, and disbelief. Ethan confronts Vanessa about the breach of trust, the impact of her actions on his life and career, and reflects on the complexities of their past relationship. It's a raw, unfiltered attempt to address the pain caused by the betrayal and to seek some semblance of closure or understanding.

Discovery Journal - 1 minute [Set Timer]
___
___
___
___
___
___

WORKOUT COMPLETED [ ]

Acting is the perfect idiot's profession.
Katharine Hepburn

VOCAL WORK - 3 minutes [Set timer]
Lip Trills: Close your lips together lightly, like you're going to blow a raspberry. Then, blow air through your closed lips while making sounds. You should feel a tickling sensation. Pick a song and Lip Trill along with it. **Tip**: Stretch your range as much as you can and pick a song you've never listened to.

VERBAL IMPROV - 10 Minutes [Set Timer]

Find a space where you are comfortable and free to express yourself. Take a moment to **let this situation, character and prompt, sink in**. Then let your imagination run wild: **Picture who you are talking to** then **begin with *the prompt*** and **continue to verbalize everything** this character would say. **Tip**: This is exploration! There is no "getting it right". BE BRAVE to explore and discover.

Character: Morgan has just learned that their close friend, Alex, has been using serious drugs. Alex was recently found unconscious and hospitalized due to an overdose. Morgan's cousin died recently of the same thing.

Prompt: "Alex, I just found out about what's going on. You need to stop."

Who are you talking to:

Describe them in two specific words:

Discovery Journal - 2 minutes [Set Timer]

_____
_____
_____
_____
_____
_____
_____
_____

WORKOUT COMPLETED [ ]

In acting, every eye blink counts.
Wes Bentley

SELF AWARENESS

The more you understand yourself, the more you are able to understand and develop your characters. Like you, your characters have thoughts, beliefs, traumas, passions etc. When you become aware of your own and start to see how those experiences and beliefs have shaped your life, how you operate and view the world, then you can develop your characters that are much more rich and vivid.

PHYSICAL WARMUP - 2 minutes [Set Timer]

Freeform Dance: Put on some music and engage in freeform dancing. Allow your body to move spontaneously and without inhibition. This can help you tap into your creative instincts and develop physical expressiveness. **Tip**: Try music you've never listened to.

CURRENT EMOTIONAL INVENTORY - 3 Minutes [Set Timer]

Write down and **record your current emotions**. Identify what you're feeling at this moment and why. **Tip**: Be as specific as you can, **don't disregard anything.** You can also **scan your body** to see how and where your current emotion is affecting you. Your posture, the way you walk, bouncing foot, sore neck etc

CURRENT EMOTIONAL STATE:

SELF DISCOVERY QUESTIONS - 10 Minutes [Set Timer]

I suggest a journal or writing it in your phone's notes so you don't run out of space here.

How do I show resilience in tough situations?

What are the most significant relationships in my life, and why?

WORKOUT COMPLETED [ ]

Age is no barrier. It's a limitation you put on your mind.
Jackie Joyner-Kersee

IMAGINATION

We have a lot of tools in our arsenal as actors but I believe imagination is the most powerful. "If you hook into the character's belief system and you believe it 100%, there is no way the audience won't." - Meryl Streep. Everyone has an Imagination but it must be worked out to get stronger. Think of your imagination as a limitless playground. In this space, you can be anyone, go anywhere, and do anything. **Have the courage to allow yourself to play!**

VOCAL WORK - 2 Minutes - [Set timer]

Lip Trills: Close your lips together lightly, like you're going to blow a raspberry. Then, blow air through your closed lips while making sounds. You should feel a tickling sensation. Pick a song and Lip Trill along with it. **Tip**: Stretch your range as much as you can and pick a song you've never listened to.

IMPROVISED STORYTELLING - 5 Minutes [Set Timer]

Speak out the scenario provided and continue the story! Focus on vivid details, character development and how the main character overcomes the main obstacle. **Tip**: Try not to stop speaking so you don't have time to "think". Allow your imagination to keep moving forward without interruption. **Tip**: Record these stories on your device, in case it's great but more importantly to see your progress as you go on.

STARTING POINT: You are Taylor, an aspiring writer, who comes across a vintage typewriter in a quaint antique shop. When you start typing on it, you realize that your written words begin to craft the reality around you. This typewriter allows you to rewrite past events or create future scenarios but with consequences and ethical dilemmas.

IMAGINARY WORLD EXPLORATION - 6 Minutes [Set Timer]

Find a quiet space to relax and focus. **Close your eyes** and let your imagination run wild. **Tip:** Engage all your senses to explore this environment. Touch, taste, smell etc and allow your emotions to guide you. **Extra:** After you explore this world with your senses, you could introduce characters and have a dialogue with them. Are they friends or foes?

IMAGINARY WORLD: COMMUTER'S DAYDREAM - A routine commute on a crowded subway train takes an unexpected turn when the train suddenly becomes a time machine.

JOURNAL YOUR EXPERIENCE - 2 Minutes [Set Timer]

_____
_____
_____
_____
_____
_____

WORKOUT COMPLETED [ ]

The best actors do not let the wheels show.
Henry Fonda

ANCHORING INTO YOUR CHARACTER COLOUR & MUSIC

Anchoring yourself into your character is vital. It's one of the most freeing feelings when you understand their *essence* because everything they do, how they do it and what their purpose is, becomes so clear to you and the audience. Every choice you make after you find your *anchor*, feels easy, because you're acting from who and what your character is at the core. You can call it an essence, an aura, vibe, energy etc. We all have it and feel it from everyone around us. There are many ways into your character but music and colour are my favourite. Music can inform the script, your character, even each scene. Colours, I think you will find, can work incredibly because we as humans respond to colours like frequencies. Colours evoke many feelings and if you pay attention closely, you can see everyone has their own 'colour' that defines their core. An essence that informs how they operate and move through the world.

THEIR COLOUR - 2 Minutes [Set Timer]
Think of **someone you know**, and **define them with a colour**. **Tip**: Trust yourself. Your initial colour is usually close. **Tip**: Start with basic colours then eventually become much more specific. **Example**: Corinna is an earthy green with rays of sunlight flowing through the green. **Extra**: Ask someone who knows *that person* as well, what they think this person's colour is and why. See how close your answers are or not.

YOUR CHARACTERS COLOUR
Read the given character description just as you would an audition, **assign a colour to that character.** Now take that colour you chose and **allow it to infuse into your entire body**, affecting your every move, your speaking, the way you see the world etc. **Take any book** you have, flip to a random page and **read the text as this Colour/Character**. **Tip**: Be specific, choose a colour that excites you and don't be afraid to get creative.

CHARACTER DESCRIPTION: [RILEY] Riley is a young, ambitious urban planner, passionate about creating sustainable, people-friendly cities. Their office is a blend of maps, models, and innovative designs, reflecting a vision for the future. Riley is often seen in smart, functional attire, equipped with a tablet full of ideas and sketches. An idealist at heart, frequently clashing with the more traditional and profit-driven approaches in their field. Riley's character is a mix of optimism and practicality, driven by a strong belief in community and environmental stewardship.

CHOOSE THEIR COLOUR - 4 Minutes [Set Timer]
THEIR COLOUR:

CHOOSE THEIR SONG - 4 Minutes [Set Timer]
THEIR SONG:

READ PASSAGE FROM BOOK - 2 Minutes [Set Timer]

FREEFORM DANCE - 2 minutes - [Set Timer]
Put on the selected music and **engage in freeform dancing, anchored in your colour/ character,** Allow your body to move spontaneously and without inhibition. This can help you tap into your creative instincts and develop physical expressiveness *while staying in character.* **Tip**: Journal about the differences as opposed to how you normally dance.

JOURNAL YOUR EXPERIENCE - 1 Minute [Set Timer]

WORKOUT COMPLETED [ ]

To survive as an actor, you have to love the artform.
Samuel L. Jackson

HISTORICAL RESEARCH

We are in the information era and have access to the world and its rich history at our fingertips. This exploration is not about 'learning facts'; it's a journey to the heart of human experience. The empathy and the understanding, especially on the things you disagree with, are incredibly valuable. If you look closely, you'll find the way people think, at different times in history, their attitudes, choices, and the way they move their bodies can teach you so much about us, right now. Fill your toolbox so it's overflowing with information and ideas to pull from so your imagination has so much to play with.

PHYSICAL WARMUP - 2 minutes - [Set Timer]
Freeform Dance: Put on some music and engage in freeform dancing. Allow your body to move spontaneously and without inhibition. This can help you tap into your creative instincts and develop physical expressiveness. **Tip**: Try music you've never listened to.

RESEARCH - 13 Minutes [Set Timer]
YouTube, streaming platforms, the internet or books, **research the given era/person/moment in time,** journal or make notes on your device, so when you want to find this information, it's organized and readily accessible. As you go, **write anything and everything _you_ find fascinating. Tip:** If the topic doesn't interest you, choose your own, or take a chance and still research it, but from a different perspective. Physicalities, voice, ideals, etc. Trust your body that when you see something interesting, you'll know. **Extra**: Speak it out and copy their movements. Our memory recall is massively affected by our bodies. Be specific and when you re-read your notes, you'll be amazed by how much your mind and body remember.

TOPIC:
Marlene Dietrich (1901-1992): A German-American actress and singer whose career spanned from the 1910s to the 1980s. Known for her distinctive voice, glamorous persona, and trailblazing style, Dietrich was a major figure in the world of film and music. Extensive footage of her performances and interviews are available for study.

WORKOUT COMPLETED [ ]

I love acting. It is so much more real than life.
Oscar Wilde

BELIEF

Beliefs are the convictions that something exists or is true, especially without proof. That is also the definition of what we do as actors. We play make-believe. Our beliefs shape our world, especially our beliefs about ourselves and it works for the characters you play. Understand your beliefs and how they influence your mind, body and spirit, then you will be able to better understand others, so you can embody them. Allow the beliefs of your character to colour your perception of your world and your interaction with everything in it. "Acting is the best magic trick in the world. We applaud performances not because it's real, but because you made us believe."

VOCAL WORK - 2 Minutes - [Set timer]
Lip Trills: Close your lips together lightly, like you're going to blow a raspberry. Then, blow air through your closed lips while making sounds. You should feel a tickling sensation. Pick a song and Lip Trill along with it. **Tip**: Stretch your range as much as you can and pick a song you've never listened to.

BELIEF WORKOUT
Get your journal or write in here. **Define your personal belief/view** on the given subject. **Grab any book you own,** flip to a random page and **read it out loud,** colouring the words and intention with your belief system. **Tip:** Write trigger words you can hook into in the future: **Optimism-** Always smiling, grateful, opportunity, sunshine yellow.

YOUR PERSONAL BELIEF
Success- 7 Minutes [Set Timer]

_____
_____
_____
_____

READ WITH BELIEF - 2 Minutes [Set Timer]

CHARACTERS BELIEF
Success

Success, to me, is purely the result of luck and circumstance. Hard work often goes unrewarded, and failure is an inevitable result of trying to fight against the odds. I see no point in striving when the outcome is mostly determined by factors beyond my control.

READ WITH CHARACTERS BELIEF - 2 Minutes [Set Timer]
Forget your personal view and **fully embrace the character's belief. Read out loud again.**

JOURNAL YOUR EXPERIENCE - 2 Minutes [Set Timer]

_____
_____
_____

WORKOUT COMPLETED [ ]

PERFORMANCE STRATEGY

14 DAY REVIEW

TAKE A MOMENT OF REFLECTION AND BREAKDOWN WHERE YOU ARE RIGHT NOW IN YOUR CAREER AND AS AN ACTOR. THE MORE SPECIFIC YOU ARE THE MORE CLEAR YOU CAN SEE WHERE YOU ARE NOW SO YOU CAN GET TO WHERE YOU WANT TO GO FASTER

★ ★ ★ ★ ★

Anna Mary Robertson Moses, better known as "Grandma Moses," began painting in her late 70s after arthritis made it impossible to continue with embroidery. Her folk art paintings became highly popular and celebrated, earning her international acclaim.

DATE:

MY WHY
WHY ARE YOU DOING WHAT YOU ARE DOING
BE SPECIFIC

MY MAIN GOALS
IN-ORDER OF IMPORTANCE

1.

   Action Step(s):

2.

   Action Step(s):

3.

   Action Step(s):

FROM THE LAST 14 DAYS ☆☆☆☆☆
5 STAR RATING

YOUR KEY POINTS AND TAKEAWAYS - WHY THAT AMOUNT OF STAR RATING, LIKES, DISLIKES, THE BIGGEST LESSON YOU LEARNED, GOOD OR BAD:

STRENGTHS:

WEAKNESSES:

IMPROVEMENT STRATEGY
HOW CAN YOU IMPROVE ON THESE AREAS FOR THE NEXT 14 DAYS:

GOAL FROM LAST :
DID YOU ACHIEVE IT?

WHY OR WHY NOT?

GOAL FOR THE NEXT 14 EXERCISES
THE MORE SPECIFIC YOU ARE THE GREATER THE RESULT

   Action Step(s):

If you want something you've never had,
you must be willing to do something you've
never done.
Thomas Jefferson

MY WHY:

GOAL(s):

PHYSICAL WARMUP - 1 minute [Set Timer]
Colour Dance: Choose a colour and dance how it makes you feel. Let the colour's energy guide your movement. **Tip:** Pick an odd colour even a mixture. Allow your creativity to play. Visualize the colour radiating from your body as you dance.

VOCAL WORK - 3 minutes [Set Timer]
Humming Slides: Start with a comfortable pitch, and hum gently, sliding up and down through your range. Feel the vibration in your chest, lips, and head. **Tip:** Keep it smooth, like a siren going up and down.

EMOTIONAL RECALL - 5 minutes [Set Timer]
Seething Jealousy: Think of a time when jealousy burned within you. Notice how this emotion might constrict your body or provoke certain actions. **Tip:** Allow your facial expressions to reflect the internal turmoil.

ANIMAL WORK - OWL
Research - 2 minutes [Set Timer]
Focus on the owl's silent flight, head rotation, and nocturnal hunting.

Animal Exercise - 3 minutes [Set Timer]
Imitate the owl's perching and turning head motion. As you evolve, maintain its observant stillness and piercing gaze.

Discovery Journal - 1 Minute [Set Timer]
3 Main Characteristics: (Whatever stands out to YOU to embody the essence)

_____
_____
_____
_____
_____
_____
_____

WORKOUT COMPLETED [ ]

The art of acting consists in keeping people
from coughing.
Benjamin Franklin

SCRIPT ANALYSIS for **RELATIONSHIPS & SPECIFICITY** - 15 minutes [Set Timer]
Choose your character, circle everything in this script you have a relationship with. Including people, places, things, smells, time of day etc. **Write what your relationship with those items are and be specific.** The more specific and fun you have with your relationships, the more interesting your characters will be and the more fun the audience has. **Tip:** Everything isn't in the scene. Use your imagination to create details, only if it's contextually appropriate. **Extra:** Write your > **Objective, win or lose? Consequence of failing?** The **Who What Where When Why.**

Title: **Beyond the Veil**
INT. SECRET RESEARCH FACILITY - NIGHT

A high-tech, secretive research facility. Fluorescent lights flicker. A large, open area, AGENT WREN (highly skilled, focused) is crouched behind a console, holding a mysterious device. The sound of approaching footsteps. DR. LARSON (dark, genius scientist) enters, escorted by armed guards.

DR. LARSON
Agent Wren, I'm glad you could see this before the launch. It's really a masterpiece.

AGENT WREN
It's over, Larson. You can't control this technology.

DR. LARSON
On the contrary, I'm the only one who can.

AGENT WREN
You're playing with forces you don't understand.

DR. LARSON
What a disappointment you've become. Understanding is a matter of perspective, Agent.

Wren activates the device, creating a pulsating energy field. The guards are thrown back.

AGENT WREN
This ends now!

Dr. Larson activates a remote control, and the facility begins to transform, revealing hidden weaponry.

DR. LARSON
You think you can stop this? I am this facility!

AGENT WREN
Then I'll have to bring down the entire place.

Wren starts running towards a central control panel, dodging laser fire. BANG! He's hit hard but keeps moving forward. Larson follows.

DR. LARSON
You're too late, Wren. The process has begun. You press that now, we all die.

Reaching the control panel, Wren starts entering a sequence. The facility's core begins to glow.

AGENT WREN
Not on my watch... And Larson, *you* were the disappointment.

DR. LARSON
No!!!

The facility rumbles, building to a climax. Larson tries to escape, but it's too late. Wren finishes the code and presses CONFIRM. The facility implodes in a blinding light.

WORKOUT COMPLETED [ ]

You have to expect things of yourself before
you can do them.
Michael Jordan

IMAGINATION

We have a lot of tools in our arsenal as actors but **I believe imagination is the most powerful.** "If you hook into the character's belief system and you believe it 100%, there is no way the audience won't." - Meryl Streep "Imagination is more important than knowledge for knowledge is limited. - Einstein. Everyone has an Imagination but it must be worked out to get stronger. Think of your imagination as a limitless playground. In this space, you can be anyone, go anywhere, and do anything. **Have the courage to allow yourself to play!**

Solo Imaginary World Exploration - 6 Minutes [Set Timer]

Find a quiet space to relax and focus. **Close your eyes** and **let your imagination run wild. Tip:** Engage all your senses to explore this environment. Touch, taste, smell etc. Allow your emotions to guide you. **Extra:** After you establish this world in your imagination, you could introduce characters and have a dialogue with them. Are they friends or foes?

IMAGINARY WORLD: Ancient Mythical Olympus: Explore the legendary home of the gods, filled with divine wonders and mythical beasts.

JOURNAL YOUR EXPERIENCE - 2 Minutes [Set Timer]

_____
_____
_____
_____
_____

Your Characters Filter - 5 Minutes [Set Timer]

Everyone including the characters you play see the world through their own specific perspective/filter. I like to use the word filter because you can take out a filter, clean it, change its style, colour, an optimist or a pessimist, comedian or a nihilist, etc. **Find a quiet space** to focus. **Close your eyes and let go of your personal thoughts and emotions** to make space for your characters. **Open your eyes, and allow the filter provided to effect everything around you. Tip**: Explore wherever you are and interact with the objects. **Extra:** How does *this* character walk and move in their world?

FILTER: Skeptical Scientist: Analyzes and questions everything logically.

JOURNAL YOUR EXPERIENCE - 2 Minutes [Set Timer]

_____
_____
_____
_____
_____

WORKOUT COMPLETED [ ]

The actor's art is the art of stopping time.
Peter Brook

CHARACTER STUDY "PEOPLE WATCHING"

Actors are required to portray characters that are believable and relatable. You don't have to agree with them but you have to understand them. Walk like them, talk like them, see the world like them. So, in order to fill our toolbox, we have to **go out into the world and study**. Then practice them over and over so we can "walk in their shoes', comfortably and confidently. Study their movements, mannerisms, the "vibe" they give off, the clothes they wear etc. **Fill your toolbox with the rhythms and idiosyncrasies of human behaviour.**

OBSERVATION CHARACTER STUDY - 15 Minutes [Set Timer]

Find a busy place where you can **sit and observe.** Choose anyone you find interesting. **Write down what stands out about them.** *The way they sit, drink their coffee, walk, talk, interact with others etc.* **Tip: Mirror them immediately.** This will help memorize the feeling of that character so whenever you come back to these characters you're discovering, your body will remember. **Extra**: Before you go to sleep, read over the characters from today and reenact their movements.

_____
_____
_____
_____
_____
_____
_____
_____
_____
_____
_____
_____
_____
_____
_____
_____
_____
_____
_____
_____

COLOURS: We as humans respond to colours like frequencies. If you pay attention closely, you can see everyone has their own 'colour' that defines their core. An essence that informs how they operate and move through the world.

WHAT COLOUR ARE THEY:

WORKOUT COMPLETED [ ]

To grasp the full significance of life is the actor's duty, to interpret it his problem, and to express it his dedication.
Marlon Brando

VOICE & DICTION

I wish I had learned this at the beginning of my career. The confidence to communicate clearly and powerfully is a game-changer for you as an actor. **Think of your voice as a musical instrument that needs regular tuning. This workout is your daily tuning session,** ensuring that your instrument is always ready. "The word 'theatre' comes from the Greeks. It means the seeing place. It is the place people come to see the truth about life and the social situation." - Stella Adler. Embrace this workout as a key to unlocking and portraying *that* truth by letting your voice be the vehicle that transports your audience into the heart of your story.

READ PASSAGE - 30 Seconds [Set Timer]
Speak the passage and take note of its quality. **Tip**: Record Audio to compare afterward.

"The marketplace is alive with energy and noise. Vendors call out their wares, shoppers haggle over prices, and the air is thick with the aromas of spices and fresh produce. Colours blend in a vibrant tapestry, capturing the essence of bustling commerce."

RELAXATION - 1 Minute [Set Timer]
Deep Breathing: Sit and Inhale deeply through your nose, filling your lungs, then exhale slowly through your mouth. Imagine stress leaving your body with each breath.

Nay Nay Nay - 1 Minute [Set Timer]
Pick a song and sing the word "Nay" repeatedly. Start with a comfortable pitch and gradually move the sound from your nose to your chest, ensuring each "Nay" is clear and resonant. Stretch your range as best you can to strengthen.

Sustained 'S' - 2 Minutes [Set Timer]
Inhale deeply and then exhale slowly, making a continuous 's' sound. Keep the sound as even and steady as you can. Always push a little longer than you think you can.

Vowel Pronunciation Drill - 2 Minutes [Set Timer]
Slowly go through each vowel sound **(A, E, I, O, U)**, **holding and exaggerating each sound. Combine them with consonants** (e.g., ba, be, bi, bo, bu). Pay attention to the clarity and sharpness of each sound. Repeat a few times before moving to the next.

Lip Trills - 3 minutes - [Set timer]
Close your lips together lightly, like you're going to blow a raspberry. Then, blow air through your closed lips while making sounds. You should feel a tickling sensation. Pick a song and Lip Trill the whole along with it. **Tip**: Stretch your range as much as you can and pick a song you've never listened to.

The Cork Exercise - 4 Minutes [Set Timer]
Place a cork between your teeth and try to read a passage aloud. This forces your articulation muscles to work harder. If you don't have a cork, bite down gently on your thumb. You can use the following text for this exercise:

READ PASSAGE AGAIN - 30 Seconds [Set Timer]
Speak the passage and take note of its quality. **Tip**: Record Audio to compare.

Discovery Journal - 1 Minute [Set Timer]

WORKOUT COMPLETED [ ]

II have not failed. I've just found 10,000 ways that won't work.
Thomas Edison

SUBTEXT

Subtext is what lies beneath the surface of our words. It's the hidden layer of meaning, driven by the character's internal thoughts, emotions, desires, and motivations. Subtext is one of my favourite things as an actor because so much can be said with one simple line of dialogue. The power of "Hello" can be exciting if you told that person years ago "If I ever see you again, I'll kill you. Maybe it's the most beautiful person you've ever seen. Now, say "hello". *Subtext* shows the audience what your relationship with the characters/places/situations are, without having to explain it. We experience it every day and it is our job to create characters that interact as we do.

VOCAL WORK - 3 minutes - [Set Timer]
Lip Trills: Close your lips together lightly, like you're going to blow a raspberry. Then, blow air through your closed lips while making sounds. You should feel a tickling sensation. Pick a song and Lip Trill along with it. **Tip**: Stretch your range as much as you can and pick a song you've never listened to.

SUBTEXT PRACTICE
Use the line of dialogue provided and practice each of these subtexts **out loud.** Move on to the next, only when you believe yourself. Trust that you will know when *that* is. Before you begin, **pick a spot to look at and imagine** in detail, **who you are speaking with**. **Tip**: *Sometimes* we mean exactly what we are saying. Look for that too. **Extra**: Substitute someone you have a strong relationship with in real life, good or bad, and see it's affect.

Initial Line: "Please. Don't do it."
Your Response Line: "You're asking a lot. You know how much this means to me, even if it's hard for you to understand. Why are you so against it? What's really going on with you?"
SUBTEXTS - 6 Minutes [Set Timer]

[ ] Determined: You're set on a path despite their pleas.
[ ] Torn: Their request makes you question your decision.
[ ] Frustrated: You feel misunderstood and constrained by their concerns.
[ ] Conflicted: Their reaction is causing you to feel a mix of guilt and defiance.
[ ] Resolute: You're convinced that this is the right thing to do, no matter what.
[ ] Your Own Subtext

RELATIONSHIP SUBTEXTS - 6 Minutes [Set Timer]
[ ] The Protective Parent: Their worry is steeped in love, but feels overbearing.
[ ] The Ex-Partner: They still have a hold on you, making decisions complex.
[ ] The Close Friend: Their opposition is unexpected and shakes your resolve.
[ ] The Sibling Rival: You're used to competing, but this feels different.
[ ] The Influential Mentor: Their guidance always mattered in the past. But now...
[ ] Your Own Subtext

Discovery Journal
_____
_____
_____
_____

WORKOUT COMPLETED [ ]

The hallmark of purposeful or deliberate practice is that you try to do something you cannot do — that takes you out of your comfort zone — and that you practice it repeatedly, honing in on the aspects that are not working until you finally get it right.
Anders Ericsson

EMOTIONS

The 'moment before', **the emotional preparation, is the most important key to a great scene.** If you start any scene <u>without</u> an emotional preparation it feels like trying to drive a car in neutral. The preparation is the uphill climb of every rollercoaster; Once you grind all the way to the top, the chains let go and the rest of the ride takes care of itself. "No one wants to see a play or a movie and look at technical proficiency. You want to be moved, you want a human experience, you want to feel less alone" - Viola Davis. **Practice your emotions over and over** so when it's time, you aren't worried "Will I get there?" **You're imagination and emotions should be a tinderbox, so easy to light up. All it take is half a spark.**

EULOGY - 12 Minutes [Set Timer]

Find a quiet comfortable space. Choose someone in your life who is alive and important to you. Create an imaginary reason for why they have died. Now start from the point of the phone call— Imagine who calls, what they say and what you say. Eventually find yourself at the funeral, about to begin the eulogy. See the casket, is it open or closed?? What is that person wearing and any other details for yourself. Before you begin to speak, look into the audience and see who is there- Family, friends etc **Then begin the eulogy. Tip:** <u>Be as specific as you can with everything.</u> **Inside of specificity is where you will find the triggers to your heart.** Let your imagination take you wherever you want in this exercise. **Example:** Placing her favourite sheep stuffed animal in the casket, tucked under her arm like she always held it, then kissing her goodbye one last time.

DISCOVERY JOURNAL - 3 Minutes [Set Timer]

Make sure to **include the specific triggers** you experience because you can use these **TRIGGER MOMENTS** in the future instead of repeating the *entire* exercise.

WORKOUT COMPLETED [ ]

An actor has to burn inside with an outer ease.
Michael Chekhov

THE CORK EXERCISE - 4 Minutes [Set Timer]
Place a cork between your teeth and read a passage aloud. This forces your articulation muscles to work harder. If you don't have a cork, bite down gently on your thumb. You can use the following text for this exercise:

"On the tranquil lakeshore, the water is still, mirroring the sky. Ducks glide gracefully, leaving ripples in their wake. The peacefulness of the scene is a balm to the soul, inviting quiet reflection."

WRITE A LETTER - 10 Minutes [Set Timer]
Get a piece of paper or write this in your device. **Take a moment** to let this situation and relationship sink in. Then let your imagination run wild and **write them a letter.**

Your Character: Isabel, a dedicated environmental activist and leader of a grassroots movement.
Other Character: Aaron, Isabel's co-founder and former best friend, who publicly discredited Isabel's work and defected to a corporation known for its environmentally harmful practices.

Relationship: Isabel and Aaron started their activism journey together, fuelled by a shared passion for environmental causes and a deep-seated friendship. Aaron's abrupt shift not only undermines the movement they built together but also feels like a personal attack on Isabel's values and efforts.

Context of the Letter: Feeling betrayed and heartbroken by Aaron's actions, Isabel writes a letter to confront this seismic shift in their relationship. The letter is a mix of personal pain, a sense of betrayal, and an attempt to understand Aaron's motivations. It's also a reflection on their shared past, the ideals they once fought for together, and Isabel's resolve to continue the fight despite Aaron's betrayal.

Discovery Journal - 1 minute [Set Timer]
_____
_____
_____
_____
_____
_____

WORKOUT COMPLETED [ ]

Acting is happy agony.
Alec Guinness

VOCAL WORK - 3 minutes [Set timer]
Lip Trills: Close your lips together lightly, like you're going to blow a raspberry. Then, blow air through your closed lips while making sounds. You should feel a tickling sensation. Pick a song and Lip Trill along with it. **Tip**: Stretch your range as much as you can and pick a song you've never listened to.

VERBAL IMPROV - 10 Minutes [Set Timer]

Find a space where you are comfortable and free to express yourself. Take a moment to **let this situation, character and prompt, sink in**. Then let your imagination run wild: **Picture who you are talking to** then **begin with *the prompt*** and **continue to verbalize everything** this character would say. **Tip**: This is exploration! There is no "getting it right". BE BRAVE to explore and discover.

Character: Jordan, just discovered that their teenager, Taylor, is involved in a dangerous online game that has recently led to a teen's death. You haven't gone to the police yet. You confront Taylor first and consider covering it up to protect her.

Prompt: "Taylor, I saw the messages on your phone about The Game. I know what you've done."

Who are you talking to:

Describe them in two specific words:

Discovery Journal - 2 minutes [Set Timer]

_____
_____
_____
_____
_____
_____
_____
_____

WORKOUT COMPLETED [ ]

I've missed more than 9000 shots in my career. I've lost almost 300 games. Twenty-six times, I've been trusted to take the game-winning shot and missed. I've failed over and over and over again in my life. And that is why I succeed.
Michael Jordan

SELF AWARENESS

The more you understand yourself, the more you are able to understand and develop your characters. Like you, your characters have thoughts, beliefs, traumas, passions etc. When you become aware of your own and start to see how those experiences and beliefs have shaped your life, how you operate and view the world, then you can develop your characters that are much more rich and vivid.

PHYSICAL WARMUP - 2 minutes [Set Timer]

Freeform Dance: Put on some music and engage in freeform dancing. Allow your body to move spontaneously and without inhibition. This can help you tap into your creative instincts and develop physical expressiveness. **Tip**: Try music you've never listened to.

CURRENT EMOTIONAL INVENTORY - 3 Minutes [Set Timer]

Write down and **record your current emotions**. Identify what you're feeling at this moment and why. **Tip**: Be as specific as you can, **don't disregard anything.** You can also **scan your body** to see how and where your current emotion is affecting you. Your posture, the way you walk, bouncing foot, sore neck etc

CURRENT EMOTIONAL STATE:

SELF DISCOVERY QUESTIONS - 10 Minutes [Set Timer]

I suggest a journal or writing it in your phone's notes so you don't run out of space here.

What are my strongest triggers/pet peeves? (Extra: What value do you have that makes this trigger so powerful)

What am I most passionate about?

WORKOUT COMPLETED [ ]

Acting is not about dressing up. Acting is about stripping bare.
Glenda Jackson

IMAGINATION

We have a lot of tools in our arsenal as actors but I believe imagination is the most powerful. "If you hook into the character's belief system and you believe it 100%, there is no way the audience won't." - Meryl Streep. Everyone has an Imagination but it must be worked out to get stronger. Think of your imagination as a limitless playground. In this space, you can be anyone, go anywhere, and do anything. **Have the courage to allow yourself to play!**

VOCAL WORK - 2 Minutes - [Set timer]
Lip Trills: Close your lips together lightly, like you're going to blow a raspberry. Then, blow air through your closed lips while making sounds. You should feel a tickling sensation. Pick a song and Lip Trill along with it. **Tip**: Stretch your range as much as you can and pick a song you've never listened to.

IMPROVISED STORYTELLING - 5 Minutes [Set Timer]
Speak out the scenario provided and continue the story! Focus on vivid details, character development and how the main character overcomes the main obstacle. **Tip**: Try not to stop speaking so you don't have time to "think". Allow your imagination to keep moving forward without interruption. **Tip:** Record these stories on your device, in case it's great but more importantly to see your progress as you go on.

STARTING POINT: You are Morgan, an amateur chess player, who discovers an ornate, antique chess set in the attic of your family home. When you play a game on this set, you find that each move influences real-world events. The chess pieces seem to represent actual people and scenarios in your life.

IMAGINARY WORLD EXPLORATION - 6 Minutes [Set Timer]

Find a quiet space to relax and focus. **Close your eyes** and let your imagination run wild. **Tip:** Engage all your senses to explore this environment. Touch, taste, smell etc and allow your emotions to guide you. **Extra:** After you explore this world with your senses, you could introduce characters and have a dialogue with them. Are they friends or foes?

IMAGINARY WORLD: OFFICE ODYSSEY - A typical day at the office takes a surreal twist when your computer screen begins to glow and transforms into a portal to a parallel dimension... You hear sounds you've never heard before. You're terrified as your boss approaches your desk you—

JOURNAL YOUR EXPERIENCE - 2 Minutes [Set Timer]

_____
_____
_____
_____
_____
_____
_____
_____

WORKOUT COMPLETED [ ]

Believe you can and you're halfway there.
Theodore Roosevelt

ANCHORING INTO YOUR CHARACTER COLOUR & MUSIC

Anchoring yourself into your character is vital. It's one of the most freeing feelings when you understand their *essence* because everything they do, how they do it and what their purpose is, becomes so clear to you and the audience. Every choice you make after you find your *anchor*, feels easy, because you're acting from who and what your character is at the core. You can call it an essence, an aura, vibe, energy etc. We all have it and feel it from everyone around us. There are many ways into your character but music and colour are my favourite. Music can inform the script, your character, even each scene. Colours, I think you will find, can work incredibly because we as humans respond to colours like frequencies. Colours evoke many feelings and if you pay attention closely, you can see everyone has their own 'colour' that defines their core. An essence that informs how they operate and move through the world.

THEIR COLOUR - 2 Minutes [Set Timer]
Think of **someone you know**, and **define them with a colour**. **Tip**: Trust yourself. Your initial colour is usually close. **Tip**: Start with basic colours then eventually become much more specific. **Example**: Corinna is an earthy green with rays of sunlight flowing through the green. **Extra**: Ask someone who knows *that person* as well, what they think this person's colour is and why. See how close your answers are or not.

YOUR CHARACTERS COLOUR
Read the given character description just as you would an audition, **assign a colour to that character.** Now take that colour you chose and **allow it to infuse into your entire body**, affecting your every move, your speaking, the way you see the world etc. **Take any book** you have, flip to a random page and **read the text as this Colour/Character**. **Tip**: Be specific, choose a colour that excites you and don't be afraid to get creative.

CHARACTER DESCRIPTION: [LANE] Lane is a talented graffiti artist who transforms the city's abandoned spaces into vibrant canvases. Wearing a hooded sweatshirt and a mask to conceal their identity, Lane works under the cover of night, leaving behind stunning murals that spark public intrigue and debate. Despite their anonymity, Lane has a loyal following on social media, where they subtly showcase their work. Driven by a desire to challenge societal norms and provoke thought through art, Lane navigates the fine line between vandalism and artistic expression. Their character embodies the rebellious spirit of street art, coupled with a quest for personal expression.

CHOOSE THEIR COLOUR - 4 Minutes [Set Timer]
THEIR COLOUR:

CHOOSE THEIR SONG - 4 Minutes [Set Timer]
THEIR SONG:

READ PASSAGE FROM BOOK - 2 Minutes [Set Timer]

FREEFORM DANCE - 2 minutes - [Set Timer]
Put on the selected music and **engage in freeform dancing, anchored in your colour/character,** Allow your body to move spontaneously and without inhibition. This can help you tap into your creative instincts and develop physical expressiveness <u>while staying in character.</u> **Tip**: Journal about the differences as opposed to how you normally dance.

JOURNAL YOUR EXPERIENCE - 1 Minute [Set Timer]

WORKOUT COMPLETED [ ]

I regard the theatre as the greatest of all art forms, the most immediate way in which a human being can share with another the sense of what it is to be a human being.
Oscar Wilde

HISTORICAL RESEARCH

We are in the information era and have access to the world and its rich history at our fingertips. This exploration is not about 'learning facts'; it's a journey to the heart of human experience. The empathy and the understanding, especially on the things you disagree with, are incredibly valuable. If you look closely, you'll find the way people think, at different times in history, their attitudes, choices, and the way they move their bodies can teach you so much about us, right now. Fill your toolbox so it's overflowing with information and ideas to pull from so your imagination has so much to play with.

PHYSICAL WARMUP - 2 minutes - [Set Timer]
Freeform Dance: Put on some music and engage in freeform dancing. Allow your body to move spontaneously and without inhibition. This can help you tap into your creative instincts and develop physical expressiveness. **Tip**: Try music you've never listened to.

RESEARCH - 13 Minutes [Set Timer]
YouTube, streaming platforms, the internet or books, **research the given era/person/moment in time,** journal or make notes on your device, so when you want to find this information, it's organized and readily accessible. As you go, **write anything and everything _you_ find fascinating. Tip:** If the topic doesn't interest you, choose your own, or take a chance and still research it, but from a different perspective. Physicalities, voice, ideals, etc. Trust your body that when you see something interesting, you'll know. **Extra**: Speak it out and copy their movements. Our memory recall is massively affected by our bodies. Be specific and when you re-read your notes, you'll be amazed by how much your mind and body remember.

TOPIC:
Frida Kahlo (1907-1954): A Mexican painter known for her many portraits, self-portraits, and works inspired by the nature and artifacts of Mexico. Her life was marked by physical and emotional pain, which she channelled into her deeply personal and vibrant art. Documentary footage and photographs, along with her artworks, offer a deep dive into her unique perspective and life experiences.

___
___
___
___
___
___
___
___
___
___
___
___
___
___
___

WORKOUT COMPLETED [ ]

The most important thing is to try and inspire people so that they can be great in whatever they want to do.
Kobe Bryant

BELIEF

Beliefs are the convictions that something exists or is true, especially without proof. That is also the definition of what we do as actors. We play make-believe. Our beliefs shape our world, especially our beliefs about ourselves and it works for the characters you play. Understand your beliefs and how they influence your mind, body and spirit, then you will be able to better understand others, so you can embody them. Allow the beliefs of your character to colour your perception of your world and your interaction with everything in it. "Acting is the best magic trick in the world. We applaud performances not because it's real, but because you made us believe."

VOCAL WORK - 2 Minutes - [Set timer]
Lip Trills: Close your lips together lightly, like you're going to blow a raspberry. Then, blow air through your closed lips while making sounds. You should feel a tickling sensation. Pick a song and Lip Trill along with it. **Tip**: Stretch your range as much as you can and pick a song you've never listened to.

BELIEF WORKOUT
Get your journal or write in here. **Define your personal belief/view** on the given subject. **Grab any book you own,** flip to a random page and **read it out loud,** colouring the words and intention with your belief system. **Tip**: Write trigger words you can hook into in the future: **Optimism-** Always smiling, grateful, opportunity, sunshine yellow.

YOUR PERSONAL BELIEF
Family - 7 Minutes [Set Timer]

_____
_____
_____
_____

READ WITH BELIEF - 2 Minutes [Set Timer]

CHARACTERS BELIEF
Family
It's like a theatrical play. Wear our family masks, playing parts of the doting son, the overbearing mother, the rebellious sibling... It's ridiculous but entertaining. Like a performance where the script is unwritten, yet everyone seems to know their lines.

READ WITH CHARACTERS BELIEF - 2 Minutes [Set Timer]
Forget your personal view and **fully embrace the character's belief.** Read out loud again.

JOURNAL YOUR EXPERIENCE - 2 Minutes [Set Timer]

_____
_____
_____
_____

WORKOUT COMPLETED [ ]

PERFORMANCE STRATEGY

14 DAY REVIEW

TAKE A MOMENT OF REFLECTION AND BREAKDOWN WHERE YOU ARE RIGHT NOW IN YOUR CAREER AND AS AN ACTOR.
THE MORE SPECIFIC YOU ARE THE MORE CLEAR YOU CAN SEE WHERE YOU ARE NOW SO YOU CAN GET TO WHERE YOU WANT TO GO FASTER

★ ★ ★ ★ ★

Jim Carrey, before his rise to fame as a Hollywood star, faced numerous challenges. He grew up in poverty, his family lived in a van at one point and he even worked as a janitor to help support them. Carrey's unwavering belief in his dream of becoming a comedian and actor, coupled with his unique brand of humour, eventually led him to become one of the most recognized and beloved comedic actors of his time

DATE:

MY WHY
WHY ARE YOU DOING WHAT YOU ARE DOING
BE SPECIFIC

MY MAIN GOALS
IN-ORDER OF IMPORTANCE

1.

    Action Step(s):

2.

    Action Step(s):

3.

    Action Step(s):

FROM THE LAST 14 DAYS   ☆☆☆☆☆
5 STAR RATING

YOUR KEY POINTS AND TAKEAWAYS - WHY THAT AMOUNT OF STAR RATING, LIKES, DISLIKES, THE BIGGEST LESSON YOU LEARNED, GOOD OR BAD:

STRENGTHS:

WEAKNESSES:

IMPROVEMENT STRATEGY
HOW CAN YOU IMPROVE ON THESE AREAS FOR THE NEXT 14 DAYS:

GOAL FROM LAST :
DID YOU ACHIEVE IT?

WHY OR WHY NOT?

GOAL FOR THE NEXT 14 EXERCISES
THE MORE SPECIFIC YOU ARE THE GREATER THE RESULT

    Action Step(s):

The hardest battle is to be nobody but yourself in a world that's doing its best to make you somebody else.
E.E. Cummings

MY WHY:

GOAL(s):

PHYSICAL WARMUP - 1 minute [Set Timer]
Puppet Strings: Imagine strings attached to different parts of your body being pulled in various directions by an unseen puppeteer. **Tip:** Allow this to lead to unexpected movements and resistances.

VOCAL WORK - 3 minutes [Set Timer]
Sighing Glissandos: Inhale deeply and then release a sigh, sliding from the top of your register down to the bottom on an "ah" sound. **Tip:** Imagine letting go of all your stress with each sigh.

EMOTIONAL RECALL - 5 minutes [Set Timer]
Heart-Wrenching Sadness: Think back to a loss that tore at your heartstrings. Allow yourself to grieve that loss again, noticing how your body naturally wants to react. **Tip:** Use your breath to guide you deeper into the emotion.

ANIMAL WORK - DOLPHIN
Research - 2 minutes [Set Timer]
Investigate the dolphin's playfulness and their way of communicating through sounds.

Animal Exercise - 3 minutes [Set Timer]
Imitate the dolphin's leaps and clicks. Transition to human, retaining the creature's joyfulness and social connectivity.

Discovery Journal - 1 Minute [Set Timer]
3 Main Characteristics: (Whatever stands out to YOU to embody the essence)

_____
_____
_____
_____
_____
_____
_____

WORKOUT COMPLETED [ ]

There are no small parts, only small actors.
Constantin Stanislavski

SCRIPT ANALYSIS for RELATIONSHIPS & SPECIFICITY - 15 minutes [Set Timer]
Choose your character, circle everything in this script you have a relationship with. Including people, places, things, smells, time of day etc. **Write what your relationship with those items are and be specific.** The more specific and fun you have with your relationships, the more interesting your characters will be and the more fun the audience has. **Tip:** Everything isn't in the scene. Use your imagination to create details, *only if* it's contextually appropriate. **Extra:** Write your > **Objective, win or lose? Consequence of failing?** The **Who What Where When Why.**

EXT. BRETT'S HOUSE - KITCHEN - LATE NIGHT

Brett and his father do the dishes.

JACK
So, what am I buying? Hockey Stick or ballet shoes?

BRETT
Who are you kidding, you'll be buying a hockey stick either way. We want it to be a surprise.

LAURA (O.S.)
You want it to be a surprise.

BRETT
We're finding out in a couple of weeks.

JACK
(Smiles)
Get used to it, Son. My father would roll over in his grave if he saw me doing dishes, right now.

He realizes what just slipped out.

BRETT
Pop'--

JACK
It's nothing. I just don't like to talk about him.

BRETT
It's not nothing.

JACK
Yes, it is.

Jack starts to leave.

BRETT
Dad. Dad, look at me.

JACK
I'm asking you to stop. (then) Kristen.

KRISTEN
Is everything--

JACK
Everything's fine. I'm just tired.

Jack heads out. Kristen grabs Brett's arms.

KRISTEN
You know your father.

She leaves. Michael and Laura wave as they watch them drive off.

LAURA
You done working now, Detective?

WORKOUT COMPLETED [ ]

If you never push yourself beyond your comfort zone, you will never improve.
Anders Ericsson

IMAGINATION

We have a lot of tools in our arsenal as actors but **I believe imagination is the most powerful.** "If you hook into the character's belief system and you believe it 100%, there is no way the audience won't." - Meryl Streep "Imagination is more important than knowledge for knowledge is limited. - Einstein. Everyone has an Imagination but it must be worked out to get stronger. Think of your imagination as a limitless playground. In this space, you can be anyone, go anywhere, and do anything. **Have the courage to allow yourself to play!**

Solo Imaginary World Exploration - 6 Minutes [Set Timer]

Find a quiet space to relax and focus. **Close your eyes** and **let your imagination run wild. Tip:** Engage all your senses to explore this environment. Touch, taste, smell etc. Allow your emotions to guide you. **Extra:** After you establish this world in your imagination, you could introduce characters and have a dialogue with them. Are they friends or foes?

IMAGINARY WORLD: Dreamlike Surreal City: Navigate a Salvador Dali-inspired city where reality is fluid and physics is skewed.

JOURNAL YOUR EXPERIENCE - 2 Minutes [Set Timer]

_____
_____
_____
_____
_____
_____
_____

Your Characters Filter - 5 Minutes [Set Timer]

Everyone including the characters you play see the world through their own specific perspective/filter. I like to use the word filter because you can take out a filter, clean it, change its style, colour, an optimist or a pessimist, comedian or a nihilist, etc. **Find a quiet space** to focus. **Close your eyes and let go of your personal thoughts and emotions** to make space for your characters. **Open your eyes, and allow the filter provided to effect everything around you. Tip**: Explore wherever you are and interact with the objects. **Extra:** How does *this* character walk and move in their world?

FILTER: Intuitive Empath: _Deeply_ feels the emotions and energies around them. Everything has an energy.

JOURNAL YOUR EXPERIENCE - 2 Minutes [Set Timer]

_____
_____
_____
_____
_____
_____

WORKOUT COMPLETED [ ]

You must have chaos within you to give
birth to a dancing star.
Friedrich Nietzsche

CHARACTER STUDY "PEOPLE WATCHING"

Actors are required to portray characters that are believable and relatable. You don't have to agree with them but you have to understand them. Walk like them, talk like them, see the world like them. So, in order to fill our toolbox, we have to **go out into the world and study**. Then practice them over and over so we can "walk in their shoes', comfortably and confidently. Study their movements, mannerisms, the "vibe" they give off, the clothes they wear etc. **Fill your toolbox with the rhythms and idiosyncrasies of human behaviour.**

OBSERVATION CHARACTER STUDY - 15 Minutes [Set Timer]

Find a busy place where you can **sit and observe.** Choose anyone you find interesting. **Write down what stands out about them.** *The way they sit, drink their coffee, walk, talk, interact with others etc.* **Tip: Mirror them immediately.** This will help memorize the feeling of that character so whenever you come back to these characters you're discovering, your body will remember. **Extra**: Before you go to sleep, read over the characters from today and reenact their movements.

_____
_____
_____
_____
_____
_____
_____
_____
_____
_____
_____
_____
_____
_____
_____
_____
_____
_____
_____
_____

COLOURS: We as humans respond to colours like frequencies. If you pay attention closely, you can see everyone has their own 'colour' that defines their core. An essence that informs how they operate and move through the world.

WHAT COLOUR ARE THEY:

WORKOUT COMPLETED [ ]

If you want to find the secrets of the universe, think in terms of energy, frequency, and vibration.
Nikola Tesla

VOICE & DICTION

I wish I had learned this at the beginning of my career. The confidence to communicate clearly and powerfully is a game-changer for you as an actor. **Think of your voice as a musical instrument that needs regular tuning. This workout is your daily tuning session,** ensuring that your instrument is always ready. "The word 'theatre' comes from the Greeks. It means the seeing place. It is the place people come to see the truth about life and the social situation." - Stella Adler. Embrace this workout as a key to unlocking and portraying *that* truth by letting your voice be the vehicle that transports your audience into the heart of your story.

READ PASSAGE - 30 Seconds [Set Timer]
Speak the passage and take note of its quality. **Tip**: Record Audio to compare afterward.

"An enchanted evening descends upon us. Streetlights cast a soft glow, shadows dance along the pavements and the gentle hum of nightlife begins. The moon, a silent guardian overhead, bathes us in a silver embrace."

RELAXATION - 1 Minute [Set Timer]
Deep Breathing: Sit and Inhale deeply through your nose, filling your lungs, then exhale slowly through your mouth. Imagine stress leaving your body with each breath.

Nay Nay Nay - 1 Minute [Set Timer]
Pick a song and sing the word "Nay" repeatedly. Start with a comfortable pitch and gradually move the sound from your nose to your chest, ensuring each "Nay" is clear and resonant. Stretch your range as best you can to strengthen.

Sustained 'S' - 2 Minutes [Set Timer]
Inhale deeply and then exhale slowly, making a continuous 's' sound. Keep the sound as even and steady as you can. Always push a little longer than you think you can.

Vowel Pronunciation Drill - 2 Minutes [Set Timer]
Slowly go through each vowel sound **(A, E, I, O, U), holding and exaggerating each sound. Combine them with consonants** (e.g., ba, be, bi, bo, bu). Pay attention to the clarity and sharpness of each sound. Repeat a few times before moving to the next.

Lip Trills - 3 minutes - [Set timer]
Close your lips together lightly, like you're going to blow a raspberry. Then, blow air through your closed lips while making sounds. You should feel a tickling sensation. Pick a song and Lip Trill the whole along with it. **Tip**: Stretch your range as much as you can and pick a song you've never listened to.

The Cork Exercise - 4 Minutes [Set Timer]
Place a cork between your teeth and try to read a passage aloud. This forces your articulation muscles to work harder. If you don't have a cork, bite down gently on your thumb. You can use the following text for this exercise:

READ PASSAGE AGAIN - 30 Seconds [Set Timer]
Speak the passage and take note of its quality. **Tip**: Record Audio to compare.

Discovery Journal - 1 Minute [Set Timer]

WORKOUT COMPLETED [ ]

The only way to do great work is to love what you do. If you haven't found it yet, keep looking. Don't settle.
Steve Jobs

SUBTEXT

Subtext is what lies beneath the surface of our words. It's the hidden layer of meaning, driven by the character's internal thoughts, emotions, desires, and motivations. Subtext is one of my favourite things as an actor because so much can be said with one simple line of dialogue. The power of "Hello" can be exciting if you told that person years ago "If I ever see you again, I'll kill you. Maybe it's the most beautiful person you've ever seen. Now, say "hello". *Subtext* shows the audience what your relationship with the characters/places/situations are, without having to explain it. We experience it every day and it is our job to create characters that interact as we do.

VOCAL WORK - 3 minutes - [Set Timer]
Lip Trills: Close your lips together lightly, like you're going to blow a raspberry. Then, blow air through your closed lips while making sounds. You should feel a tickling sensation. Pick a song and Lip Trill along with it. **Tip**: Stretch your range as much as you can and pick a song you've never listened to.

SUBTEXT PRACTICE
Use the line of dialogue provided and practice each of these subtexts **out loud.** Move on to the next, only when you believe yourself. Trust that you will know when *that* is. Before you begin, **pick a spot to look at and imagine** in detail, **who you are speaking with**. **Tip**: *Sometimes* we mean exactly what we are saying. Look for that too. **Extra**: Substitute someone you have a strong relationship with in real life, good or bad, and see it's affect.

Initial Line: "Hi, how can I help you?"
Your Response Line: "Oh, hi. I'm just... Well, I'm a bit lost, actually. Not just here, but you know, in general. It's been one of those days. Or maybe one of those years."

SUBTEXTS - 6 Minutes [Set Timer]
[ ] Overwhelmed: You're grappling with more than just the immediate situation.
[ ] Seeking Guidance: You're at a crossroads and in need of some direction.
[ ] Vulnerable: You're more open about your feelings than you usually are.
[ ] Disoriented: You're struggling to find your footing in a broader sense.
[ ] Wistful: You're reflecting on how things have changed for you lately.
[ ] Your Own Subtext

RELATIONSHIP SUBTEXTS - 6 Minutes [Set Timer]
[ ] The Friendly Stranger: Their kindness is a rare comfort in your chaotic life.
[ ] The Distant Acquaintance: You unexpectedly find solace in this casual interaction.
[ ] The Former Classmate: Surprisingly, they become a source of unexpected advice.
[ ] Her/Him: You've seen them in your dreams for years... But you've never met.
[ ] The Neighbor You Barely Know: This conversation starts to bridge the gap.
[ ] Your Own Subtext

Discovery Journal

_____
_____
_____
_____
_____

WORKOUT COMPLETED [ ]

You are never too old to set another goal or
to dream a new dream.
C.S. Lewis

EMOTIONS

The 'moment before', **the emotional preparation, is the most important key to a great scene.** If you start any scene *without* an emotional preparation it feels like trying to drive a car in neutral. The preparation is the uphill climb of every rollercoaster; Once you grind all the way to the top, the chains let go and the rest of the ride takes care of itself. "No one wants to see a play or a movie and look at technical proficiency. You want to be moved, you want a human experience, you want to feel less alone" - Viola Davis. **Practice your emotions over and over** so when it's time, you aren't worried "Will I get there?" **You're imagination and emotions should be a tinderbox, so easy to light up. All it take is half a spark.**

EULOGY - 12 Minutes [Set Timer]

Find a quiet comfortable space. Choose someone in your life who is alive and important to you. Create an imaginary reason for why they have died. Now start from the point of the phone call— Imagine who calls, what they say and what you say. Eventually find yourself at the funeral, about to begin the eulogy. See the casket, is it open or closed?? What is that person wearing and any other details for yourself. Before you begin to speak, look into the audience and see who is there- Family, friends etc **Then begin the eulogy. Tip**: Be as specific as you can with everything. **Inside of specificity is where you will find the triggers to your heart.** Let your imagination take you wherever you want in this exercise. **Example**: Placing her favourite sheep stuffed animal in the casket, tucked under her arm like she always held it, then kissing her goodbye one last time.

DISCOVERY JOURNAL - 3 Minutes [Set Timer]

Make sure to **include the specific triggers** you experience because you can use these **TRIGGER MOMENTS** in the future instead of repeating the *entire* exercise.

___
___
___
___
___
___
___
___
___
___
___
___
___
___
___
___
___
___
___
___
___

WORKOUT COMPLETED [ ]

Acting is a sport. On stage, you must be ready to move like a tennis player on his toes. Your concentration must be acute.
Robert Stack

THE CORK EXERCISE - 4 Minutes [Set Timer]
Place a cork between your teeth and read a passage aloud. This forces your articulation muscles to work harder. If you don't have a cork, bite down gently on your thumb. You can use the following text for this exercise:

> "At the bustling marketplace, vendors shout their wares, and the aroma of spices fills the air. Colourful stalls display an array of goods, from fresh fruits to handmade crafts, each telling a story of culture and tradition."

WRITE A LETTER - 10 Minutes [Set Timer]
Get a piece of paper or write this in your device. **Take a moment** to let this situation and relationship sink in. Then let your imagination run wild and **write them a letter.**

Your Character: Leo, a seasoned detective who has dedicated their life to law enforcement.
Other Character: Mia, Leo's partner on the force, was recently exposed as a mole, working for a criminal organization that Leo has been trying to bring down.

Relationship: Leo and Mia were more than just partners; they were close friends who had each other's backs in the most dangerous situations. Leo trusted Mia implicitly, valuing their insight and bravery. Mia's betrayal has not only endangered Leo's life's work but also left a deep personal wound.

Context of the Letter: Struggling with a sense of anger, betrayal, and disbelief, Leo writes to Mia. The letter is a way for Leo to confront the pain and confusion caused by Mia's actions, to question why Mia chose this path, and to express the sense of loss for a partnership and friendship that Leo treasured.

Discovery Journal - 1 minute [Set Timer]
_____
_____
_____
_____
_____
_____

WORKOUT COMPLETED [ ]

I am not a product of my circumstances. I
am a product of my decisions
Stephen Covey

VOCAL WORK - 3 minutes [Set timer]

Lip Trills: Close your lips together lightly, like you're going to blow a raspberry. Then, blow air through your closed lips while making sounds. You should feel a tickling sensation. Pick a song and Lip Trill along with it. **Tip**: Stretch your range as much as you can and pick a song you've never listened to.

VERBAL IMPROV - 10 Minutes [Set Timer]

Find a space where you are comfortable and free to express yourself. Take a moment to **let this situation, character and prompt, sink in**. Then let your imagination run wild: **Picture who you are talking to** then **begin with the prompt** and **continue to verbalize everything** this character would say. **Tip**: This is exploration! There is no "getting it right". BE BRAVE to explore and discover.

Character: Alex, who lives alone, has recently been noticing strange occurrences around their home; items being moved and unexplained noises at night. After setting up a camera, Alex sees footage of their neighbour entering their house at odd hours. You don't go to the police. You confront your neighbour.

Prompt: "I saw the footage of you coming into my house at night."

Discovery Journal - 2 minutes [Set Timer]

Who are you talking to:

Describe them in two specific words:

Discovery Journal - 2 minutes [Set Timer]

_____
_____
_____
_____
_____
_____
_____
_____

WORKOUT COMPLETED [ ]

Acting is not about being famous, it's about exploring the human soul.
Annette Bening

SELF AWARENESS

The more you understand yourself, the more you are able to understand and develop your characters. Like you, your characters have thoughts, beliefs, traumas, passions etc. When you become aware of your own and start to see how those experiences and beliefs have shaped your life, how you operate and view the world, then you can develop your characters that are much more rich and vivid.

PHYSICAL WARMUP - 2 minutes [Set Timer]
Freeform Dance: Put on some music and engage in freeform dancing. Allow your body to move spontaneously and without inhibition. This can help you tap into your creative instincts and develop physical expressiveness. **Tip**: Try music you've never listened to.

CURRENT EMOTIONAL INVENTORY - 3 Minutes [Set Timer]
Write down and **record your current emotions**. Identify what you're feeling at this moment and why. **Tip**: Be as specific as you can, **don't disregard anything.** You can also **scan your body** to see how and where your current emotion is affecting you. Your posture, the way you walk, bouncing foot, sore neck etc

CURRENT EMOTIONAL STATE:

SELF DISCOVERY QUESTIONS - 10 Minutes [Set Timer]
I suggest a journal or writing it in your phone's notes so you don't run out of space here.

What aspects of my life would I like to improve? (Extra: What will that do if you improve it)

How do I handle failure or rejection? (Extra: What happens physically to my body when these moments happen)

WORKOUT COMPLETED [ ]

To uncover your true potential, you must first find your own limits and then you have to have the courage to blow past them.
Picabo Street

IMAGINATION

We have a lot of tools in our arsenal as actors but I believe imagination is the most powerful. "If you hook into the character's belief system and you believe it 100%, there is no way the audience won't." - Meryl Streep. Everyone has an Imagination but it must be worked out to get stronger. Think of your imagination as a limitless playground. In this space, you can be anyone, go anywhere, and do anything. **Have the courage to allow yourself to play!**

VOCAL WORK - 2 Minutes - [Set timer]
Lip Trills: Close your lips together lightly, like you're going to blow a raspberry. Then, blow air through your closed lips while making sounds. You should feel a tickling sensation. Pick a song and Lip Trill along with it. **Tip**: Stretch your range as much as you can and pick a song you've never listened to.

IMPROVISED STORYTELLING - 5 Minutes [Set Timer]
Speak out the scenario provided and continue the story! Focus on vivid details, character development and how the main character overcomes the main obstacle. **Tip**: Try not to stop speaking so you don't have time to "think". Allow your imagination to keep moving forward without interruption. **Tip**: Record these stories on your device, in case it's great but more importantly to see your progress as you go on.

STARTING POINT: You are Jordan, a hobbyist painter, who buys an antique easel from a mysterious old art store. After setting it up in your studio, you notice that whatever you paint on it begins to manifest in real life,

IMAGINARY WORLD EXPLORATION - 6 Minutes [Set Timer]

Find a quiet space to relax and focus. **Close your eyes** and let your imagination run wild. **Tip:** Engage all your senses to explore this environment. Touch, taste, smell etc and allow your emotions to guide you. **Extra:** After you explore this world with your senses, you could introduce characters and have a dialogue with them. Are they friends or foes?

IMAGINARY WORLD: GENTLE RAINBOW VALLEY - A valley where gentle rains produce endless, vibrant rainbows that arch gracefully across the sky. The air is filled with the fresh scent of rain. You have a strong feeling, this is where dreams are made.

JOURNAL YOUR EXPERIENCE - 2 Minutes [Set Timer]

_____
_____
_____
_____
_____
_____
_____

WORKOUT COMPLETED [ ]

There is no point at which performance maxes out and additional practice does not lead to further improvement.
Anders Ericsson

ANCHORING INTO YOUR CHARACTER COLOUR & MUSIC

Anchoring yourself into your character is vital. It's one of the most freeing feelings when you understand their *essence* because everything they do, how they do it and what their purpose is, becomes so clear to you and the audience. Every choice you make after you find your *anchor*, feels easy, because you're acting from who and what your character is at the core. You can call it an essence, an aura, vibe, energy etc. We all have it and feel it from everyone around us. There are many ways into your character but music and colour are my favourite. Music can inform the script, your character, even each scene. Colours, I think you will find, can work incredibly because we as humans respond to colours like frequencies. Colours evoke many feelings and if you pay attention closely, you can see everyone has their own 'colour' that defines their core. An essence that informs how they operate and move through the world.

THEIR COLOUR - 2 Minutes [Set Timer]
Think of **someone you know**, and **define them with a colour**. **Tip**: Trust yourself. Your initial colour is usually close. **Tip**: Start with basic colours then eventually become much more specific. **Example**: Corinna is an earthy green with rays of sunlight flowing through the green. **Extra**: Ask someone who knows *that person* as well, what they think this person's colour is and why. See how close your answers are or not.

YOUR CHARACTERS COLOUR
Read the given character description just as you would an audition, **assign a colour to that character.** Now take that colour you chose and **allow it to infuse into your entire body**, affecting your every move, your speaking, the way you see the world etc. **Take any book** you have, flip to a random page and **read the text as this Colour/Character**. **Tip**: Be specific, choose a colour that excites you and don't be afraid to get creative.

CHARACTER DESCRIPTION: [ELLIOT] Elliot is a young prodigy in the world of competitive chess, often underestimated due to their unassuming appearance. Their small apartment serves as a strategic haven, walls lined with chess books and historic game boards. Elliot's attire is usually casual, but their eyes reveal a fierce intensity and focus. Beneath their quiet demeanour lies a whirlwind of strategic thinking and a burning desire to prove themselves among the greats. Elliot's character is a compelling fusion of youthful ambition, intellectual prowess, and the emotional weight of competition.

CHOOSE THEIR COLOUR - 4 Minutes [Set Timer]
THEIR COLOUR:

CHOOSE THEIR SONG - 4 Minutes [Set Timer]
THEIR SONG:

READ PASSAGE FROM BOOK - 2 Minutes [Set Timer]

FREEFORM DANCE - 2 minutes - [Set Timer]
Put on the selected music and **engage in freeform dancing, anchored in your colour/character,** Allow your body to move spontaneously and without inhibition. This can help you tap into your creative instincts and develop physical expressiveness *while staying in character.* **Tip**: Journal about the differences as opposed to how you normally dance.

JOURNAL YOUR EXPERIENCE - 1 Minute [Set Timer]

WORKOUT COMPLETED [ ]

Hold fast to dreams, for if dreams die, life is a broken-winged bird that cannot fly.
Langston Hughes

HISTORICAL RESEARCH

We are in the information era and have access to the world and its rich history at our fingertips. This exploration is not about 'learning facts'; it's a journey to the heart of human experience. The empathy and the understanding, especially on the things you disagree with, are incredibly valuable. If you look closely, you'll find the way people think, at different times in history, their attitudes, choices, and the way they move their bodies can teach you so much about us, right now. Fill your toolbox so it's overflowing with information and ideas to pull from so your imagination has so much to play with.

PHYSICAL WARMUP - 2 minutes - [Set Timer]
Freeform Dance: Put on some music and engage in freeform dancing. Allow your body to move spontaneously and without inhibition. This can help you tap into your creative instincts and develop physical expressiveness. **Tip**: Try music you've never listened to.

RESEARCH - 13 Minutes [Set Timer]
YouTube, streaming platforms, the internet or books, **research the given era/person/moment in time,** journal or make notes on your device, so when you want to find this information, it's organized and readily accessible. As you go, **write anything and everything _you_ find fascinating. Tip:** If the topic doesn't interest you, choose your own, or take a chance and still research it, but from a different perspective. Physicalities, voice, ideals, etc. Trust your body that when you see something interesting, you'll know. **Extra**: Speak it out and copy their movements. Our memory recall is massively affected by our bodies. Be specific and when you re-read your notes, you'll be amazed by how much your mind and body remember.

TOPIC:
Charlie Chaplin (1889-1977): An iconic figure in the silent film era, known for his character "The Tramp." Chaplin's unique physical comedy style and expressive acting make him a fascinating subject for actors. There is extensive footage of his films available, providing insights into early cinematic techniques and non-verbal storytelling.

WORKOUT COMPLETED [ ]

There will occasionally be times
when a seemingly mundane action is
perfect correct for a scene.
A practical handbook for the actor

BELIEF

Beliefs are the convictions that something exists or is true, especially without proof. That is also the definition of what we do as actors. We play make-believe. Our beliefs shape our world, especially our beliefs about ourselves and it works for the characters you play. Understand your beliefs and how they influence your mind, body and spirit, then you will be able to better understand others, so you can embody them. Allow the beliefs of your character to colour your perception of your world and your interaction with everything in it. "Acting is the best magic trick in the world. We applaud performances not because it's real, but because you made us believe."

VOCAL WORK - 2 Minutes - [Set timer]
Lip Trills: Close your lips together lightly, like you're going to blow a raspberry. Then, blow air through your closed lips while making sounds. You should feel a tickling sensation. Pick a song and Lip Trill along with it. **Tip**: Stretch your range as much as you can and pick a song you've never listened to.

BELIEF WORKOUT
Get your journal or write in here. **Define your personal belief/view** on the given subject. **Grab any book you own,** flip to a random page and **read it out loud,** colouring the words and intention with your belief system. **Tip:** Write trigger words you can hook into in the future: **Optimism-** Always smiling, grateful, opportunity, sunshine yellow.

YOUR PERSONAL BELIEF
A Higher Power - 7 Minutes [Set Timer]

_____
_____
_____
_____

READ WITH BELIEF - 2 Minutes [Set Timer]

CHARACTERS BELIEF
A Higher Power
I believe that life is part of a grand design, guided by a higher power. This belief gives my life purpose and direction, and I see every event as part of a larger, divine plan. God is with me always. It almost feels like I'm walking with my best friend who inspires and protects me every step I take of every day.

READ WITH CHARACTERS BELIEF - 2 Minutes [Set Timer]
Forget your personal view and **fully embrace the character's belief**. Read out loud again.

JOURNAL YOUR EXPERIENCE - 2 Minutes [Set Timer]

_____
_____
_____

WORKOUT COMPLETED [ ]

PERFORMANCE STRATEGY
14 DAY REVIEW

TAKE A MOMENT OF REFLECTION AND BREAKDOWN WHERE YOU ARE RIGHT NOW IN YOUR CAREER AND AS AN ACTOR.
THE MORE SPECIFIC YOU ARE THE MORE CLEAR YOU CAN SEE WHERE YOU ARE NOW SO YOU CAN GET TO WHERE YOU WANT TO GO FASTER

★ ★ ★ ★ ★

Soichiro Honda: After being turned down for an engineering job at Toyota, he started making scooters at home and eventually founded Honda Motor Company.

DATE:

MY WHY
WHY ARE YOU DOING WHAT YOU ARE DOING
BE SPECIFIC

MY MAIN GOALS
IN-ORDER OF IMPORTANCE

1.

   Action Step(s):

2.

   Action Step(s):

3.

   Action Step(s):

FROM THE LAST 14 DAYS ☆☆☆☆☆
5 STAR RATING

YOUR KEY POINTS AND TAKEAWAYS - WHY THAT AMOUNT OF STAR RATING, LIKES, DISLIKES, THE BIGGEST LESSON YOU LEARNED, GOOD OR BAD:

STRENGTHS:

WEAKNESSES:

IMPROVEMENT STRATEGY
HOW CAN YOU IMPROVE ON THESE AREAS FOR THE NEXT 14 DAYS:

GOAL FROM LAST :
DID YOU ACHIEVE IT?

WHY OR WHY NOT?

GOAL FOR THE NEXT 14 EXERCISES
THE MORE SPECIFIC YOU ARE THE GREATER THE RESULT

   Action Step(s):

The best performers set goals that are not about the outcome but about the process of reaching the outcome.
Anders Ericsson

MY WHY:

GOAL(s):

PHYSICAL WARMUP - 1 minute [Set Timer]
Colour Dance: Choose a colour and dance how it makes you feel. Let the colour's energy guide your movement. **Tip**: Visualize the colour radiating from your body as you dance.

VOCAL WORK - 3 minutes [Set timer]
Lip Trills: Close your lips together lightly, like you're going to blow a raspberry. Then, blow air through your closed lips while making sounds. You should feel a tickling sensation.

EMOTIONAL RECALL - 5 minutes [Set Timer]
Courageous Act: Bring to mind a moment when you had to gather all your courage to face a fear or challenge. **Tip**: Stand firm and breathe deeply, embodying the strength you found in that moment.

ANIMAL WORK - HORSE

Research - 2 minutes [Set Timer]
Study the horse's powerful yet graceful gait and social herd behaviour.

Animal Exercise - 3 minutes [Set Timer]
Emulate the trotting and galloping, and then as a human, conserve the horse's noble composure and sense of freedom.

Discovery Journal - 1 Minute [Set Timer]
3 Main Characteristics: (Whatever stands out to YOU to embody the essence)

_____
_____
_____
_____
_____
_____
_____
_____
_____

WORKOUT COMPLETED [ ]

Twenty years from now you will be more disappointed by the things you didn't do than by the ones you did.
Mark Twain

SCRIPT ANALYSIS for **RELATIONSHIPS & SPECIFICITY** - 15 minutes [Set Timer]
Choose your character, circle everything in this script you have a relationship with. Including people, places, things, smells, time of day etc. **Write what your relationship with those items are** and **be specific**. The more specific and fun you have with your relationships, the more interesting your characters will be and the more fun the audience has. **Tip:** Everything isn't in the scene. Use your imagination to create details, only if it's contextually appropriate. **Extra:** Write your > **Objective, win or lose? Consequence of failing?** The **Who What Where When Why.**

Title: **Echoes of Time**

INT. ABANDONED WAREHOUSE - NIGHT

A vast, dimly lit warehouse. Complex machinery fills the space. DR. ADAIR (mid-40s, brilliant and enigmatic) stands near a sophisticated, otherworldly device. KAI (early 30s, inquisitive and cautious) enters, taking in the surreal scene.

KAI
Dr. Adair? What is this place?

DR. ADAIR
This is where realities converge, Kai. A laboratory for studying the fabric of time itself.

KAI
And this machine?

DR. ADAIR
It's a gateway. A means to traverse alternate timelines, to witness the impact of choices made and unmade.

KAI
That sounds impossible.

DR. ADAIR
In our line of work, 'impossible' is a matter of perspective.

KAI
What's the purpose? What are you trying to find?

DR. ADAIR
Answers to questions we're afraid to ask. To see the consequences of our actions across the tapestry of time.

KAI
Isn't that dangerous? Meddling with time?

DR. ADAIR
All discovery is dangerous, Kai. But the greater risk is ignorance.

KAI
But how can you control it? How do you know what changes to make?

DR. ADAIR
Control is an illusion. It's not about changing the past but understanding it. We're observers, not gods.

KAI
And if something goes wrong?

DR. ADAIR
Then we face the consequences. Time is unforgiving, and we must be prepared to meet its challenges.

Kai steps closer to the device, a mix of fear and awe in their eyes.

KAI
What if we're not ready for what we find?

DR. ADAIR
Then we learn, we adapt. That's the essence of our existence, Kai. To continually evolve, even in the face of the unknown.

WORKOUT COMPLETED [ ]

I'm a skilled professional actor. Whether or not I've any talent is beside the point.
Michael Caine

IMAGINATION

We have a lot of tools in our arsenal as actors but **I believe imagination is the most powerful.** "If you hook into the character's belief system and you believe it 100%, there is no way the audience won't." - Meryl Streep "Imagination is more important than knowledge for knowledge is limited. - Einstein. Everyone has an Imagination but it must be worked out to get stronger. Think of your imagination as a limitless playground. In this space, you can be anyone, go anywhere, and do anything. **Have the courage to allow yourself to play!**

Solo Imaginary World Exploration - 6 Minutes [Set Timer]

Find a quiet space to relax and focus. **Close your eyes** and **let your imagination run wild. Tip:** Engage all your senses to explore this environment. Touch, taste, smell etc. Allow your emotions to guide you. **Extra:** After you establish this world in your imagination, you could introduce characters and have a dialogue with them. Are they friends or foes?

IMAGINARY WORLD: Space Station Orbiting a Black Hole: Experience the isolation and mystery of a space station near a black hole.

JOURNAL YOUR EXPERIENCE - 2 Minutes [Set Timer]

_____
_____
_____
_____
_____
_____

Your Characters Filter - 5 Minutes [Set Timer]

Everyone including the characters you play see the world through their own specific perspective/filter. I like to use the word filter because you can take out a filter, clean it, change its style, colour, an optimist or a pessimist, comedian or a nihilist, etc. **Find a quiet space** to focus. **Close your eyes and let go of your personal thoughts and emotions** to make space for your characters. **Open your eyes, and allow the filter provided to effect everything around you. Tip**: Explore wherever you are and interact with the objects. **Extra:** How does _this_ character walk and move in their world?

FILTER: Hardened Survivor: Views every situation as a challenge to overcome.

JOURNAL YOUR EXPERIENCE - 2 Minutes [Set Timer]

_____
_____
_____
_____
_____
_____

WORKOUT COMPLETED [ ]

I'm reflective only in the sense that I learn to move forward. I reflect with a purpose.
Kobe Bryant

CHARACTER STUDY "PEOPLE WATCHING"

Actors are required to portray characters that are believable and relatable. You don't have to agree with them but you have to understand them. Walk like them, talk like them, see the world like them. So, in order to fill our toolbox, we have to **go out into the world and study**. Then practice them over and over so we can "walk in their shoes', comfortably and confidently. Study their movements, mannerisms, the "vibe" they give off, the clothes they wear etc. **Fill your toolbox with the rhythms and idiosyncrasies of human behaviour.**

OBSERVATION CHARACTER STUDY - 15 Minutes [Set Timer]

Find a busy place where you can **sit and observe.** Choose anyone you find interesting. **Write down what stands out about them.** *The way they sit, drink their coffee, walk, talk, interact with others etc.* **Tip: Mirror them immediately.** This will help memorize the feeling of that character so whenever you come back to these characters you're discovering, your body will remember. **Extra**: Before you go to sleep, read over the characters from today and reenact their movements.

_____
_____
_____
_____
_____
_____
_____
_____
_____
_____
_____
_____
_____
_____
_____
_____
_____
_____
_____
_____
_____
_____

COLOURS: We as humans respond to colours like frequencies. If you pay attention closely, you can see everyone has their own 'colour' that defines their core. An essence that informs how they operate and move through the world.

WHAT COLOUR ARE THEY:

WORKOUT COMPLETED [ ]

The secret to film is that it's an illusion.
George Lucas

VOICE & DICTION

I wish I had learned this at the beginning of my career. The confidence to communicate clearly and powerfully is a game-changer for you as an actor. **Think of your voice as a musical instrument that needs regular tuning. This workout is your daily tuning session,** ensuring that your instrument is always ready. "The word 'theatre' comes from the Greeks. It means the seeing place. It is the place people come to see the truth about life and the social situation." - Stella Adler. Embrace this workout as a key to unlocking and portraying *that* truth by letting your voice be the vehicle that transports your audience into the heart of your story.

READ PASSAGE - 30 Seconds [Set Timer]
Speak the passage and take note of its quality. **Tip**: Record Audio to compare afterward.

"The harbour awakens at dawn. Boats rock gently, seagulls screech overhead and the breeze carries the promise of journeys afar. Fishermen prepare their nets, their silhouettes etched against the rising sun."

RELAXATION - 1 Minute [Set Timer]
Deep Breathing: Sit and Inhale deeply through your nose, filling your lungs, then exhale slowly through your mouth. Imagine stress leaving your body with each breath.

Nay Nay Nay - 1 Minute [Set Timer]
Pick a song and sing the word "Nay" repeatedly. Start with a comfortable pitch and gradually move the sound from your nose to your chest, ensuring each "Nay" is clear and resonant. Stretch your range as best you can to strengthen.

Sustained 'S' - 2 Minutes [Set Timer]
Inhale deeply and then exhale slowly, making a continuous 's' sound. Keep the sound as even and steady as you can. Always push a little longer than you think you can.

Vowel Pronunciation Drill - 2 Minutes [Set Timer]
Slowly go through each vowel sound **(A, E, I, O, U)**, **holding and exaggerating each sound. Combine them with consonants** (e.g., ba, be, bi, bo, bu). Pay attention to the clarity and sharpness of each sound. Repeat a few times before moving to the next.

Lip Trills - 3 minutes - [Set timer]
Close your lips together lightly, like you're going to blow a raspberry. Then, blow air through your closed lips while making sounds. You should feel a tickling sensation. Pick a song and Lip Trill the whole along with it. **Tip**: Stretch your range as much as you can and pick a song you've never listened to.

The Cork Exercise - 4 Minutes [Set Timer]
Place a cork between your teeth and try to read a passage aloud. This forces your articulation muscles to work harder. If you don't have a cork, bite down gently on your thumb. You can use the following text for this exercise:

READ PASSAGE AGAIN - 30 Seconds [Set Timer]
Speak the passage and take note of its quality. **Tip**: Record Audio to compare.

Discovery Journal - 1 Minute [Set Timer]

WORKOUT COMPLETED [ ]

I failed my way to success.
Thomas Edison

SUBTEXT

Subtext is what lies beneath the surface of our words. It's the hidden layer of meaning, driven by the character's internal thoughts, emotions, desires, and motivations. Subtext is one of my favourite things as an actor because so much can be said with one simple line of dialogue. The power of "Hello" can be exciting if you told that person years ago "If I ever see you again, I'll kill you. Maybe it's the most beautiful person you've ever seen. Now, say "hello". *Subtext* shows the audience what your relationship with the characters/places/situations are, without having to explain it. We experience it every day and it is our job to create characters that interact as we do.

VOCAL WORK - 3 minutes - [Set Timer]
Lip Trills: Close your lips together lightly, like you're going to blow a raspberry. Then, blow air through your closed lips while making sounds. You should feel a tickling sensation. Pick a song and Lip Trill along with it. **Tip**: Stretch your range as much as you can and pick a song you've never listened to.

SUBTEXT PRACTICE
Use the line of dialogue provided and practice each of these subtexts **out loud.** Move on to the next, only when you believe yourself. Trust that you will know when *that* is. Before you begin, **pick a spot to look at and imagine** in detail, **who you are speaking with**. **Tip**: *Sometimes* we mean exactly what we are saying. Look for that too. **Extra**: Substitute someone you have a strong relationship with in real life, good or bad, and see it's affect.

Initial Line: "Where have you been?"
Your Response Line: "Around. It's just… Life's been pulling me in a thousand directions. It's hard to keep track of time, you know?"

SUBTEXTS - 6 Minutes [Set Timer]
[ ] Pressured: You're feeling the weight of various responsibilities and expectations.
[ ] Isolated: Despite being busy, you feel disconnected from others.
[ ] Defensive: You're trying to justify your absence without revealing too much.
[ ] Regretful: You wish you had stayed more connected and involved.
[ ] Overwhelmed: Juggling everything has been more challenging than anticipated.
[ ] Your Own Subtext

RELATIONSHIP SUBTEXTS - 6 Minutes [Set Timer]
[ ] The Concerned Friend: They're worried but might not understand the full picture.
[ ] The Forgotten Partner: Your absence has put a strain on your relationship.
[ ] The Family Member Who Feels Neglected: They've missed your presence in their life.
[ ] The Co-Worker Who Depends on You: They're frustrated by your unavailability.
[ ] The Old Friend Who Feels Left Behind: They're trying to rekindle a fading connection.
[ ] Your Own Subtext

Discovery Journal

_____
_____
_____
_____
_____

WORKOUT COMPLETED [ ]

Everything negative - pressure, challenges - is all an opportunity for me to rise.
Kobe Bryant

EMOTIONS

The 'moment before', **the emotional preparation, is the most important key to a great scene.** If you start any scene <u>without</u> an emotional preparation it feels like trying to drive a car in neutral. The preparation is the uphill climb of every rollercoaster; Once you grind all the way to the top, the chains let go and the rest of the ride takes care of itself. "No one wants to see a play or a movie and look at technical proficiency. You want to be moved, you want a human experience, you want to feel less alone" - Viola Davis. **Practice your emotions over and over** so when it's time, you aren't worried "Will I get there?" **You're imagination and emotions should be a tinderbox, so easy to light up. All it take is half a spark.**

EULOGY - 12 Minutes [Set Timer]

Find a quiet comfortable space. Choose someone in your life who is alive and important to you. Create an imaginary reason for why they have died. Now start from the point of the phone call— Imagine who calls, what they say and what you say. Eventually find yourself at the funeral, about to begin the eulogy. See the casket, is it open or closed?? What is that person wearing and any other details for yourself. Before you begin to speak, look into the audience and see who is there- Family, friends etc **Then begin the eulogy. Tip:** <u>Be as specific as you can with everything.</u> **Inside of specificity is where you will find the triggers to your heart.** Let your imagination take you wherever you want in this exercise. **Example**: Placing her favourite sheep stuffed animal in the casket, tucked under her arm like she always held it, then kissing her goodbye one last time.

DISCOVERY JOURNAL - 3 Minutes [Set Timer]

Make sure to **include the specific triggers** you experience because you can use these **TRIGGER MOMENTS** in the future instead of repeating the *entire* exercise.

_____
_____
_____
_____
_____
_____
_____
_____
_____
_____
_____
_____
_____
_____
_____
_____
_____
_____

WORKOUT COMPLETED [ ]

You can't put a limit on anything. The more you dream, the farther you get.
Michael Phelps

THE CORK EXERCISE - 4 Minutes [Set Timer]
Place a cork between your teeth and read a passage aloud. This forces your articulation muscles to work harder. If you don't have a cork, bite down gently on your thumb. You can use the following text for this exercise:

"In the ancient library, rows of books hold the wisdom of ages. The scent of old paper and ink permeates the air. Each shelf is a doorway to another world, waiting to be explored and cherished."

WRITE A LETTER - 10 Minutes [Set Timer]
Get a piece of paper or write this in your device. **Take a moment** to let this situation and relationship sink in. Then let your imagination run wild and **write them a letter.**

Your Character: Sophia, a well-respected chef and owner of a popular restaurant.
Other Character: Luca, Sophia's former protégé and head chef, who abruptly left to open a rival restaurant using Sophia's recipes and culinary concepts.

Relationship: Sophia and Luca shared a bond that went beyond the typical mentor-protégé dynamic. Sophia saw Luca as a culinary kindred spirit and invested heavily in their development. Luca's departure and subsequent betrayal not only shocked Sophia but also threatened the integrity and success of her own restaurant.

Context of the Letter: Facing the sting of Luca's betrayal and the challenges posed to her business, Sophia writes a letter to Luca. In this letter, she confronts the feelings of betrayal and disappointment, questions Luca's motives, and expresses the deep sense of personal and professional hurt caused by Luca's actions.

Discovery Journal - 1 minute [Set Timer]

_____
_____
_____
_____
_____
_____
_____

WORKOUT COMPLETED [ ]

It's amazing how words can ruin what you really want to say.
Victor Zinck Jr

VOCAL WORK - 3 minutes [Set timer]

Lip Trills: Close your lips together lightly, like you're going to blow a raspberry. Then, blow air through your closed lips while making sounds. You should feel a tickling sensation. Pick a song and Lip Trill along with it. **Tip**: Stretch your range as much as you can and pick a song you've never listened to.

VERBAL IMPROV - 10 Minutes [Set Timer]

Find a space where you are comfortable and free to express yourself. Take a moment to **let this situation, character and prompt, sink in**. Then let your imagination run wild: **Picture who you are talking to** then **begin with the prompt** and **continue to verbalize everything** this character would say. **Tip**: This is exploration! There is no "getting it right". BE BRAVE to explore and discover.

Character: Riley, has been saving and planning for years to buy a family home. Recently, Riley discovered that their trusted financial advisor, a long-time friend, has been making risky investments with their savings without consent, resulting in a significant financial loss.

Prompt: "I trusted you with my life savings, and you've nearly lost it all. How could you do that?"

Who are you talking to:

Describe them in two specific words:

Discovery Journal - 2 minutes [Set Timer]

_____
_____
_____
_____
_____
_____
_____
_____

WORKOUT COMPLETED [ ]

Make sure your worst enemy doesn't live
between your own two ears.
Laird Hamilton

SELF AWARENESS

The more you understand yourself, the more you are able to understand and develop your characters. Like you, your characters have thoughts, beliefs, traumas, passions etc. When you become aware of your own and start to see how those experiences and beliefs have shaped your life, how you operate and view the world, then you can develop your characters that are much more rich and vivid.

PHYSICAL WARMUP - 2 minutes [Set Timer]

Freeform Dance: Put on some music and engage in freeform dancing. Allow your body to move spontaneously and without inhibition. This can help you tap into your creative instincts and develop physical expressiveness. **Tip**: Try music you've never listened to.

CURRENT EMOTIONAL INVENTORY - 3 Minutes [Set Timer]

Write down and **record your current emotions**. Identify what you're feeling at this moment and why. **Tip**: Be as specific as you can, **don't disregard anything.** You can also **scan your body** to see how and where your current emotion is affecting you. Your posture, the way you walk, bouncing foot, sore neck etc

CURRENT EMOTIONAL STATE:

SELF DISCOVERY QUESTIONS - 10 Minutes [Set Timer]

I suggest a journal or writing it in your phone's notes so you don't run out of space here.

What are my long-term goals and dreams?

Describe how will feel to receive/accomplish them

WORKOUT COMPLETED [ ]

It does not do to dwell on dreams
and forget to live.
J.K. Rowling

IMAGINATION

We have a lot of tools in our arsenal as actors but I believe imagination is the most powerful. "If you hook into the character's belief system and you believe it 100%, there is no way the audience won't." - Meryl Streep. Everyone has an Imagination but it must be worked out to get stronger. Think of your imagination as a limitless playground. In this space, you can be anyone, go anywhere, and do anything. **Have the courage to allow yourself to play!**

VOCAL WORK - 2 Minutes - [Set timer]
Lip Trills: Close your lips together lightly, like you're going to blow a raspberry. Then, blow air through your closed lips while making sounds. You should feel a tickling sensation. Pick a song and Lip Trill along with it. **Tip**: Stretch your range as much as you can and pick a song you've never listened to.

IMPROVISED STORYTELLING - 5 Minutes [Set Timer]
Speak out the scenario provided and continue the story! Focus on vivid details, character development and how the main character overcomes the main obstacle. **Tip**: Try not to stop speaking so you don't have time to "think". Allow your imagination to keep moving forward without interruption. **Tip**: Record these stories on your device, in case it's great but more importantly to see your progress as you go on.

STARTING POINT: You are Casey, a novice gardener who plants an unknown seed found in an old, dusty packet in the back of a garden shop. Surprisingly, the plant that grows is unlike any other; it thrives rapidly and seems to communicate through its movements and the patterns on its leaves.

IMAGINARY WORLD EXPLORATION - 6 Minutes [Set Timer]

Find a quiet space to relax and focus. **Close your eyes** and let your imagination run wild. **Tip:** Engage all your senses to explore this environment. Touch, taste, smell etc and allow your emotions to guide you. **Extra:** After you explore this world with your senses, you could introduce characters and have a dialogue with them. Are they friends or foes?

IMAGINARY WORLD: SONG OF THE TIDAL COVE - A tranquil cove where the rhythmic lapping of ocean waves creates a melody you know well. Redbirds, bigger than eagles, glide overhead, moving to the sound. Rain clouds approach.

JOURNAL YOUR EXPERIENCE - 2 Minutes [Set Timer]

___

___

___

___

___

___

___

WORKOUT COMPLETED [ ]

If you're an actor, even a successful one,
you're still waiting for the phone to ring.
Kevin Bacon

ANCHORING INTO YOUR CHARACTER COLOUR & MUSIC

Anchoring yourself into your character is vital. It's one of the most freeing feelings when you understand their *essence* because everything they do, how they do it and what their purpose is, becomes so clear to you and the audience. Every choice you make after you find your *anchor*, feels easy, because you're acting from who and what your character is at the core. You can call it an essence, an aura, vibe, energy etc. We all have it and feel it from everyone around us. There are many ways into your character but music and colour are my favourite. Music can inform the script, your character, even each scene. Colours, I think you will find, can work incredibly because we as humans respond to colours like frequencies. Colours evoke many feelings and if you pay attention closely, you can see everyone has their own 'colour' that defines their core. An essence that informs how they operate and move through the world.

THEIR COLOUR - 2 Minutes [Set Timer]
Think of **someone you know**, and **define them with a colour**. **Tip**: Trust yourself. Your initial colour is usually close. **Tip**: Start with basic colours then eventually become much more specific. **Example**: Corinna is an earthy green with rays of sunlight flowing through the green. **Extra**: Ask someone who knows *that person* as well, what they think this person's colour is and why. See how close your answers are or not.

YOUR CHARACTERS COLOUR
Read the given character description just as you would an audition, **assign a colour to that character.** Now take that colour you chose and **allow it to infuse into your entire body**, affecting your every move, your speaking, the way you see the world etc. **Take any book** you have, flip to a random page and **read the text as this Colour/Character**. **Tip**: Be specific, choose a colour that excites you and don't be afraid to get creative.

CHARACTER DESCRIPTION: [HARPER] Harper is a seasoned private investigator specializing in cold cases. Their small, cluttered office is a testament to years spent unravelling mysteries others have long abandoned. Known for wearing a classic trench coat and fedora, Harper's style echoes a bygone era of detective work. Beneath a cynical exterior lies a sharp, analytical mind and a surprisingly compassionate heart. Harper's pursuit of truth is relentless, often leading them down dark paths and into moral grey areas. Their character blends old-school grit with modern cunning, driven by a personal code.

CHOOSE THEIR COLOUR - 4 Minutes [Set Timer]
THEIR COLOUR:

CHOOSE THEIR SONG - 4 Minutes [Set Timer]
THEIR SONG:

READ PASSAGE FROM BOOK - 2 Minutes [Set Timer]

FREEFORM DANCE - 2 minutes - [Set Timer]
Put on the selected music and **engage in freeform dancing, anchored in your colour/character,** Allow your body to move spontaneously and without inhibition. This can help you tap into your creative instincts and develop physical expressiveness <u>while staying in character.</u> **Tip**: Journal about the differences as opposed to how you normally dance.

JOURNAL YOUR EXPERIENCE - 1 Minute [Set Timer]

WORKOUT COMPLETED [ ]

I don't think there's any artist of any value who doesn't doubt what they're doing.
Francis Ford Coppola

HISTORICAL RESEARCH

We are in the information era and have access to the world and its rich history at our fingertips. This exploration is not about 'learning facts'; it's a journey to the heart of human experience. The empathy and the understanding, especially on the things you disagree with, are incredibly valuable. If you look closely, you'll find the way people think, at different times in history, their attitudes, choices, and the way they move their bodies can teach you so much about us, right now. Fill your toolbox so it's overflowing with information and ideas to pull from so your imagination has so much to play with.

PHYSICAL WARMUP - 2 minutes - [Set Timer]
Freeform Dance: Put on some music and engage in freeform dancing. Allow your body to move spontaneously and without inhibition. This can help you tap into your creative instincts and develop physical expressiveness. **Tip**: Try music you've never listened to.

RESEARCH - 13 Minutes [Set Timer]
YouTube, streaming platforms, the internet or books, **research the given era/person/moment in time,** journal or make notes on your device, so when you want to find this information, it's organized and readily accessible. As you go, **write anything and everything _you_ find fascinating. Tip:** If the topic doesn't interest you, choose your own, or take a chance and still research it, but from a different perspective. Physicalities, voice, ideals, etc. Trust your body that when you see something interesting, you'll know. **Extra**: Speak it out and copy their movements. Our memory recall is massively affected by our bodies. Be specific and when you re-read your notes, you'll be amazed by how much your mind and body remember.

TOPIC:
Watergate Scandal (1972-1974): This major American political scandal involved the Nixon administration's continuous attempts to cover up its involvement in the June 1972 break-in at the Democratic National Committee headquarters in the Watergate office. The scandal led to the resignation of President Richard Nixon.

WORKOUT COMPLETED [ ]

Genius is one percent inspiration and
ninety-nine percent perspiration.
Thomas Edison

BELIEF

Beliefs are the convictions that something exists or is true, especially without proof. That is also the definition of what we do as actors. We play make-believe. Our beliefs shape our world, especially our beliefs about ourselves and it works for the characters you play. Understand your beliefs and how they influence your mind, body and spirit, then you will be able to better understand others, so you can embody them. Allow the beliefs of your character to colour your perception of your world and your interaction with everything in it. "Acting is the best magic trick in the world. We applaud performances not because it's real, but because you made us believe."

VOCAL WORK - 2 Minutes - [Set timer]
Lip Trills: Close your lips together lightly, like you're going to blow a raspberry. Then, blow air through your closed lips while making sounds. You should feel a tickling sensation. Pick a song and Lip Trill along with it. **Tip**: Stretch your range as much as you can and pick a song you've never listened to.

BELIEF WORKOUT
Get your journal or write in here. **Define your personal belief/view** on the given subject. **Grab any book you own,** flip to a random page and **read it out loud,** colouring the words and intention with your belief system. **Tip**: Write trigger words you can hook into in the future: **Optimism-** Always smiling, grateful, opportunity, sunshine yellow.

YOUR PERSONAL BELIEF
Time - 7 Minutes [Set Timer]

_____
_____
_____
_____

READ WITH BELIEF - 2 Minutes [Set Timer]

CHARACTERS BELIEF
Time
I see time as a burning candle, a constant reminder that life is fleeting and every moment is precious. "Time" pushes me to seize opportunities, take risks, and live aggressively. It's a race against the clock, where hesitating or waiting means missing out. In my eyes, time is not just passing; it's a challenge to make the most of every second before the candle is out.

READ WITH CHARACTERS BELIEF - 2 Minutes [Set Timer]
Forget your personal view and **fully embrace the character's belief. Read out loud again.**

JOURNAL YOUR EXPERIENCE - 2 Minutes [Set Timer]

_____
_____
_____
_____

WORKOUT COMPLETED [ ]

PERFORMANCE STRATEGY
14 DAY REVIEW

TAKE A MOMENT OF REFLECTION AND BREAKDOWN WHERE YOU ARE RIGHT NOW IN YOUR CAREER AND AS AN ACTOR.
THE MORE SPECIFIC YOU ARE THE MORE CLEAR YOU CAN SEE WHERE YOU ARE NOW SO YOU CAN GET TO WHERE YOU WANT TO GO FASTER

★   ★   ★   ★   ★

Stephen King: His first novel, "Carrie," was rejected multiple times. He threw away the manuscript, but his wife retrieved it and encouraged him to resubmit it.

DATE:

MY WHY
WHY ARE YOU DOING WHAT YOU ARE DOING
BE SPECIFIC

MY MAIN GOALS
IN-ORDER OF IMPORTANCE

1.

   Action Step(s):

2.

   Action Step(s):

3.

   Action Step(s):

FROM THE LAST 14 DAYS
5 STAR RATING

☆☆☆☆☆

YOUR KEY POINTS AND TAKEAWAYS - WHY THAT AMOUNT OF STAR RATING, LIKES, DISLIKES, THE BIGGEST LESSON YOU LEARNED, GOOD OR BAD:

STRENGTHS:

WEAKNESSES:

IMPROVEMENT STRATEGY
HOW CAN YOU IMPROVE ON THESE AREAS FOR THE NEXT 14 DAYS:

GOAL FROM LAST :
DID YOU ACHIEVE IT?

WHY OR WHY NOT?

GOAL FOR THE NEXT 14 EXERCISES
THE MORE SPECIFIC YOU ARE THE GREATER THE RESULT

   Action Step(s):

We don't make movies to make money, we make money to make more movies.
Walt Disney

MY WHY:

GOAL(s):

PHYSICAL WARMUP - 1 minute [Set Timer]
Freeform Dance: Put on some music and engage in freeform dancing. Allow your body to move spontaneously and without inhibition. This can help you tap into your creative instincts and develop physical expressiveness. **Tip:** Try music you've never listened to.

VOCAL WARMUP - 3 minutes [Set Timer]
Laughter Scale: Laugh in a scale pattern, going from low to high notes, like "ha-ha-ha-ha-ha" up and down the scales. **Tip**: Let the laughter be natural and feel how it resonates in your body.

EMOTIONAL RECALL - 5 minutes [Set Timer]
Excitement Surge: Select a memory where you felt a surge of excitement, such as the moments before a performance or a surprise. **Tip**: Feel the adrenaline in your system and let that energy inform your movements.

ANIMAL WORK - SQUIRREL

Research - 2 minutes [Set Timer]
Note the squirrel's agility, quick movements, and alertness.

Animal Exercise - 3 minutes [Set Timer]
Channel the squirrel's scurrying and foraging. As you morph back, maintain its lively energy and resourcefulness.

Discovery Journal - 1 Minute [Set Timer]
3 Main Characteristics: (Whatever stands out to YOU to embody the essence)

_____
_____
_____
_____
_____
_____
_____

WORKOUT COMPLETED [ ]

Simplicity is the ultimate sophistication.
Leonardo da Vinci

SCRIPT ANALYSIS for **RELATIONSHIPS & SPECIFICITY** - 15 minutes [Set Timer]
Choose your character, circle everything in this script you have a relationship with. Including people, places, things, smells, time of day etc. **Write what your relationship with those items are** and **be specific**. The more specific and fun you have with your relationships, the more interesting your characters will be and the more fun the audience has. **Tip:** Everything isn't in the scene. Use your imagination to create details, only if it's contextually appropriate. **Extra:** Write your > **Objective, win or lose? Consequence of failing?** The **Who What Where When Why.**

Title: **Unspoken Legacies**
INT. OLD BOOKSTORE - AFTERNOON
A quaint, cluttered bookstore. Shelves laden with books create a maze-like atmosphere. LUCAS (rugged, introspective) browses. His sister, EMILY (Ielegant, composed), enters the store.

EMILY
Lucas?
Lucas turns, surprised and slightly uneasy.
LUCAS
Emily... What are you doing here?
EMILY
I could ask you the same. I thought you left town years ago.
LUCAS
I did. Just back to settle some... old affairs.
EMILY
Like you settled them when you left us?
LUCAS
I had my reasons. You wouldn't understand.
EMILY
Try me. We're your family, Lucas. You owed us an explanation.
LUCAS
Family? Our family was broken long before I left.
EMILY
And you leaving fixed it? Or did it just fix things for you?
LUCAS
It wasn't like that. Dad's debts, the threats, I had to get away.
EMILY
And what about me? Did you think about what you were leaving behind?
LUCAS
Every day, Em. I thought I was protecting you.
EMILY
Protecting me? You abandoned me, Lucas. In a house full of ghosts and debts.
LUCAS
I'm sorry, Emily. I truly am.
EMILY
Sorry doesn't change the past. But maybe it's a start.
Lucas reaches out tentatively. Emily hesitates, then takes his hand.
LUCAS
Let me make it right, Emily. Let me be your brother again.

WORKOUT COMPLETED [ ]

I don't believe in art. I believe in artists.
Marcel Duchamp

IMAGINATION

We have a lot of tools in our arsenal as actors but **I believe imagination is the most powerful.** "If you hook into the character's belief system and you believe it 100%, there is no way the audience won't." - Meryl Streep "Imagination is more important than knowledge for knowledge is limited. - Einstein. Everyone has an Imagination but it must be worked out to get stronger. Think of your imagination as a limitless playground. In this space, you can be anyone, go anywhere, and do anything. **Have the courage to allow yourself to play!**

Solo Imaginary World Exploration - 6 Minutes [Set Timer]

Find a quiet space to relax and focus. **Close your eyes** and **let your imagination run wild. Tip:** Engage all your senses to explore this environment. Touch, taste, smell etc. Allow your emotions to guide you. **Extra:** After you establish this world in your imagination, you could introduce characters and have a dialogue with them. Are they friends or foes?

IMAGINARY WORLD: Medieval Kingdom in Turmoil: Immerse in a world of castles and dragons amid political intrigue and power struggles.

JOURNAL YOUR EXPERIENCE - 2 Minutes [Set Timer]

_____
_____
_____
_____
_____
_____

Your Characters Filter - 5 Minutes [Set Timer]

Everyone including the characters you play see the world through their own specific perspective/filter. I like to use the word filter because you can take out a filter, clean it, change its style, colour, an optimist or a pessimist, comedian or a nihilist, etc. **Find a quiet space** to focus. **Close your eyes and let go of your personal thoughts and emotions** to make space for your characters. **Open your eyes, and allow the filter provided to effect everything around you. Tip:** Explore wherever you are and interact with the objects. **Extra:** How does *this* character walk and move in their world?

FILTER: Passionate Artist: Sees the world as a canvas for beauty and expression.

JOURNAL YOUR EXPERIENCE - 2 Minutes [Set Timer]

_____
_____
_____
_____
_____
_____

WORKOUT COMPLETED [ ]

My first initial response is they are so good because they're not faking it, but that's 100% wrong. They are 100% faking it, they're just doing it so well. They've done their homework, emotionally understanding the material and they are vibrantly alive in the moment.
Victor Zinck Jr

CHARACTER STUDY "PEOPLE WATCHING"

Actors are required to portray characters that are believable and relatable. You don't have to agree with them but you have to understand them. Walk like them, talk like them, see the world like them. So, in order to fill our toolbox, we have to **go out into the world and study**. Then practice them over and over so we can "walk in their shoes', comfortably and confidently. Study their movements, mannerisms, the "vibe" they give off, the clothes they wear etc. **Fill your toolbox with the rhythms and idiosyncrasies of human behaviour.**

OBSERVATION CHARACTER STUDY - 15 Minutes [Set Timer]

Find a busy place where you can **sit and observe.** Choose anyone you find interesting. **Write down what stands out about them.** *The way they sit, drink their coffee, walk, talk, interact with others etc.* **Tip**: **Mirror them immediately.** This will help memorize the feeling of that character so whenever you come back to these characters you're discovering, your body will remember. **Extra**: Before you go to sleep, read over the characters from today and reenact their movements.

_____
_____
_____
_____
_____
_____
_____
_____
_____
_____
_____
_____
_____
_____
_____
_____
_____
_____
_____
_____

COLOURS: We as humans respond to colours like frequencies. If you pay attention closely, you can see everyone has their own 'colour' that defines their core. An essence that informs how they operate and move through the world.

WHAT COLOUR ARE THEY:

WORKOUT COMPLETED [ ]

The role of the artist is to ask questions, not answer them.
Anton Chekhov

VOICE & DICTION

I wish I had learned this at the beginning of my career. The confidence to communicate clearly and powerfully is a game-changer for you as an actor. **Think of your voice as a musical instrument that needs regular tuning. This workout is your daily tuning session,** ensuring that your instrument is always ready. "The word 'theatre' comes from the Greeks. It means the seeing place. It is the place people come to see the truth about life and the social situation." - Stella Adler. Embrace this workout as a key to unlocking and portraying *that* truth by letting your voice be the vehicle that transports your audience into the heart of your story.

READ PASSAGE - 30 Seconds [Set Timer]
Speak the passage and take note of its quality. **Tip**: Record Audio to compare afterward.

> "Over the whispering waves, under the singing stars, a symphony of dreams weaves through the night's embrace, echoing in the heart of the eternal dance."

RELAXATION - 1 Minute [Set Timer]
Deep Breathing: Sit and Inhale deeply through your nose, filling your lungs, then exhale slowly through your mouth. Imagine stress leaving your body with each breath.

Nay Nay Nay - 1 Minute [Set Timer]
Pick a song and sing the word "Nay" repeatedly. Start with a comfortable pitch and gradually move the sound from your nose to your chest, ensuring each "Nay" is clear and resonant. Stretch your range as best you can to strengthen.

Sustained 'S' - 2 Minutes [Set Timer]
Inhale deeply and then exhale slowly, making a continuous 's' sound. Keep the sound as even and steady as you can. Always push a little longer than you think you can.

Vowel Pronunciation Drill - 2 Minutes [Set Timer]
Slowly go through each vowel sound **(A, E, I, O, U), holding and exaggerating each sound. Combine them with consonants** (e.g., ba, be, bi, bo, bu). Pay attention to the clarity and sharpness of each sound. Repeat a few times before moving to the next.

Lip Trills - 3 minutes - [Set timer]
Close your lips together lightly, like you're going to blow a raspberry. Then, blow air through your closed lips while making sounds. You should feel a tickling sensation. Pick a song and Lip Trill the whole along with it. **Tip**: Stretch your range as much as you can and pick a song you've never listened to.

The Cork Exercise - 4 Minutes [Set Timer]
Place a cork between your teeth and try to read a passage aloud. This forces your articulation muscles to work harder. If you don't have a cork, bite down gently on your thumb. You can use the following text for this exercise:

READ PASSAGE AGAIN - 30 Seconds [Set Timer]
Speak the passage and take note of its quality. **Tip**: Record Audio to compare.

Discovery Journal - 1 Minute [Set Timer]

WORKOUT COMPLETED [ ]

We keep moving forward, opening new doors, and doing new things, because we're curious and curiosity keeps leading us down new paths.
Walt Disney

SUBTEXT

Subtext is what lies beneath the surface of our words. It's the hidden layer of meaning, driven by the character's internal thoughts, emotions, desires, and motivations. Subtext is one of my favourite things as an actor because so much can be said with one simple line of dialogue. The power of "Hello" can be exciting if you told that person years ago "If I ever see you again, I'll kill you. Maybe it's the most beautiful person you've ever seen. Now, say "hello". *Subtext* shows the audience what your relationship with the characters/places/situations are, without having to explain it. We experience it every day and it is our job to create characters that interact as we do.

VOCAL WORK - 3 minutes - [Set Timer]
Lip Trills: Close your lips together lightly, like you're going to blow a raspberry. Then, blow air through your closed lips while making sounds. You should feel a tickling sensation. Pick a song and Lip Trill along with it. **Tip**: Stretch your range as much as you can and pick a song you've never listened to.

SUBTEXT PRACTICE
Use the line of dialogue provided and practice each of these subtexts **out loud.** Move on to the next, only when you believe yourself. Trust that you will know when *that* is. Before you begin, **pick a spot to look at and imagine** in detail, **who you are speaking with**. **Tip**: *Sometimes* we mean exactly what we are saying. Look for that too. **Extra**: Substitute someone you have a strong relationship with in real life, good or bad, and see it's affect.

Initial Line: "Hello."
Your Response Line: " Hi. "

SUBTEXTS - 6 Minutes [Set Timer]
[ ] Furious: Your ex who cheated on you with your best friend.
[ ] Cynical: You know their tone means they have bad news.
[ ] Indifferent: You acknowledge the greeting but can't be bothered.
[ ] Inquisitive: You know they must have some big news if they are here, talking to you.
[ ] Untrustworthy: You don't know this person and don't trust new people.
[ ] Your Own Subtext

RELATIONSHIP SUBTEXTS - 6 Minutes [Set Timer]
[ ] Stranger: But they look at you like they've known you for years...
[ ] Racist co-worker who makes horrible jokes constantly and you're stuck in an elevator.
[ ] Unfocused friend: They are always on their phone and not present when you hang out.
[ ] "That Friend": They've had seven jobs in the last year and owe you 5,000 $
[ ] The Love of your life. They are married and today you're going to tell them how you feel.
[ ] Your Own Subtext

Discovery Journal
_____
_____
_____
_____

WORKOUT COMPLETED [ ]

I am my own experiment. I am my own work of art.
Salvador Dali

EMOTIONS

The 'moment before', **the emotional preparation, is the most important key to a great scene.** If you start any scene *without* an emotional preparation it feels like trying to drive a car in neutral. The preparation is the uphill climb of every rollercoaster; Once you grind all the way to the top, the chains let go and the rest of the ride takes care of itself. "No one wants to see a play or a movie and look at technical proficiency. You want to be moved, you want a human experience, you want to feel less alone" - Viola Davis. **Practice your emotions over and over** so when it's time, you aren't worried "Will I get there?" **You're imagination and emotions should be a tinderbox, so easy to light up. All it take is half a spark.**

EULOGY - 12 Minutes [Set Timer]

Find a quiet comfortable space. Choose someone in your life who is alive and important to you. Create an imaginary reason for why they have died. Now start from the point of the phone call— Imagine who calls, what they say and what you say. Eventually find yourself at the funeral, about to begin the eulogy. See the casket, is it open or closed?? What is that person wearing and any other details for yourself. Before you begin to speak, look into the audience and see who is there- Family, friends etc **Then begin the eulogy. Tip:** Be as specific as you can with everything. **Inside of specificity is where you will find the triggers to your heart.** Let your imagination take you wherever you want in this exercise. **Example**: Placing her favourite sheep stuffed animal in the casket, tucked under her arm like she always held it, then kissing her goodbye one last time.

DISCOVERY JOURNAL - 3 Minutes [Set Timer]

Make sure to **include the specific triggers** you experience because you can use these **TRIGGER MOMENTS** in the future instead of repeating the *entire* exercise.

WORKOUT COMPLETED [ ]

The role of the artist is to not look away.
Akira Kurosawa

THE CORK EXERCISE - 4 Minutes [Set Timer]
Place a cork between your teeth and read a passage aloud. This forces your articulation muscles to work harder. If you don't have a cork, bite down gently on your thumb. You can use the following text for this exercise:

"As night envelops the forest, nocturnal creatures emerge. Owls hoot softly, their eyes glowing in the darkness. The moon casts a silver light through the trees, creating a serene and mystical world."

WRITE A LETTER - 10 Minutes [Set Timer]
Get a piece of paper or write this in your device. **Take a moment** to let this situation and relationship sink in. Then let your imagination run wild and **write them a letter.**

Your Character: Emma, a promising young athlete on the verge of breaking into professional sports.
Other Character: Chris, Emma's former coach and mentor, who was recently implicated in a doping scandal involving several athletes, including allegations against Emma.

Relationship: Emma always saw Chris as a guiding force, instrumental in her development and success. Their relationship was built on hard work, mutual respect, and trust. However, the scandal has not only cast a shadow over Emma's career but also left her feeling betrayed and manipulated by someone she once admired and trusted implicitly.

Context of the Letter: Reeling from the accusations and the tarnishing of her reputation, Emma writes to Chris. This letter is her way of confronting the situation, expressing her sense of betrayal, confusion, and anger. It's a search for truth amidst the chaos and a way to regain control over her narrative and future.

Discovery Journal - 1 minute [Set Timer]
_____
_____
_____
_____
_____
_____

WORKOUT COMPLETED [ ]

If a million people see my movie, I hope they see a million different movies.
Quentin Tarantino

VOCAL WORK - 3 minutes [Set timer]
Lip Trills: Close your lips together lightly, like you're going to blow a raspberry. Then, blow air through your closed lips while making sounds. You should feel a tickling sensation. Pick a song and Lip Trill along with it. **Tip**: Stretch your range as much as you can and pick a song you've never listened to.

VERBAL IMPROV - 10 Minutes [Set Timer]

Find a space where you are comfortable and free to express yourself. Take a moment to **let this situation, character and prompt, sink in**. Then let your imagination run wild: **Picture who you are talking to** then **begin with *the prompt*** and **continue to verbalize everything** this character would say. **Tip**: This is exploration! There is no "getting it right". BE BRAVE to explore and discover.

Character: Sam, a dedicated volunteer at a local animal shelter, who has been tirelessly working to rehabilitate a particularly abused dog. Just as the dog begins to show improvement, Sam discovers that another volunteer, who seemed compassionate, has been mistreating the animal when no one else is around.

Prompt: "I found out what's been happening with the dog when I'm not here. How could you treat an animal like that?"

Who are you talking to:

Describe them in two specific words:

Discovery Journal - 2 minutes [Set Timer]
_____
_____
_____
_____
_____
_____

WORKOUT COMPLETED [ ]

Remember that the AS IF is purely a metro device. A way of sparking yourself to invest fully in the scene. Under no circumstances should you ever play the AS IF onstage. It is not a substitute for the play. It is something you've created for yourself to both personalize the action and get your motor going.
A practical handbook for the actor

SELF AWARENESS

The more you understand yourself, the more you are able to understand and develop your characters. Like you, your characters have thoughts, beliefs, traumas, passions etc. When you become aware of your own and start to see how those experiences and beliefs have shaped your life, how you operate and view the world, then you can develop your characters that are much more rich and vivid.

PHYSICAL WARMUP - 2 minutes [Set Timer]
Freeform Dance: Put on some music and engage in freeform dancing. Allow your body to move spontaneously and without inhibition. This can help you tap into your creative instincts and develop physical expressiveness. **Tip**: Try music you've never listened to.

CURRENT EMOTIONAL INVENTORY - 3 Minutes [Set Timer]
Write down and **record your current emotions**. Identify what you're feeling at this moment and why. **Tip**: Be as specific as you can, **don't disregard anything.** You can also **scan your body** to see how and where your current emotion is affecting you. Your posture, the way you walk, bouncing foot, sore neck etc

CURRENT EMOTIONAL STATE:

SELF DISCOVERY QUESTIONS - 10 Minutes [Set Timer]
I suggest a journal or writing it in your phone's notes so you don't run out of space here.

What are my biggest regrets, and why?

How do I define success, and do I feel successful?

WORKOUT COMPLETED [ ]

The future belongs to those who believe
in the beauty of their dreams.
Eleanor Roosevelt

IMAGINATION

We have a lot of tools in our arsenal as actors but I believe imagination is the most powerful. "If you hook into the character's belief system and you believe it 100%, there is no way the audience won't." - Meryl Streep. Everyone has an Imagination but it must be worked out to get stronger. Think of your imagination as a limitless playground. In this space, you can be anyone, go anywhere, and do anything. **Have the courage to allow yourself to play!**

VOCAL WORK - 2 Minutes - [Set timer]
Lip Trills: Close your lips together lightly, like you're going to blow a raspberry. Then, blow air through your closed lips while making sounds. You should feel a tickling sensation. Pick a song and Lip Trill along with it. **Tip**: Stretch your range as much as you can and pick a song you've never listened to.

IMPROVISED STORYTELLING - 5 Minutes [Set Timer]
Speak out the scenario provided and continue the story! Focus on vivid details, character development and how the main character overcomes the main obstacle. **Tip**: Try not to stop speaking so you don't have time to "think". Allow your imagination to keep moving forward without interruption. **Tip**: Record these stories on your device, in case it's great but more importantly to see your progress as you go on.

STARTING POINT: You are Harper, an urban explorer who discovers a hidden underground city beneath your bustling metropolis. This subterranean world is frozen in time and as you explore, you realize that the city is not simply a relic but is inhabited by echoes of its former residents, who reveal their stories and secrets.

IMAGINARY WORLD EXPLORATION - 6 Minutes [Set Timer]

Find a quiet space to relax and focus. **Close your eyes** and let your imagination run wild. **Tip:** Engage all your senses to explore this environment. Touch, taste, smell etc and allow your emotions to guide you. **Extra:** After you explore this world with your senses, you could introduce characters and have a dialogue with them. Are they friends or foes?

IMAGINARY WORLD: ECHOING CANYON - A canyon with towering red rock formations that seem to echo your every word. The sound of your voice reverberates through the majestic landscape, creating a unique and captivating experience.

JOURNAL YOUR EXPERIENCE - 2 Minutes [Set Timer]

___
___
___
___
___
___
___

WORKOUT COMPLETED [ ]

I think audiences get too comfortable and familiar in today's movies. They believe everything they're hearing and seeing. I like to shake that up.
Christopher Nolan

ANCHORING INTO YOUR CHARACTER COLOUR & MUSIC

Anchoring yourself into your character is vital. It's one of the most freeing feelings when you understand their *essence* because everything they do, how they do it and what their purpose is, becomes so clear to you and the audience. Every choice you make after you find your *anchor*, feels easy, because you're acting from who and what your character is at the core. You can call it an essence, an aura, vibe, energy etc. We all have it and feel it from everyone around us. There are many ways into your character but music and colour are my favourite. Music can inform the script, your character, even each scene. Colours, I think you will find, can work incredibly because we as humans respond to colours like frequencies. Colours evoke many feelings and if you pay attention closely, you can see everyone has their own 'colour' that defines their core. An essence that informs how they operate and move through the world.

THEIR COLOUR - 2 Minutes [Set Timer]
Think of **someone you know**, and **define them with a colour**. **Tip**: Trust yourself. Your initial colour is usually close. **Tip**: Start with basic colours then eventually become much more specific. **Example**: Corinna is an earthy green with rays of sunlight flowing through the green. **Extra**: Ask someone who knows *that person* as well, what they think this person's colour is and why. See how close your answers are or not.

YOUR CHARACTERS COLOUR
Read the given character description just as you would an audition, **assign a colour to that character.** Now take that colour you chose and **allow it to infuse into your entire body**, affecting your every move, your speaking, the way you see the world etc. **Take any book** you have, flip to a random page and **read the text as this Colour/Character**. **Tip**: Be specific, choose a colour that excites you and don't be afraid to get creative.

CHARACTER DESCRIPTION: [PHOENIX] Phoenix is an underground street racer, known for their fearless driving and rebellious spirit. The streets at night are their domain, where they command respect with a souped-up car that's as bold and unpredictable as they are. Phoenix wears a custom leather jacket, a symbol of their free-spirited and risk-taking nature. Beneath the adrenaline-fuelled exterior lies a backstory of defiance against a restrictive upbringing. Phoenix's character is an electrifying blend of speed, defiance, and the pursuit of freedom, driven by an unyielding desire to live life on their own terms.

CHOOSE THEIR COLOUR - 4 Minutes [Set Timer]
THEIR COLOUR:

CHOOSE THEIR SONG - 4 Minutes [Set Timer]
THEIR SONG:

READ PASSAGE FROM BOOK - 2 Minutes [Set Timer]

FREEFORM DANCE - 2 minutes - [Set Timer]
Put on the selected music and **engage in freeform dancing, anchored in your colour/character,** Allow your body to move spontaneously and without inhibition. This can help you tap into your creative instincts and develop physical expressiveness <u>while staying in character.</u> **Tip**: Journal about the differences as opposed to how you normally dance.

JOURNAL YOUR EXPERIENCE - 1 Minute [Set Timer]

WORKOUT COMPLETED [ ]

We applaud performances not because it is real, but because you made us believe.
Victor Zinck Jr

HISTORICAL RESEARCH

We are in the information era and have access to the world and its rich history at our fingertips. This exploration is not about 'learning facts'; it's a journey to the heart of human experience. The empathy and the understanding, especially on the things you disagree with, are incredibly valuable. If you look closely, you'll find the way people think, at different times in history, their attitudes, choices, and the way they move their bodies can teach you so much about us, right now. Fill your toolbox so it's overflowing with information and ideas to pull from so your imagination has so much to play with.

PHYSICAL WARMUP - 2 minutes - [Set Timer]
Freeform Dance: Put on some music and engage in freeform dancing. Allow your body to move spontaneously and without inhibition. This can help you tap into your creative instincts and develop physical expressiveness. **Tip**: Try music you've never listened to.

RESEARCH - 13 Minutes [Set Timer]
YouTube, streaming platforms, the internet or books, **research the given era/person/moment in time,** journal or make notes on your device, so when you want to find this information, it's organized and readily accessible. As you go, **write anything and everything _you_ find fascinating. Tip:** If the topic doesn't interest you, choose your own, or take a chance and still research it, but from a different perspective. Physicalities, voice, ideals, etc. Trust your body that when you see something interesting, you'll know. **Extra**: Speak it out and copy their movements. Our memory recall is massively affected by our bodies. Be specific and when you re-read your notes, you'll be amazed by how much your mind and body remember.

TOPIC:
The Green Children of Woolpit: This medieval legend from the 12th century tells of two children, a brother and sister, who mysteriously appeared in the village of Woolpit in Suffolk, England. The children had green-tinted skin and spoke an unknown language. According to the accounts, they eventually learned to speak English and explained that they came from a place called St. Martin's Land, where the sun never shone and everything was green. The story of the Green Children of Woolpit has been the subject of much speculation and analysis, with theories ranging from extraterrestrial origins to a folk memory of historical events.

WORKOUT COMPLETED [ ]

The most important thing is that you believe
that you're meant to be an actor.
Then you will be.
Kate Winslet

BELIEF

Beliefs are the convictions that something exists or is true, especially without proof. That is also the definition of what we do as actors. We play make-believe. Our beliefs shape our world, especially our beliefs about ourselves and it works for the characters you play. Understand your beliefs and how they influence your mind, body and spirit, then you will be able to better understand others, so you can embody them. Allow the beliefs of your character to colour your perception of your world and your interaction with everything in it. "Acting is the best magic trick in the world. We applaud performances not because it's real, but because you made us believe."

VOCAL WORK - 2 Minutes - [Set timer]

Lip Trills: Close your lips together lightly, like you're going to blow a raspberry. Then, blow air through your closed lips while making sounds. You should feel a tickling sensation. Pick a song and Lip Trill along with it. **Tip**: Stretch your range as much as you can and pick a song you've never listened to.

BELIEF WORKOUT

Get your journal or write in here. **Define your personal belief/view** on the given subject. **Grab any book you own,** flip to a random page and **read it out loud,** colouring the words and intention with your belief system. **Tip**: Write trigger words you can hook into in the future: **Optimism-** Always smiling, grateful, opportunity, sunshine yellow.

YOUR PERSONAL BELIEF

Money - 7 Minutes [Set Timer]

_____
_____
_____
_____

READ WITH BELIEF - 2 Minutes [Set Timer]

CHARACTERS BELIEF

Money

I'm a shark. I'm on the hunt every day for it. It keeps me alive. Everything I do I always have this 3rd eye, looking for an opportunity. I love that about myself. I respect that about others. I am a shark. The world is an ocean.

READ WITH CHARACTERS BELIEF - 2 Minutes [Set Timer]

Forget your personal view and **fully embrace the character's belief. Read out loud again.**

JOURNAL YOUR EXPERIENCE - 2 Minutes [Set Timer]

_____
_____
_____

WORKOUT COMPLETED [ ]

PERFORMANCE STRATEGY
14 DAY REVIEW

TAKE A MOMENT OF REFLECTION AND BREAKDOWN WHERE YOU ARE RIGHT NOW IN YOUR CAREER AND AS AN ACTOR.
THE MORE SPECIFIC YOU ARE THE MORE CLEAR YOU CAN SEE WHERE YOU ARE NOW SO YOU CAN GET TO WHERE YOU WANT TO GO FASTER

★ ★ ★ ★ ★

Vera Wang: Began her career in fashion at age 40 after failing to make the US Olympic figure-skating team and being passed over for an editor-in-chief position at Vogue.

DATE:

MY WHY
WHY ARE YOU DOING WHAT YOU ARE DOING
BE SPECIFIC

MY MAIN GOALS
IN-ORDER OF IMPORTANCE

1.

   Action Step(s):

2.

   Action Step(s):

3.

   Action Step(s):

FROM THE LAST 14 DAYS ☆☆☆☆☆
5 STAR RATING

YOUR KEY POINTS AND TAKEAWAYS - WHY THAT AMOUNT OF STAR RATING, LIKES, DISLIKES, THE BIGGEST LESSON YOU LEARNED, GOOD OR BAD:

STRENGTHS:

WEAKNESSES:

IMPROVEMENT STRATEGY
HOW CAN YOU IMPROVE ON THESE AREAS FOR THE NEXT 14 DAYS:

GOAL FROM LAST :
DID YOU ACHIEVE IT?

WHY OR WHY NOT?

GOAL FOR THE NEXT 14 EXERCISES
THE MORE SPECIFIC YOU ARE THE GREATER THE RESULT

   Action Step(s):

When people ask me if I went to film school, I tell them, 'No, I went to films.'
Quentin Tarantino

MY WHY:

GOAL(s):

PHYSICAL WARMUP - 1 minute [Set Timer]
Colour Dance: Choose a colour and dance how it makes you feel. Let the colour's energy guide your movement. **Tip**: Visualize the colour radiating from your body as you dance.

VOCAL WARMUP - 3 minutes [Set Timer]
Fluttered Lip Trills: With relaxed lips, blow air through them to create a trilling sound, like a horse. **Tip**: Keep the breath steady and the lips as loose as possible to improve flexibility.

EMOTIONAL RECALL - 5 minutes [Set Timer]
Comforting Embrace: Think of a moment when you received or gave a hug that provided deep comfort or solace. **Tip**: Embrace the warmth of the memory and how it eases your muscles and breathing.

ANIMAL WORK - PEACOCK
Research - 2 minutes [Set Timer]
Observe the peacock's display, colour, and the way it struts.

Animal Exercise - 3 minutes [Set Timer]
Adopt the peacock's prideful showmanship, then smoothly transition into human, keeping a flair of flamboyance and confidence.

Discovery Journal - 1 Minute [Set Timer]
3 Main Characteristics: (Whatever stands out to YOU to embody the essence)

_____
_____
_____
_____
_____
_____
_____
_____

WORKOUT COMPLETED [ ]

Acting touches nerves you have absolutely
no control over.
Alan Rickman

SCRIPT ANALYSIS for **RELATIONSHIPS & SPECIFICITY** - 15 minutes [Set Timer]
Choose your character, circle everything in this script you have a relationship with. Including people, places, things, smells, time of day etc. **Write what your relationship with those items are** and **be specific**. The more specific and fun you have with your relationships, the more interesting your characters will be and the more fun the audience has. **Tip:** Everything isn't in the scene. Use your imagination to create details, only if it's contextually appropriate. **Extra:** Write your > **Objective, win or lose? Consequence of failing?** The **Who What Where When Why.**

Title: **Ambition's Edge**
INT. UNIVERSITY LABORATORY - EVENING
A modern laboratory, filled with advanced equipment. DR. HELENA (brilliant and authoritative) stands, examining data on a screen. ALEX (ambitious student) Enters quickly

ALEX
Dr. Helena, we need to talk about the research findings.
DR. HELENA
Alex, this isn't a good time.
ALEX
It's never a good time! You've been avoiding this discussion.
DR. HELENA
I'm not avoiding anything. The data just isn't ready.
ALEX
I think it is. And I think you know it could change everything in our field.
DR. HELENA
Change everything? Or just elevate your career?
ALEX
This isn't about my career. It's about the truth!
DR. HELENA
Truth is a luxury in science. What we need is certainty.
ALEX
But the evidence is clear. We can't ignore it because it's inconvenient.
DR. HELENA
You're young, Alex. You don't understand the implications.
ALEX
I understand more than you think. I know about the funding pressures.
DR. HELENA
And yet you seem ready to jeopardize everything we've built here.
ALEX
What's the point of building anything if we're not honest about our findings?
DR. HELENA
Sometimes, honesty isn't black and white, Alex. It's about the bigger picture.
ALEX
And what about integrity? Does that not matter anymore?
DR. HELENA
Of course, it does. But we must be strategic about how we present our discoveries.
ALEX
Strategic or cautious? There's a difference.
DR. HELENA
You have much to learn. Not everything is as simple as it seems in academia.
ALEX
I'm not naïve, Dr. Helena. I know what's at stake.
DR. HELENA
Then you must also understand the risks of moving too fast.
Alex stands firm, meeting her gaze with determination.
ALEX
And you must understand the risks of not moving at all.

WORKOUT COMPLETED [ ]

I'll do whatever it takes to win games, whether it's sitting on a bench waving a towel, handing a cup of water to a teammate, or hitting the game-winning shot.
Kobe Bryant

IMAGINATION

We have a lot of tools in our arsenal as actors but **I believe imagination is the most powerful.** "If you hook into the character's belief system and you believe it 100%, there is no way the audience won't." - Meryl Streep "Imagination is more important than knowledge for knowledge is limited. - Einstein. Everyone has an Imagination but it must be worked out to get stronger. Think of your imagination as a limitless playground. In this space, you can be anyone, go anywhere, and do anything. **Have the courage to allow yourself to play!**

Solo Imaginary World Exploration - 6 Minutes [Set Timer]

Find a quiet space to relax and focus. **Close your eyes** and **let your imagination run wild. Tip:** Engage all your senses to explore this environment. Touch, taste, smell etc. Allow your emotions to guide you. **Extra:** After you establish this world in your imagination, you could introduce characters and have a dialogue with them. Are they friends or foes?

IMAGINARY WORLD: Post-Apocalyptic Wasteland: Endure in a collapsed civilization with desolate landscapes and lawless societies.

JOURNAL YOUR EXPERIENCE - 2 Minutes [Set Timer]

_____
_____
_____
_____
_____
_____

Your Characters Filter - 5 Minutes [Set Timer]

Everyone including the characters you play see the world through their own specific perspective/filter. I like to use the word filter because you can take out a filter, clean it, change its style, colour, an optimist or a pessimist, comedian or a nihilist, etc. **Find a quiet space** to focus. **Close your eyes and let go of your personal thoughts and emotions** to make space for your characters. **Open your eyes, and allow the filter provided to effect everything around you. Tip**: Explore wherever you are and interact with the objects. **Extra:** How does _this_ character walk and move in their world?

FILTER: Innocent Child: Experiences everything with wonder and naiveté.

JOURNAL YOUR EXPERIENCE - 2 Minutes [Set Timer]

_____
_____
_____
_____
_____
_____

WORKOUT COMPLETED [ ]

To live truthfully onstage and effectively
perform your action you must learn to
embrace each moment as it actually
occurs, NOT as you would like it to be.
A practical handbook for the actor

CHARACTER STUDY "PEOPLE WATCHING"

Actors are required to portray characters that are believable and relatable. You don't have to agree with them but you have to understand them. Walk like them, talk like them, see the world like them. So, in order to fill our toolbox, we have to **go out into the world and study**. Then practice them over and over so we can "walk in their shoes', comfortably and confidently. Study their movements, mannerisms, the "vibe" they give off, the clothes they wear etc. **Fill your toolbox with the rhythms and idiosyncrasies of human behaviour.**

OBSERVATION CHARACTER STUDY - 15 Minutes [Set Timer]

Find a busy place where you can **sit and observe.** Choose anyone you find interesting. **Write down what stands out about them.** *The way they sit, drink their coffee, walk, talk, interact with others etc.* **Tip**: **Mirror them immediately.** This will help memorize the feeling of that character so whenever you come back to these characters you're discovering, your body will remember. **Extra**: Before you go to sleep, read over the characters from today and reenact their movements.

___

COLOURS: We as humans respond to colours like frequencies. If you pay attention closely, you can see everyone has their own 'colour' that defines their core. An essence that informs how they operate and move through the world.

WHAT COLOUR ARE THEY:

WORKOUT COMPLETED [ ]

Film is incredibly democratic and accessible, it's probably the best option if you actually want to change the world, not just re-decorate it.
Banksy

VOICE & DICTION

I wish I had learned this at the beginning of my career. The confidence to communicate clearly and powerfully is a game-changer for you as an actor. **Think of your voice as a musical instrument that needs regular tuning. This workout is your daily tuning session,** ensuring that your instrument is always ready. "The word 'theatre' comes from the Greeks. It means the seeing place. It is the place people come to see the truth about life and the social situation." - Stella Adler. Embrace this workout as a key to unlocking and portraying *that* truth by letting your voice be the vehicle that transports your audience into the heart of your story.

READ PASSAGE - 30 Seconds [Set Timer]
Speak the passage and take note of its quality. **Tip**: Record Audio to compare afterward.

> "In the old library, time stands still. Shelves of books tower from floor to ceiling, the scent of aged paper fills the air, and every whisper echoes in the hallowed halls. The quiet sanctuary holds the wisdom of ages, waiting to be discovered."

RELAXATION - 1 Minute [Set Timer]
Deep Breathing: Sit and Inhale deeply through your nose, filling your lungs, then exhale slowly through your mouth. Imagine stress leaving your body with each breath.

Nay Nay Nay - 1 Minute [Set Timer]
Pick a song and sing the word "Nay" repeatedly. Start with a comfortable pitch and gradually move the sound from your nose to your chest, ensuring each "Nay" is clear and resonant. Stretch your range as best you can to strengthen.

Sustained 'S' - 2 Minutes [Set Timer]
Inhale deeply and then exhale slowly, making a continuous 's' sound. Keep the sound as even and steady as you can. Always push a little longer than you think you can.

Vowel Pronunciation Drill - 2 Minutes [Set Timer]
Slowly go through each vowel sound **(A, E, I, O, U), holding and exaggerating each sound. Combine them with consonants** (e.g., ba, be, bi, bo, bu). Pay attention to the clarity and sharpness of each sound. Repeat a few times before moving to the next.

Lip Trills - 3 minutes - [Set timer]
Close your lips together lightly, like you're going to blow a raspberry. Then, blow air through your closed lips while making sounds. You should feel a tickling sensation. Pick a song and Lip Trill the whole along with it. **Tip**: Stretch your range as much as you can and pick a song you've never listened to.

The Cork Exercise - 4 Minutes [Set Timer]
Place a cork between your teeth and try to read a passage aloud. This forces your articulation muscles to work harder. If you don't have a cork, bite down gently on your thumb. You can use the following text for this exercise:

READ PASSAGE AGAIN - 30 Seconds [Set Timer]
Speak the passage and take note of its quality. **Tip**: Record Audio to compare.

Discovery Journal - 1 Minute [Set Timer]

WORKOUT COMPLETED [ ]

A film is never really good unless the camera is an eye in the head of a poet.
Orson Welles

SUBTEXT

Subtext is what lies beneath the surface of our words. It's the hidden layer of meaning, driven by the character's internal thoughts, emotions, desires, and motivations. Subtext is one of my favourite things as an actor because so much can be said with one simple line of dialogue. The power of "Hello" can be exciting if you told that person years ago "If I ever see you again, I'll kill you. Maybe it's the most beautiful person you've ever seen. Now, say "hello". *Subtext* shows the audience what your relationship with the characters/places/situations are, without having to explain it. We experience it every day and it is our job to create characters that interact as we do.

VOCAL WORK - 3 minutes - [Set Timer]
Lip Trills: Close your lips together lightly, like you're going to blow a raspberry. Then, blow air through your closed lips while making sounds. You should feel a tickling sensation. Pick a song and Lip Trill along with it. **Tip**: Stretch your range as much as you can and pick a song you've never listened to.

SUBTEXT PRACTICE
Use the line of dialogue provided and practice each of these subtexts **out loud.** Move on to the next, only when you believe yourself. Trust that you will know when *that* is. Before you begin, **pick a spot to look at and imagine** in detail, **who you are speaking with**. **Tip**: *Sometimes* we mean exactly what we are saying. Look for that too. **Extra**: Substitute someone you have a strong relationship with in real life, good or bad, and see it's affect.

Initial Line: "I want to kiss you right now."
Your Response Line: "I'm not sure what to say…"

SUBTEXTS - 6 Minutes [Set Timer]
[ ] Annoyed: Again?!
[ ] Excited: I never believed in love at first sight until now.
[ ] Worrying: I have feelings for you but I don't want to ruin our friendship.
[ ] Indifferent: It doesn't really matter to you either way.
[ ] Horny and Conflicted: Sexy stranger but you're in a serious relationship.
[ ] Your Own Subtext

RELATIONSHIP SUBTEXTS - 6 Minutes [Set Timer]
[ ] Your biggest crush you thought didn't like you.
[ ] Second cousin.
[ ] Close friend of 15 years… Never has done this before.
[ ] Competitive Fellow Actor: Trying to mess with you before an audition
[ ] Homeless man at a bus stop.
[ ] Your Own Subtext

Discovery Journal

_____
_____
_____
_____

WORKOUT COMPLETED [ ]

The difference between ordinary and extraordinary is that little extra.
Jimmy Johnson

EMOTIONS
The 'moment before', **the emotional preparation, is the most important key to a great scene.** If you start any scene *without* an emotional preparation it feels like trying to drive a car in neutral. The preparation is the uphill climb of every rollercoaster; Once you grind all the way to the top, the chains let go and the rest of the ride takes care of itself. "No one wants to see a play or a movie and look at technical proficiency. You want to be moved, you want a human experience, you want to feel less alone" - Viola Davis. **Practice your emotions over and over** so when it's time, you aren't worried "Will I get there?" **You're imagination and emotions should be a tinderbox, so easy to light up. All it take is half a spark.**

EULOGY - 12 Minutes [Set Timer]
Find a quiet comfortable space. Choose someone in your life who is alive and important to you. Create an imaginary reason for why they have died. Now start from the point of the phone call— Imagine who calls, what they say and what you say. Eventually find yourself at the funeral, about to begin the eulogy. See the casket, is it open or closed?? What is that person wearing and any other details for yourself. Before you begin to speak, look into the audience and see who is there- Family, friends etc **Then begin the eulogy. Tip**: Be as specific as you can with everything. **Inside of specificity is where you will find the triggers to your heart.** Let your imagination take you wherever you want in this exercise. **Example**: Placing her favourite sheep stuffed animal in the casket, tucked under her arm like she always held it, then kissing her goodbye one last time.

DISCOVERY JOURNAL - 3 Minutes [Set Timer]
Make sure to **include the specific triggers** you experience because you can use these **TRIGGER MOMENTS** in the future instead of repeating the *entire* exercise.

___
___
___
___
___
___
___
___
___
___
___
___
___
___
___
___
___
___
___
___

WORKOUT COMPLETED [ ]

Not having to work requires a lot of hard work.
S. Miers

THE CORK EXERCISE - 4 Minutes [Set Timer]
Place a cork between your teeth and read a passage aloud. This forces your articulation muscles to work harder. If you don't have a cork, bite down gently on your thumb. You can use the following text for this exercise:

> "In the quiet countryside, fields of green stretch towards the horizon. Farm animals graze peacefully, and a gentle stream meanders through. The scent of fresh earth and growing things fills the air, bringing a sense of calm."

WRITE A LETTER - 10 Minutes [Set Timer]
Get a piece of paper or write this in your device. **Take a moment** to let this situation and relationship sink in. Then let your imagination run wild and **write them a letter.**

Your Character: Max, an investigative journalist known for uncovering major scandals.
Other Character: Kendall, Max's mentor and trusted confidant, was revealed to be involved in one of the biggest scandals Max has ever uncovered.

Relationship: Max always looked up to Kendall, gaining invaluable insights and guidance from them. Their bond went beyond a typical mentor-mentee relationship; it was one of deep mutual respect and trust. However, this trust was shattered when Max's latest investigation revealed Kendall's direct involvement in corrupt activities they had been reporting against.

Context of the Letter: Struggling with a sense of betrayal and disillusionment, Max writes to Kendall. The letter is a confrontation of the painful truth, an expression of deep disappointment, and a search for answers as to why Kendall, a once-respected figure in Max's life, chose such a path.

Discovery Journal - 1 minute [Set Timer]
_____
_____
_____
_____
_____

WORKOUT COMPLETED [ ]

An athlete cannot run with money in his pockets. He must run with hope in his heart and dreams in his head.
Emil Zatopek

VOCAL WORK - 3 minutes [Set timer]

Lip Trills: Close your lips together lightly, like you're going to blow a raspberry. Then, blow air through your closed lips while making sounds. You should feel a tickling sensation. Pick a song and Lip Trill along with it. **Tip**: Stretch your range as much as you can and pick a song you've never listened to.

VERBAL IMPROV - 10 Minutes [Set Timer]

Find a space where you are comfortable and free to express yourself. Take a moment to **let this situation, character and prompt, sink in**. Then let your imagination run wild: **Picture who you are talking to** then **begin with *the prompt*** and **continue to verbalize everything** this character would say. **Tip**: This is exploration! There is no "getting it right". BE BRAVE to explore and discover.

Character: Taylor, an enthusiastic member of a local book club, has been excitedly organizing a special meeting with a famous author. Just before the event, Taylor learns that their co-organizer, a trusted friend from the club, has cancelled the author's appearance without consulting them, out of jealousy over Taylor receiving all the credit for the event.

Prompt: "Why did you cancel the author's appearance for our book club meeting without telling me?"

Who are you talking to:

Describe them in two specific words:

Discovery Journal - 2 minutes [Set Timer]

_____
_____
_____
_____
_____
_____
_____
_____

WORKOUT COMPLETED [ ]

The most honest form of filmmaking is to make a film for yourself.
Peter Jackson

SELF AWARENESS

The more you understand yourself, the more you are able to understand and develop your characters. Like you, your characters have thoughts, beliefs, traumas, passions etc. When you become aware of your own and start to see how those experiences and beliefs have shaped your life, how you operate and view the world, then you can develop your characters that are much more rich and vivid.

PHYSICAL WARMUP - 2 minutes [Set Timer]

Freeform Dance: Put on some music and engage in freeform dancing. Allow your body to move spontaneously and without inhibition. This can help you tap into your creative instincts and develop physical expressiveness. **Tip**: Try music you've never listened to.

CURRENT EMOTIONAL INVENTORY - 3 Minutes [Set Timer]

Write down and **record your current emotions**. Identify what you're feeling at this moment and why. **Tip**: Be as specific as you can, **don't disregard anything.** You can also **scan your body** to see how and where your current emotion is affecting you. Your posture, the way you walk, bouncing foot, sore neck etc

CURRENT EMOTIONAL STATE:

SELF DISCOVERY QUESTIONS - 10 Minutes [Set Timer]

I suggest a journal or writing it in your phone's notes so you don't run out of space here.

What are my coping mechanisms for dealing with pain or discomfort?

How do I deal with anger or frustration?

What brings me genuine joy and happiness?

WORKOUT COMPLETED [ ]

Be so good they can't ignore you.
Steve Martin

IMAGINATION

We have a lot of tools in our arsenal as actors but I believe imagination is the most powerful. "If you hook into the character's belief system and you believe it 100%, there is no way the audience won't." - Meryl Streep. Everyone has an Imagination but it must be worked out to get stronger. Think of your imagination as a limitless playground. In this space, you can be anyone, go anywhere, and do anything. **Have the courage to allow yourself to play!**

VOCAL WORK - 2 Minutes - [Set timer]
Lip Trills: Close your lips together lightly, like you're going to blow a raspberry. Then, blow air through your closed lips while making sounds. You should feel a tickling sensation. Pick a song and Lip Trill along with it. **Tip**: Stretch your range as much as you can and pick a song you've never listened to.

IMPROVISED STORYTELLING - 5 Minutes [Set Timer]
Speak out the scenario provided and continue the story! Focus on vivid details, character development and how the main character overcomes the main obstacle. **Tip**: Try not to stop speaking so you don't have time to "think". Allow your imagination to keep moving forward without interruption. **Tip**: Record these stories on your device, in case it's great but more importantly to see your progress as you go on.

STARTING POINT: You are Sam, a linguist who receives an ancient, unreadable manuscript rumoured to be a lost language. As you begin to decipher it, you find that the manuscript is magical. It not only holds secrets of the past but also seems to predict future events, making your quest both exhilarating and fraught with responsibility.

IMAGINARY WORLD EXPLORATION - 6 Minutes [Set Timer]

Find a quiet space to relax and focus. **Close your eyes** and let your imagination run wild. **Tip:** Engage all your senses to explore this environment. Touch, taste, smell etc and allow your emotions to guide you. **Extra:** After you explore this world with your senses, you could introduce characters and have a dialogue with them. Are they friends or foes?

IMAGINARY WORLD: MOONLIT BEACH - A tranquil beach bathed in the soft, silvery light of the moon. The gentle lapping of waves and the cool, sandy shore invite you to relax and contemplate the mysteries of the night.

JOURNAL YOUR EXPERIENCE - 2 Minutes [Set Timer]

_____
_____
_____
_____
_____
_____
_____
_____

WORKOUT COMPLETED [ ]

The true sign of intelligence is not knowledge but imagination.
Albert Einstein

ANCHORING INTO YOUR CHARACTER COLOUR & MUSIC

Anchoring yourself into your character is vital. It's one of the most freeing feelings when you understand their *essence* because everything they do, how they do it and what their purpose is, becomes so clear to you and the audience. Every choice you make after you find your *anchor*, feels easy, because you're acting from who and what your character is at the core. You can call it an essence, an aura, vibe, energy etc. We all have it and feel it from everyone around us. There are many ways into your character but music and colour are my favourite. Music can inform the script, your character, even each scene. Colours, I think you will find, can work incredibly because we as humans respond to colours like frequencies. Colours evoke many feelings and if you pay attention closely, you can see everyone has their own 'colour' that defines their core. An essence that informs how they operate and move through the world.

THEIR COLOUR - 2 Minutes [Set Timer]
Think of **someone you know**, and **define them with a colour**. **Tip**: Trust yourself. Your initial colour is usually close. **Tip**: Start with basic colours then eventually become much more specific. **Example**: Corinna is an earthy green with rays of sunlight flowing through the green. **Extra**: Ask someone who knows *that person* as well, what they think this person's colour is and why. See how close your answers are or not.

YOUR CHARACTERS COLOUR
Read the given character description just as you would an audition, **assign a colour to that character.** Now take that colour you chose and **allow it to infuse into your entire body**, affecting your every move, your speaking, the way you see the world etc. **Take any book** you have, flip to a random page and **read the text as this Colour/Character.** Tip: Be specific, choose a colour that excites you and don't be afraid to get creative.

CHARACTER DESCRIPTION: [FINLEY] Finley is a gifted but reclusive sculptor, whose workshop is a hidden oasis of art, filled with clay, stone, and sculptures in various stages of completion. They work mostly at night, finding solace in the quiet hours. Finley is typically clad in a well-worn apron smeared with clay, their hands perpetually stained from their craft. Although shy and reticent in public, their art speaks volumes, revealing a profound connection to the human form and the emotions it can convey. Finley's character is a juxtaposition of solitary artistic dedication and the silent eloquence of their sculptures.

CHOOSE THEIR COLOUR - 4 Minutes [Set Timer]
THEIR COLOUR:

CHOOSE THEIR SONG - 4 Minutes [Set Timer]
THEIR SONG:

READ PASSAGE FROM BOOK - 2 Minutes [Set Timer]

FREEFORM DANCE - 2 minutes - [Set Timer]
Put on the selected music and **engage in freeform dancing**, anchored in your colour/character, Allow your body to move spontaneously and without inhibition. This can help you tap into your creative instincts and develop physical expressiveness *while staying in character.* **Tip**: Journal about the differences as opposed to how you normally dance.

JOURNAL YOUR EXPERIENCE - 1 Minute [Set Timer]

WORKOUT COMPLETED [ ]

Stop explaining yourself. Shut up and act!
Craig MacDonald

HISTORICAL RESEARCH

We are in the information era and have access to the world and its rich history at our fingertips. This exploration is not about 'learning facts'; it's a journey to the heart of human experience. The empathy and the understanding, especially on the things you disagree with, are incredibly valuable. If you look closely, you'll find the way people think, at different times in history, their attitudes, choices, and the way they move their bodies can teach you so much about us, right now. Fill your toolbox so it's overflowing with information and ideas to pull from so your imagination has so much to play with.

PHYSICAL WARMUP - 2 minutes - [Set Timer]
Freeform Dance: Put on some music and engage in freeform dancing. Allow your body to move spontaneously and without inhibition. This can help you tap into your creative instincts and develop physical expressiveness. **Tip**: Try music you've never listened to.

RESEARCH - 13 Minutes [Set Timer]
YouTube, streaming platforms, the internet or books, **research the given era/person/moment in time,** journal or make notes on your device, so when you want to find this information, it's organized and readily accessible. As you go, **write anything and everything _you_ find fascinating. Tip:** If the topic doesn't interest you, choose your own, or take a chance and still research it, but from a different perspective. Physicalities, voice, ideals, etc. Trust your body that when you see something interesting, you'll know. **Extra**: Speak it out and copy their movements. Our memory recall is massively affected by our bodies. Be specific and when you re-read your notes, you'll be amazed by how much your mind and body remember.

TOPIC:
Stanislav Petrov: a Soviet officer who potentially saved the world from nuclear war on September 26, 1983. Petrov was on duty at the Soviet Union's early-warning satellite system when the system reported a US missile was headed toward the Soviet Union. Faced with a decision that could have led to a massive retaliatory strike, Petrov judged the warning to be a false alarm. His decision, which was based on intuition and his understanding of the system's unreliability, prevented a potential nuclear disaster.

_____
_____
_____
_____
_____
_____
_____
_____
_____
_____
_____
_____
_____
_____

WORKOUT COMPLETED [ ]

No matter what anybody tells you, words
and ideas can change the world.
Dead Poets Society

BELIEF

Beliefs are the convictions that something exists or is true, especially without proof. That is also the definition of what we do as actors. We play make-believe. Our beliefs shape our world, especially our beliefs about ourselves and it works for the characters you play. Understand your beliefs and how they influence your mind, body and spirit, then you will be able to better understand others, so you can embody them. Allow the beliefs of your character to colour your perception of your world and your interaction with everything in it. "Acting is the best magic trick in the world. We applaud performances not because it's real, but because you made us believe."

VOCAL WORK - 2 Minutes - [Set timer]
Lip Trills: Close your lips together lightly, like you're going to blow a raspberry. Then, blow air through your closed lips while making sounds. You should feel a tickling sensation. Pick a song and Lip Trill along with it. **Tip:** Stretch your range as much as you can and pick a song you've never listened to.

BELIEF WORKOUT
Get your journal or write in here. **Define your personal belief/view** on the given subject. **Grab any book you own,** flip to a random page and **read it out loud,** colouring the words and intention with your belief system. **Tip:** Write trigger words you can hook into in the future: **Optimism-** Always smiling, grateful, opportunity, sunshine yellow.

YOUR PERSONAL BELIEF
Complacency - 7 Minutes [Set Timer]

_____
_____
_____
_____

READ WITH BELIEF - 2 Minutes [Set Timer]

CHARACTERS BELIEF
Complacency
My ex said I was complacent, but I love the slow pace, the quiet and simple life. Take your time. Soak every moment up. It's not "complacency", I just love my life, right here, right now and I just flow with life. I think people think they see complacency, but more often it's actually people living their life, moment to moment. Complacency is when you aren't living in the moment. It's okay not to want more and more and more. Just be here:)

READ WITH CHARACTERS BELIEF - 2 Minutes [Set Timer]
Forget your personal view and **fully embrace the character's belief. Read out loud again.**

JOURNAL YOUR EXPERIENCE - 2 Minutes [Set Timer]

_____
_____
_____

WORKOUT COMPLETED [ ]

PERFORMANCE STRATEGY
14 DAY REVIEW

TAKE A MOMENT OF REFLECTION AND BREAKDOWN WHERE YOU ARE RIGHT NOW IN YOUR CAREER AND AS AN ACTOR.
THE MORE SPECIFIC YOU ARE THE MORE CLEAR YOU CAN SEE WHERE YOU ARE NOW SO YOU CAN GET TO WHERE YOU WANT TO GO FASTER

★   ★   ★   ★   ★

Sylvester Stallone, before fame, struggled as an actor and even sold his dog for $50 to survive. He later wrote and starred in "Rocky," which became a massive success, allowing him to buy back his dog and launching his career as a renowned action star.

DATE:

MY WHY
WHY ARE YOU DOING WHAT YOU ARE DOING
BE SPECIFIC

MY MAIN GOALS
IN-ORDER OF IMPORTANCE

1.

   Action Step(s):

2.

   Action Step(s):

3.

   Action Step(s):

FROM THE LAST 14 DAYS   ☆☆☆☆☆
5 STAR RATING

YOUR KEY POINTS AND TAKEAWAYS - WHY THAT AMOUNT OF STAR RATING, LIKES, DISLIKES, THE BIGGEST LESSON YOU LEARNED, GOOD OR BAD:

STRENGTHS:

WEAKNESSES:

IMPROVEMENT STRATEGY
HOW CAN YOU IMPROVE ON THESE AREAS FOR THE NEXT 14 DAYS:

GOAL FROM LAST :
DID YOU ACHIEVE IT?

WHY OR WHY NOT?

GOAL FOR THE NEXT 14 EXERCISES
THE MORE SPECIFIC YOU ARE THE GREATER THE RESULT

   Action Step(s):

It's hard to beat a person who never gives up.
Babe Ruth

MY WHY:

GOAL(s):

PHYSICAL WARMUP - 1 minute [Set Timer]
Character Walks: Adopt the walk of different characters or personalities and let that evolve into dance. **Tip**: Let the character's backstory fuel the emotion of your movements.

VOCAL WARMUP - 3 minutes [Set Timer]
Popping P's: Emphasize the letter 'P' in phrases to strengthen your diaphragm and improve breath control. **Tip**: Pair this with powerful breaths to support the popping sound.

EMOTIONAL RECALL - 5 minutes [Set Timer]
Comedic Relief: Bring to mind a memory that always makes you laugh, no matter how many times you think about it. **Tip**: Let the laughter come naturally and notice how it changes your energy and facial expressions.

ANIMAL WORK - ELEPHANT
Research - 2 minutes [Set Timer]
Contemplate the elephant's size, family structure, and gentle nature despite its power.

Animal Exercise - 3 minutes [Set Timer]
Imitate the slow, majestic walk of an elephant and its communicative trumpeting. Retain its dignified presence as you become human again. Integrate some speech when you're ready.

Discovery Journal - 1 Minute [Set Timer]
3 Main Characteristics: (Whatever stands out to YOU to embody the essence)

_____
_____
_____
_____
_____
_____
_____

WORKOUT COMPLETED [ ]

Stay true to yourself and your artistic vision. Don't compromise your authenticity for anyone or anything.
Tom Hardy

SCRIPT ANALYSIS for RELATIONSHIPS & SPECIFICITY - 15 minutes [Set Timer]

Choose your character, circle everything in this script you have a relationship with. Including people, places, things, smells, time of day etc. **Write what your relationship with those items are and be specific.** The more specific and fun you have with your relationships, the more interesting your characters will be and the more fun the audience has. **Tip:** Everything isn't in the scene. Use your imagination to create details, only if it's contextually appropriate. **Extra:** Write your > **Objective, win or lose? Consequence of failing?** The Who What Where When Why.

Title: **Lines in the Sand**

INT. COFFEE SHOP - DAY

A cozy, crowded coffee shop. Amidst the hum of conversation and clinking of cups, RACHEL (determined lawyer) sits at a small table. Across from her is CHRIS (weary but idealistic), her childhood friend, now a witness in a high-profile case.

RACHEL
Chris, I know this is hard. But I need you to tell me everything you know.

CHRIS
Rachel, I can't. It's not just about the case. It's bigger than that.

RACHEL
This isn't just about winning or losing, Chris. It's about justice.

CHRIS
Justice? Or your career?

RACHEL
It's not that simple, and you know it.

CHRIS
I wish I could help you, I really do. But I have to think about my family.

RACHEL
And what about the truth? Does that not matter to you anymore?

CHRIS
Of course, it does. But there are consequences, Rachel. I can't ignore them.

RACHEL
I'm not asking you to ignore them. I'm asking you to trust me.

CHRIS
Trust? It's not that easy.

RACHEL
Chris, we've been through so much. Don't let this be the thing that ends us.

CHRIS
It's not about us, Rachel. It's about doing what's right.

Chris stands up, conflicted. Rachel reaches out, stopping him.

RACHEL
Please, Chris. We need your testimony. You can make a difference.

Chris looks at Rachel, torn between loyalty and fear, then slowly sits back down.

WORKOUT COMPLETED [ ]

It takes time to not be stupid.
Victor Zinck Jr

IMAGINATION

We have a lot of tools in our arsenal as actors but **I believe imagination is the most powerful.** "If you hook into the character's belief system and you believe it 100%, there is no way the audience won't." - Meryl Streep "Imagination is more important than knowledge for knowledge is limited. - Einstein. Everyone has an Imagination but it must be worked out to get stronger. Think of your imagination as a limitless playground. In this space, you can be anyone, go anywhere, and do anything. **Have the courage to allow yourself to play!**

Solo Imaginary World Exploration - 6 Minutes [Set Timer]

Find a quiet space to relax and focus. **Close your eyes** and **let your imagination run wild. Tip:** Engage all your senses to explore this environment. Touch, taste, smell etc. Allow your emotions to guide you. **Extra:** After you establish this world in your imagination, you could introduce characters and have a dialogue with them. Are they friends or foes?

IMAGINARY WORLD: Enchanted Forest: Engage with mythical creatures in a magical forest full of secrets and enchantments.

JOURNAL YOUR EXPERIENCE - 2 Minutes [Set Timer]

_____
_____
_____
_____
_____

Your Characters Filter - 5 Minutes [Set Timer]

Everyone including the characters you play see the world through their own specific perspective/filter. I like to use the word filter because you can take out a filter, clean it, change its style, colour, an optimist or a pessimist, comedian or a nihilist, etc. **Find a quiet space** to focus. **Close your eyes and let go of your personal thoughts and emotions** to make space for your characters. **Open your eyes, and allow the filter provided to effect everything around you. Tip**: Explore wherever you are and interact with the objects. **Extra:** How does *this* character walk and move in their world?

FILTER: Wise Sage: Views the world through the lens of wisdom and ancient knowledge.

JOURNAL YOUR EXPERIENCE - 2 Minutes [Set Timer]

_____
_____
_____
_____
_____

WORKOUT COMPLETED [ ]

I alway imagine that I'm going to get to set and the director's going to go, "I dont even like this scene…make it up." And I've got to be ready for that. And If I'm not ready for that, I feel very insecure arriving on the set.
Christian Bale

CHARACTER STUDY "PEOPLE WATCHING"

Actors are required to portray characters that are believable and relatable. You don't have to agree with them but you have to understand them. Walk like them, talk like them, see the world like them. So, in order to fill our toolbox, we have to **go out into the world and study**. Then practice them over and over so we can "walk in their shoes', comfortably and confidently. Study their movements, mannerisms, the "vibe" they give off, the clothes they wear etc. **Fill your toolbox with the rhythms and idiosyncrasies of human behaviour.**

OBSERVATION CHARACTER STUDY - 15 Minutes [Set Timer]

Find a busy place where you can **sit and observe.** Choose anyone you find interesting. **Write down what stands out about them.** *The way they sit, drink their coffee, walk, talk, interact with others etc.* **Tip: Mirror them immediately.** This will help memorize the feeling of that character so whenever you come back to these characters you're discovering, your body will remember. **Extra:** Before you go to sleep, read over the characters from today and reenact their movements.

_____
_____
_____
_____
_____
_____
_____
_____
_____
_____
_____
_____
_____
_____
_____
_____
_____
_____
_____
_____

COLOURS: We as humans respond to colours like frequencies. If you pay attention closely, you can see everyone has their own 'colour' that defines their core. An essence that informs how they operate and move through the world.

WHAT COLOUR ARE THEY:

WORKOUT COMPLETED [ ]

The mind is the limit. As long as the mind can envision the fact that you can do something, you can do it, as long as you really believe 100 percent.
Arnold Schwarzenegger

VOICE & DICTION

I wish I had learned this at the beginning of my career. The confidence to communicate clearly and powerfully is a game-changer for you as an actor. **Think of your voice as a musical instrument that needs regular tuning. This workout is your daily tuning session,** ensuring that your instrument is always ready. "The word 'theatre' comes from the Greeks. It means the seeing place. It is the place people come to see the truth about life and the social situation." - Stella Adler. Embrace this workout as a key to unlocking and portraying *that* truth by letting your voice be the vehicle that transports your audience into the heart of your story.

READ PASSAGE - 30 Seconds [Set Timer]
Speak the passage and take note of its quality. **Tip**: Record Audio to compare afterward.

> "The countryside spreads out in peaceful tranquillity. Fields sway in the breeze, a distant tractor hums and the sky arches high and clear. The rhythm of rural life beats slowly, in tune with the cycles of nature."

RELAXATION - 1 Minute [Set Timer]
Deep Breathing: Sit and Inhale deeply through your nose, filling your lungs, then exhale slowly through your mouth. Imagine stress leaving your body with each breath.

Nay Nay Nay - 1 Minute [Set Timer]
Pick a song and sing the word "Nay" repeatedly. Start with a comfortable pitch and gradually move the sound from your nose to your chest, ensuring each "Nay" is clear and resonant. Stretch your range as best you can to strengthen.

Sustained 'S' - 2 Minutes [Set Timer]
Inhale deeply and then exhale slowly, making a continuous 's' sound. Keep the sound as even and steady as you can. Always push a little longer than you think you can.

Vowel Pronunciation Drill - 2 Minutes [Set Timer]
Slowly go through each vowel sound **(A, E, I, O, U), holding and exaggerating each sound. Combine them with consonants** (e.g., ba, be, bi, bo, bu). Pay attention to the clarity and sharpness of each sound. Repeat a few times before moving to the next.

Lip Trills - 3 minutes - [Set timer]
Close your lips together lightly, like you're going to blow a raspberry. Then, blow air through your closed lips while making sounds. You should feel a tickling sensation. Pick a song and Lip Trill the whole along with it. **Tip**: Stretch your range as much as you can and pick a song you've never listened to.

The Cork Exercise - 4 Minutes [Set Timer]
Place a cork between your teeth and try to read a passage aloud. This forces your articulation muscles to work harder. If you don't have a cork, bite down gently on your thumb. You can use the following text for this exercise:

READ PASSAGE AGAIN - 30 Seconds [Set Timer]
Speak the passage and take note of its quality. **Tip**: Record Audio to compare.

Discovery Journal - 1 Minute [Set Timer]

WORKOUT COMPLETED [ ]

The ones who are crazy enough to think that they can change the world, are the ones who do.
Steve Jobs

SUBTEXT

Subtext is what lies beneath the surface of our words. It's the hidden layer of meaning, driven by the character's internal thoughts, emotions, desires, and motivations. Subtext is one of my favourite things as an actor because so much can be said with one simple line of dialogue. The power of "Hello" can be exciting if you told that person years ago "If I ever see you again, I'll kill you. Maybe it's the most beautiful person you've ever seen. Now, say "hello". *Subtext* shows the audience what your relationship with the characters/places/situations are, without having to explain it. We experience it every day and it is our job to create characters that interact as we do.

VOCAL WORK - 3 minutes - [Set Timer]
Lip Trills: Close your lips together lightly, like you're going to blow a raspberry. Then, blow air through your closed lips while making sounds. You should feel a tickling sensation. Pick a song and Lip Trill along with it. **Tip**: Stretch your range as much as you can and pick a song you've never listened to.

SUBTEXT PRACTICE
Use the line of dialogue provided and practice each of these subtexts **out loud.** Move on to the next, only when you believe yourself. Trust that you will know when *that* is. Before you begin, **pick a spot to look at and imagine** in detail, **who you are speaking with. Tip**: *Sometimes* we mean exactly what we are saying. Look for that too. **Extra**: Substitute someone you have a strong relationship with in real life, good or bad, and see it's affect.

Initial Line: "Have you seen my keys?"
Your Response Line: "Your keys? No, I haven't seen them. But then again, everything's been a bit of a blur lately. Maybe they're where you least expect them. You know how these things have a way of hiding in plain sight."

SUBTEXTS - 6 Minutes [Set Timer]
[ ] Distracted: Preoccupied with your own issues and barely keeping track of your life.
[ ] Nonchalant: You're not too concerned about the keys or the minor chaos.
[ ] Playful: You find a bit of humor in these everyday mishaps.
[ ] Reflective: The lost keys make you think about other things you've lost track of.
[ ] Sympathetic: You empathize with the frustration of losing something important.
[ ] Your Own Subtext

RELATIONSHIP SUBTEXTS - 6 Minutes [Set Timer]
[ ] The Roommate Who's Always Misplacing Things: A familiar, slightly exasperating routine.
[ ] Your Spouse: On the verge of getting a divorce. These things drive you insane.
[ ] Little Brother: Always have their back and lift them up no matter what's happening.
[ ] The Parent Who's Growing Forgetful: It's concerning. Alzheimers?
[ ] The close friend who's going Through a Rough Time: Their mind is elsewhere.
[ ] Your Own Subtext

Discovery Journal
_____
_____
_____

WORKOUT COMPLETED [ ]

Good artists copy, great artists steal.
Pablo Picasso

EMOTIONS

The 'moment before', **the emotional preparation, is the most important key to a great scene.** If you start any scene <u>without</u> an emotional preparation it feels like trying to drive a car in neutral. The preparation is the uphill climb of every rollercoaster; Once you grind all the way to the top, the chains let go and the rest of the ride takes care of itself. "No one wants to see a play or a movie and look at technical proficiency. You want to be moved, you want a human experience, you want to feel less alone" - Viola Davis. **Practice your emotions over and over** so when it's time, you aren't worried "Will I get there?" **You're imagination and emotions should be a tinderbox, so easy to light up. All it take is half a spark.**

EULOGY - 12 Minutes [Set Timer]

Find a quiet comfortable space. Choose someone in your life who is alive and important to you. Create an imaginary reason for why they have died. Now start from the point of the phone call— Imagine who calls, what they say and what you say. Eventually find yourself at the funeral, about to begin the eulogy. See the casket, is it open or closed?? What is that person wearing and any other details for yourself. Before you begin to speak, look into the audience and see who is there- Family, friends etc **Then begin the eulogy. Tip:** Be as specific as you can with everything. **Inside of specificity is where you will find the triggers to your heart.** Let your imagination take you wherever you want in this exercise. **Example**: Placing her favourite sheep stuffed animal in the casket, tucked under her arm like she always held it, then kissing her goodbye one last time.

DISCOVERY JOURNAL - 3 Minutes [Set Timer]

Make sure to **include the specific triggers** you experience because you can use these **TRIGGER MOMENTS** in the future instead of repeating the *entire* exercise.

_____
_____
_____
_____
_____
_____
_____
_____
_____
_____
_____
_____
_____
_____
_____
_____
_____
_____
_____

WORKOUT COMPLETED [ ]

When you hit a wall – of your own imagined limitations – just kick it in.
Sam Shepard

THE CORK EXERCISE - 4 Minutes [Set Timer]
Place a cork between your teeth and read a passage aloud. This forces your articulation muscles to work harder. If you don't have a cork, bite down gently on your thumb. You can use the following text for this exercise:

> "High in the mountains, the air is crisp and invigorating. Snow caps the majestic peaks, glistening under the sun. Pine trees whisper secrets of the ancient land, as eagles soar above, embracing the vastness of the sky."

WRITE A LETTER - 10 Minutes [Set Timer]
Get a piece of paper or write this in your device. **Take a moment** to let this situation and relationship sink in. Then let your imagination run wild and **write them a letter.**

Your Character: Riley, a successful entrepreneur who has recently launched a groundbreaking tech startup.
Other Character: Casey, a long-time friend and former business partner betrayed Riley by selling a similar startup idea to a major competitor.

Relationship: Riley and Casey have been friends since college and started their first business venture together. However, when Riley shared the concept for a new startup, Casey secretly took the idea, sold it to a competitor, and left Riley in the dark. This act of betrayal fractured what was once a strong friendship and partnership.

Context of the Letter: Despite the betrayal, Riley's startup has achieved significant success. Feeling a mix of triumph and lingering resentment, Riley writes a letter to Casey. This letter confronts the betrayal, reflects on the loss of their friendship, and expresses Riley's feelings about moving forward without Casey, who once was an integral part of Riley's professional and personal life.

Discovery Journal - 1 minute [Set Timer]

_____
_____
_____
_____
_____

WORKOUT COMPLETED [ ]

Nod, say yes, then do whatever the fu@! You were going to do in the first place.
Robert Downey Jr

VOCAL WORK - 3 minutes [Set timer]

Lip Trills: Close your lips together lightly, like you're going to blow a raspberry. Then, blow air through your closed lips while making sounds. You should feel a tickling sensation. Pick a song and Lip Trill along with it. **Tip**: Stretch your range as much as you can and pick a song you've never listened to.

VERBAL IMPROV - 10 Minutes [Set Timer]

Find a space where you are comfortable and free to express yourself. Take a moment to **let this situation, character and prompt, sink in**. Then let your imagination run wild: **Picture <u>who</u> you are talking to** then **begin with *the prompt*** and **continue to verbalize everything** this character would say. **Tip**: This is exploration! There is no "getting it right". <u>BE BRAVE</u> to explore and discover.

Character: Alex, a dedicated member of a local amateur soccer team, who has been working hard to organize a charity match. Just before the event, Alex discovers that their co-organizer and teammate has been diverting funds meant for the charity into their own account.

Prompt: "I just found out about the charity funds. Can you explain why they're in your personal account?"

Who are you talking to:

Describe them in two specific words:

Discovery Journal - 2 minutes [Set Timer]

_____
_____
_____
_____
_____
_____
_____
_____

WORKOUT COMPLETED [ ]

It always seems impossible until it is done.
Nelson Mandela

SELF AWARENESS

The more you understand yourself, the more you are able to understand and develop your characters. Like you, your characters have thoughts, beliefs, traumas, passions etc. When you become aware of your own and start to see how those experiences and beliefs have shaped your life, how you operate and view the world, then you can develop your characters that are much more rich and vivid.

PHYSICAL WARMUP - 2 minutes [Set Timer]

Freeform Dance: Put on some music and engage in freeform dancing. Allow your body to move spontaneously and without inhibition. This can help you tap into your creative instincts and develop physical expressiveness. **Tip**: Try music you've never listened to.

CURRENT EMOTIONAL INVENTORY - 3 Minutes [Set Timer]

Write down and **record your current emotions**. Identify what you're feeling at this moment and why. **Tip**: Be as specific as you can, **don't disregard anything.** You can also **scan your body** to see how and where your current emotion is affecting you. Your posture, the way you walk, bouncing foot, sore neck etc

CURRENT EMOTIONAL STATE:

SELF DISCOVERY QUESTIONS - 10 Minutes [Set Timer]

I suggest a journal or writing it in your phone's notes so you don't run out of space here.

What moments in my life have been most transformative? (Extra: How did it affect your life moving forward)

How do I express love and affection? (Extra: What type of love and affection is my favourite to receive)

WORKOUT COMPLETED [ ]

Acting is standing up naked and turning around very slowly.
Rosalind Russell

IMAGINATION

We have a lot of tools in our arsenal as actors but I believe imagination is the most powerful. "If you hook into the character's belief system and you believe it 100%, there is no way the audience won't." - Meryl Streep. Everyone has an Imagination but it must be worked out to get stronger. Think of your imagination as a limitless playground. In this space, you can be anyone, go anywhere, and do anything. **Have the courage to allow yourself to play!**

VOCAL WORK - 2 Minutes - [Set timer]

Lip Trills: Close your lips together lightly, like you're going to blow a raspberry. Then, blow air through your closed lips while making sounds. You should feel a tickling sensation. Pick a song and Lip Trill along with it. **Tip**: Stretch your range as much as you can and pick a song you've never listened to.

IMPROVISED STORYTELLING - 5 Minutes [Set Timer]

Speak out the scenario provided and continue the story! Focus on vivid details, character development and how the main character overcomes the main obstacle. **Tip**: Try not to stop speaking so you don't have time to "think". Allow your imagination to keep moving forward without interruption. **Tip:** Record these stories on your device, in case it's great but more importantly to see your progress as you go on.

STARTING POINT: You are Riley, a struggling musician who finds an old, dusty guitar in the attic of your new apartment. When you play it, you discover the guitar has the power to evoke vivid memories from its previous owners. Each chord reveals a different story, transporting you to various moments in time and allowing you to experience life through someone else's eyes. As you explore these musical journeys, you start to uncover the guitar's mysterious origin and its connection to a legendary musician.

IMAGINARY WORLD EXPLORATION - 6 Minutes [Set Timer]

Find a quiet space to relax and focus. **Close your eyes** and let your imagination run wild. **Tip:** Engage all your senses to explore this environment. Touch, taste, smell etc and allow your emotions to guide you. **Extra:** After you explore this world with your senses, you could introduce characters and have a dialogue with them. Are they friends or foes?

IMAGINARY WORLD: LAUNDROMAT LUMINANCE - While waiting for your laundry to finish, you notice that the washing machines emit a soft, otherworldly glow. Stepping closer, you discover that each machine leads to a different dreamlike world.

JOURNAL YOUR EXPERIENCE - 2 Minutes [Set Timer]

___
___
___
___
___
___
___

WORKOUT COMPLETED [ ]

What do you do when the director gives
you a note?
"I do it."
Sam Braun

ANCHORING INTO YOUR CHARACTER COLOUR & MUSIC

Anchoring yourself into your character is vital. It's one of the most freeing feelings when you understand their *essence* because everything they do, how they do it and what their purpose is, becomes so clear to you and the audience. Every choice you make after you find your *anchor*, feels easy, because you're acting from who and what your character is at the core. You can call it an essence, an aura, vibe, energy etc. We all have it and feel it from everyone around us. There are many ways into your character but music and colour are my favourite. Music can inform the script, your character, even each scene. Colours, I think you will find, can work incredibly because we as humans respond to colours like frequencies. Colours evoke many feelings and if you pay attention closely, you can see everyone has their own 'colour' that defines their core. An essence that informs how they operate and move through the world.

THEIR COLOUR - 2 Minutes [Set Timer]
Think of **someone you know**, and **define them with a colour**. **Tip**: Trust yourself. Your initial colour is usually close. **Tip**: Start with basic colours then eventually become much more specific. **Example**: Corinna is an earthy green with rays of sunlight flowing through the green. **Extra**: Ask someone who knows *that person* as well, what they think this person's colour is and why. See how close your answers are or not.

YOUR CHARACTERS COLOUR
Read the given character description just as you would an audition, **assign a colour to that character.** Now take that colour you chose and **allow it to infuse into your entire body**, affecting your every move, your speaking, the way you see the world etc. **Take any book** you have, flip to a random page and **read the text as this Colour/Character. Tip**: Be specific, choose a colour that excites you and don't be afraid to get creative.

CHARACTER DESCRIPTION: [SAGE] Sage is a nocturnal radio host with a soothing, enigmatic voice that becomes a companion to the lonely and sleepless. Their studio is a haven of dim lights and vintage records, reflecting a deep love for music and storytelling. Sage is often seen wearing comfortable, bohemian-style clothing, exuding a relaxed yet introspective vibe. Despite their calming on-air persona, Sage harbours a restless spirit, driven by a quest for deeper truths and human connections. Their character combines a philosophical outlook with a touch of mystery, weaving tales and thoughts that resonate with the night owls of the city.

CHOOSE THEIR COLOUR - 4 Minutes [Set Timer]
THEIR COLOUR:

CHOOSE THEIR SONG - 4 Minutes [Set Timer]
THEIR SONG:

READ PASSAGE FROM BOOK - 2 Minutes [Set Timer]

FREEFORM DANCE - 2 minutes - [Set Timer]
Put on the selected music and **engage in freeform dancing, anchored in your colour/character,** Allow your body to move spontaneously and without inhibition. This can help you tap into your creative instincts and develop physical expressiveness <u>while staying in character.</u> **Tip**: Journal about the differences as opposed to how you normally dance.

JOURNAL YOUR EXPERIENCE - 1 Minute [Set Timer]

WORKOUT COMPLETED [ ]

You are infectious whether you like it or not.
Choose your poison.
Victor Zinck Jr

HISTORICAL RESEARCH

We are in the information era and have access to the world and its rich history at our fingertips. This exploration is not about 'learning facts'; it's a journey to the heart of human experience. The empathy and the understanding, especially on the things you disagree with, are incredibly valuable. If you look closely, you'll find the way people think, at different times in history, their attitudes, choices, and the way they move their bodies can teach you so much about us, right now. Fill your toolbox so it's overflowing with information and ideas to pull from so your imagination has so much to play with.

PHYSICAL WARMUP - 2 minutes - [Set Timer]
Freeform Dance: Put on some music and engage in freeform dancing. Allow your body to move spontaneously and without inhibition. This can help you tap into your creative instincts and develop physical expressiveness. **Tip**: Try music you've never listened to.

RESEARCH - 13 Minutes [Set Timer]
YouTube, streaming platforms, the internet or books, **research the given era/person/moment in time,** journal or make notes on your device, so when you want to find this information, it's organized and readily accessible. As you go, **write anything and everything _you_ find fascinating. Tip:** If the topic doesn't interest you, choose your own, or take a chance and still research it, but from a different perspective. Physicalities, voice, ideals, etc. Trust your body that when you see something interesting, you'll know. **Extra**: Speak it out and copy their movements. Our memory recall is massively affected by our bodies. Be specific and when you re-read your notes, you'll be amazed by how much your mind and body remember.

TOPIC:
The Great Emu War (1932): In a surprisingly unusual conflict, the Australian military waged a "war" against a large population of emus in Western Australia. The emus, having caused immense damage to crops during the Great Depression, were targeted in a failed attempt at population control. Despite using machine guns, the soldiers were unsuccessful in significantly reducing the emu numbers, leading to the operation's termination. This event has been noted for its peculiarity and is often cited as an example of an unexpected and unconventional challenge in wildlife management.

___
___
___
___
___
___
___
___
___
___
___
___
___
___
___

WORKOUT COMPLETED [ ]

I'm a great believer in luck, and I find the harder I work, the more I have of it.
Thomas Jefferson

BELIEF

Beliefs are the convictions that something exists or is true, especially without proof. That is also the definition of what we do as actors. We play make-believe. Our beliefs shape our world, especially our beliefs about ourselves and it works for the characters you play. Understand your beliefs and how they influence your mind, body and spirit, then you will be able to better understand others, so you can embody them. Allow the beliefs of your character to colour your perception of your world and your interaction with everything in it. "Acting is the best magic trick in the world. We applaud performances not because it's real, but because you made us believe."

VOCAL WORK - 2 Minutes - [Set timer]
Lip Trills: Close your lips together lightly, like you're going to blow a raspberry. Then, blow air through your closed lips while making sounds. You should feel a tickling sensation. Pick a song and Lip Trill along with it. **Tip**: Stretch your range as much as you can and pick a song you've never listened to.

BELIEF WORKOUT
Get your journal or write in here. **Define your personal belief/view** on the given subject. **Grab any book you own,** flip to a random page and **read it out loud,** colouring the words and intention with your belief system. **Tip**: Write trigger words you can hook into in the future: **Optimism-** Always smiling, grateful, opportunity, sunshine yellow.

YOUR PERSONAL BELIEF
Taking Risks - 7 Minutes [Set Timer]

_____
_____
_____
_____
_____

READ WITH BELIEF - 2 Minutes [Set Timer]

CHARACTERS BELIEF
Taking Risks
Can't live without it and I can't stop the urge. I don't want to either, I love it and love other people who have that same look in their eyes about life. There is this thing inside of me that I have no control over and when it says go, I go. And it's almost always saying go!

READ WITH CHARACTERS BELIEF - 2 Minutes [Set Timer]
Forget your personal view and **fully embrace the character's belief. Read out loud again.**

JOURNAL YOUR EXPERIENCE - 2 Minutes [Set Timer]

_____
_____
_____

WORKOUT COMPLETED [ ]

PERFORMANCE STRATEGY
14 DAY REVIEW

TAKE A MOMENT OF REFLECTION AND BREAKDOWN WHERE YOU ARE RIGHT NOW IN YOUR CAREER AND AS AN ACTOR.
THE MORE SPECIFIC YOU ARE THE MORE CLEAR YOU CAN SEE WHERE YOU ARE NOW SO YOU CAN GET TO WHERE YOU WANT TO GO FASTER

★ ★ ★ ★ ★

Oprah Winfrey, born into poverty and faced with numerous hardships in her early life, rose to become a dominant force in the media industry. Her success as a talk show host, media executive, and philanthropist made her North America's first black multi-billionaire, inspiring millions worldwide.

DATE:

MY WHY
WHY ARE YOU DOING WHAT YOU ARE DOING
BE SPECIFIC

MY MAIN GOALS
IN-ORDER OF IMPORTANCE

1.

   Action Step(s):

2.

   Action Step(s):

3.

   Action Step(s):

FROM THE LAST 14 DAYS
5 STAR RATING

YOUR KEY POINTS AND TAKEAWAYS - WHY THAT AMOUNT OF STAR RATING, LIKES, DISLIKES, THE BIGGEST LESSON YOU LEARNED, GOOD OR BAD:

STRENGTHS:

WEAKNESSES:

IMPROVEMENT STRATEGY
HOW CAN YOU IMPROVE ON THESE AREAS FOR THE NEXT 14 DAYS:

GOAL FROM LAST :
DID YOU ACHIEVE IT?

WHY OR WHY NOT?

GOAL FOR THE NEXT 14 EXERCISES
THE MORE SPECIFIC YOU ARE THE GREATER THE RESULT

   Action Step(s):

Dreams are the touchstones of our character's.
Henry David Thoreau

MY WHY:

GOAL(s):

PHYSICAL WARMUP - 1 minute [Set Timer]
Colour Dance: Choose a colour and dance how it makes you feel. Let the colour's energy guide your movement. **Tip**: Visualize the colour radiating from your body as you dance.

VOCAL WARMUP - 3 minutes [Set Timer]
Vowel Play: Sing a series of vowels (a-e-i-o-u), holding each one for a few seconds. **Tip:** Focus on maintaining a steady pitch and experimenting with different volumes.

EMOTIONAL RECALL - 5 minutes [Set Timer]
Achievement Pride:
Think of a time when you achieved something significant and felt immense pride. **Tip:** Absorb the confidence and self-assurance from the memory and let it boost your posture and expression.

ANIMAL WORK - WOLF
Research - 2 minutes [Set Timer]
Study the social dynamics, hunting tactics, and communication of wolves.

Animal Exercise - 3 minutes [Set Timer]
Emulate the wolf's prowl and howl. Absorb its pack mentality and independence as you shift back to human, maintaining a sense of loyalty and leadership.

Discovery Journal - 1 Minute [Set Timer]
3 Main Characteristics: (Whatever stands out to YOU to embody the essence)

_____
_____
_____
_____
_____
_____
_____
_____

WORKOUT COMPLETED [ ]

Real acting is impossible to spot. Do you ever catch talents like Robert Duvall or Kathy Bates acting? No. I defy you to show me where.
William Esper

SCRIPT ANALYSIS for RELATIONSHIPS & SPECIFICITY - 15 minutes [Set Timer]
Choose your character, circle everything in this script you have a relationship with. Including people, places, things, smells, time of day etc. **Write what your relationship with those items are and be specific.** The more specific and fun you have with your relationships, the more interesting your characters will be and the more fun the audience has. **Tip:** Everything isn't in the scene. Use your imagination to create details, only if it's contextually appropriate. **Extra:** Write your > **Objective, win or lose? Consequence of failing?** The Who What Where When Why.

Title: Echoes of Time
INT. SPACECRAFT BRIDGE - ADJACENT TO A NEBULA
A sprawling nebula casts ethereal colours across the spacecraft's bridge. **CAPTAIN HAWKINS**, stoic and contemplative, gazes at a holographic star map. **DR. ELISE ROWAN**, fiercely intelligent, watches the nebula...

CAPTAIN HAWKINS
It's a long shot, Elise. You know that.

DR. ROWAN
We've been chasing long shots since we left Earth's orbit.

CAPTAIN HAWKINS
(turning to her)
This is different. The risks...

DR. ROWAN
I'm aware. But imagine if we're right.

CAPTAIN HAWKINS
And if we're wrong?

DR. ROWAN
(softly) Then we learn something new. Isn't that why we're here?
A brief silence as they both consider the stakes.

CAPTAIN HAWKINS
You think it's here? Among these stars?

DR. ROWAN
(gazing out) Where better to hide a secret than in plain sight? This nebula... It's a veil, not a barrier.

CAPTAIN HAWKINS
Alright. Set the coordinates.

DR. ROWAN
(smiling faintly) Sir? I wouldn't want to do this with anyone else.

CAPTAIN HAWKINS
What was it you said to Valesquez before our brief? "Risk is the price of progress." I like that.

DR. ROWAN
Me too... That's why I said it.
They share a brief smile then a moment of understanding, two voyagers on the edge of discovery. As the ship adjusts its course, the nebula outside is a silent testament to the mysteries of the universe and seems to beckon them closer, promising answers and perhaps, new questions.

WORKOUT COMPLETED [ ]

I saw the angel in the marble and carved
until I set him free.
Michaelangelo

IMAGINATION

We have a lot of tools in our arsenal as actors but **I believe imagination is the most powerful.** "If you hook into the character's belief system and you believe it 100%, there is no way the audience won't." - Meryl Streep "Imagination is more important than knowledge for knowledge is limited. - Einstein. Everyone has an Imagination but it must be worked out to get stronger. Think of your imagination as a limitless playground. In this space, you can be anyone, go anywhere, and do anything. **Have the courage to allow yourself to play!**

Solo Imaginary World Exploration - 6 Minutes [Set Timer]

Find a quiet space to relax and focus. **Close your eyes** and **let your imagination run wild. Tip:** Engage all your senses to explore this environment. Touch, taste, smell etc. Allow your emotions to guide you. **Extra:** After you establish this world in your imagination, you could introduce characters and have a dialogue with them. Are they friends or foes?

IMAGINARY WORLD: Haunted Victorian Mansion: Investigate a creaky mansion filled with ghostly whispers and unexplained occurrences.

JOURNAL YOUR EXPERIENCE - 2 Minutes [Set Timer]

_____
_____
_____
_____
_____
_____
_____

Your Characters Filter - 5 Minutes [Set Timer]

Everyone including the characters you play see the world through their own specific perspective/filter. I like to use the word filter because you can take out a filter, clean it, change its style, colour, an optimist or a pessimist, comedian or a nihilist, etc. **Find a quiet space** to focus. **Close your eyes and let go of your personal thoughts and emotions** to make space for your characters. **Open your eyes, and allow the filter provided to effect everything around you. Tip:** Explore wherever you are and interact with the objects. **Extra:** How does *this* character walk and move in their world?

FILTER: Playful Prankster: Finds humour and mischief in every interaction. Your life goal is to make everyone laugh.

JOURNAL YOUR EXPERIENCE - 2 Minutes [Set Timer]

_____
_____
_____
_____
_____
_____
_____

WORKOUT COMPLETED [ ]

It's supposed to be hard. If it wasn't hard, everyone would do it. The hard... is what makes it great.
Jimmy Dugan, A League of Their Own

CHARACTER STUDY "PEOPLE WATCHING"

Actors are required to portray characters that are believable and relatable. You don't have to agree with them but you have to understand them. Walk like them, talk like them, see the world like them. So, in order to fill our toolbox, we have to **go out into the world and study.** Then practice them over and over so we can "walk in their shoes', comfortably and confidently. Study their movements, mannerisms, the "vibe" they give off, the clothes they wear etc. **Fill your toolbox with the rhythms and idiosyncrasies of human behaviour.**

OBSERVATION CHARACTER STUDY - 15 Minutes [Set Timer]

Find a busy place where you can **sit and observe.** Choose anyone you find interesting. **Write down what stands out about them.** *The way they sit, drink their coffee, walk, talk, interact with others etc.* **Tip: Mirror them immediately.** This will help memorize the feeling of that character so whenever you come back to these characters you're discovering, your body will remember. **Extra:** Before you go to sleep, read over the characters from today and reenact their movements.

_____
_____
_____
_____
_____
_____
_____
_____
_____
_____
_____
_____
_____
_____
_____
_____
_____
_____
_____
_____

COLOURS: We as humans respond to colours like frequencies. If you pay attention closely, you can see everyone has their own 'colour' that defines their core. An essence that informs how they operate and move through the world.

WHAT COLOUR ARE THEY:

WORKOUT COMPLETED [ ]

The role of the director is to create a space where the actor or actress can become more than they've ever been before, more than they've dreamed of being.
Robert Altman

VOICE & DICTION

I wish I had learned this at the beginning of my career. The confidence to communicate clearly and powerfully is a game-changer for you as an actor. **Think of your voice as a musical instrument that needs regular tuning. This workout is your daily tuning session,** ensuring that your instrument is always ready. "The word 'theatre' comes from the Greeks. It means the seeing place. It is the place people come to see the truth about life and the social situation." - Stella Adler. Embrace this workout as a key to unlocking and portraying *that* truth by letting your voice be the vehicle that transports your audience into the heart of your story.

READ PASSAGE - 30 Seconds [Set Timer]
Speak the passage and take note of its quality. **Tip**: Record Audio to compare afterward.

> "Sunrise paints the beach in hues of gold and pink. The waves lap at the shore, footprints dot the sand the early morning serenity is a balm to the soul. Seashells and seaweed lie scattered, treasures of the tide."

RELAXATION - 1 Minute [Set Timer]
Deep Breathing: Sit and Inhale deeply through your nose, filling your lungs, then exhale slowly through your mouth. Imagine stress leaving your body with each breath.

Nay Nay Nay - 1 Minute [Set Timer]
Pick a song and sing the word "Nay" repeatedly. Start with a comfortable pitch and gradually move the sound from your nose to your chest, ensuring each "Nay" is clear and resonant. Stretch your range as best you can to strengthen.

Sustained 'S' - 2 Minutes [Set Timer]
Inhale deeply and then exhale slowly, making a continuous 's' sound. Keep the sound as even and steady as you can. Always push a little longer than you think you can.

Vowel Pronunciation Drill - 2 Minutes [Set Timer]
Slowly go through each vowel sound **(A, E, I, O, U)**, **holding and exaggerating each sound. Combine them with consonants** (e.g., ba, be, bi, bo, bu). Pay attention to the clarity and sharpness of each sound. Repeat a few times before moving to the next.

Lip Trills - 3 minutes - [Set timer]
Close your lips together lightly, like you're going to blow a raspberry. Then, blow air through your closed lips while making sounds. You should feel a tickling sensation. Pick a song and Lip Trill the whole along with it. **Tip**: Stretch your range as much as you can and pick a song you've never listened to.

The Cork Exercise - 4 Minutes [Set Timer]
Place a cork between your teeth and try to read a passage aloud. This forces your articulation muscles to work harder. If you don't have a cork, bite down gently on your thumb. You can use the following text for this exercise:

READ PASSAGE AGAIN - 30 Seconds [Set Timer]
Speak the passage and take note of its quality. **Tip**: Record Audio to compare.

Discovery Journal - 1 Minute [Set Timer]

WORKOUT COMPLETED [ ]

Imagination is more important than knowledge. Knowledge is limited.
Albert Einstein

SUBTEXT

Subtext is what lies beneath the surface of our words. It's the hidden layer of meaning, driven by the character's internal thoughts, emotions, desires, and motivations. Subtext is one of my favourite things as an actor because so much can be said with one simple line of dialogue. The power of "Hello" can be exciting if you told that person years ago "If I ever see you again, I'll kill you. Maybe it's the most beautiful person you've ever seen. Now, say "hello". *Subtext* shows the audience what your relationship with the characters/places/situations are, without having to explain it. We experience it every day and it is our job to create characters that interact as we do.

VOCAL WORK - 3 minutes - [Set Timer]
Lip Trills: Close your lips together lightly, like you're going to blow a raspberry. Then, blow air through your closed lips while making sounds. You should feel a tickling sensation. Pick a song and Lip Trill along with it. **Tip**: Stretch your range as much as you can and pick a song you've never listened to.

SUBTEXT PRACTICE
Use the line of dialogue provided and practice each of these subtexts **out loud.** Move on to the next, only when you believe yourself. Trust that you will know when *that* is. Before you begin, **pick a spot to look at and imagine** in detail, **who you are speaking with**. **Tip**: *Sometimes* we mean exactly what we are saying. Look for that too. **Extra**: Substitute someone you have a strong relationship with in real life, good or bad, and see it's affect.

Initial Line: "What were you thinking?"
Your Response Line: "I don't know. It seemed like a good idea at the time, or maybe I just wasn't thinking at all. It's hard to explain. You've never done something like that?"

SUBTEXTS - 6 Minutes [Set Timer]
[ ] Impulsive: You acted without thinking and are now facing the consequences.
[ ] Defensive: You feel cornered and are trying to justify your actions.
[ ] Reflective: You're questioning your judgment and the reasons behind your actions.
[ ] Regretful: You realize the mistake and wish you could undo it.
[ ] Sarcastic: You don't give a @&*!? What this person thinks.
[ ] Your Own Subtext

RELATIONSHIP SUBTEXTS - 6 Minutes [Set Timer]
[ ] Disappointed Parent: Their reaction makes you question your choices even more.
[ ] Police Officer: You were drinking and driving and totalled your car. You're in the hospital.
[ ] Boss: Hate your job because of her. Awful woman who likes to make people feel small.
[ ] The Supportive Sibling: Despite the trouble, they're there to help you through it.
[ ] The fake friend: You know you can't trust them with any personal information.
[ ] Your Own Subtext

Discovery Journal

___

WORKOUT COMPLETED [ ]

Every man's life ends the same way. It is only the details of how he lived and how he died that distinguish one man from another.
Ernest Hemingway - Midnight in Paris

EMOTIONS

The 'moment before', **the emotional preparation, is the most important key to a great scene.** If you start any scene <u>without</u> an emotional preparation it feels like trying to drive a car in neutral. The preparation is the uphill climb of every rollercoaster; Once you grind all the way to the top, the chains let go and the rest of the ride takes care of itself. "No one wants to see a play or a movie and look at technical proficiency. You want to be moved, you want a human experience, you want to feel less alone" - Viola Davis. **Practice your emotions over and over** so when it's time, you aren't worried "Will I get there?" **You're imagination and emotions should be a tinderbox, so easy to light up. All it take is half a spark.**

EULOGY - 12 Minutes [Set Timer]

Find a quiet comfortable space. Choose someone in your life who is alive and important to you. Create an imaginary reason for why they have died. Now start from the point of the phone call— Imagine who calls, what they say and what you say. Eventually find yourself at the funeral, about to begin the eulogy. See the casket, is it open or closed?? What is that person wearing and any other details for yourself. Before you begin to speak, look into the audience and see who is there- Family, friends etc **Then begin the eulogy. Tip**: <u>Be as specific as you can with everything.</u> **Inside of specificity is where you will find the triggers to your heart.** Let your imagination take you wherever you want in this exercise. **Example**: Placing her favourite sheep stuffed animal in the casket, tucked under her arm like she always held it, then kissing her goodbye one last time.

DISCOVERY JOURNAL - 3 Minutes [Set Timer]

Make sure to **include the specific triggers** you experience because you can use these **TRIGGER MOMENTS** in the future instead of repeating the *entire* exercise.

WORKOUT COMPLETED [ ]

You mustn't be afraid to dream a little bigger, darling.
Tom Hardy - Inception

THE CORK EXERCISE - 4 Minutes [Set Timer]

Place a cork between your teeth and read a passage aloud. This forces your articulation muscles to work harder. If you don't have a cork, bite down gently on your thumb. You can use the following text for this exercise:

"Beneath the ocean's surface, a hidden world thrives. Waves gently lap above, while schools of fish dart through the vibrant coral reefs. Sunlight filters through the water, creating a dance of light and shadow, revealing the mysteries of the deep."

WRITE A LETTER - 10 Minutes [Set Timer]

Get a piece of paper or write this in your device. **Take a moment** to let this situation and relationship sink in. Then let your imagination run wild and **write them a letter.**

Your Character: Sam, a seasoned journalist known for their hard-hitting reporting and unwavering dedication to the truth.

Other Character: Jamie, a close friend and fellow journalist, who has recently been accused of fabricating a story.

Relationship: Sam and Jamie have been colleagues and confidants for years, sharing both the triumphs and challenges of their profession. However, the recent scandal has shaken Sam's trust in Jamie, causing a rift in what was once an unbreakable bond.

Context of the Letter: In the midst of the scandal, Sam feels torn between loyalty to Jamie and a commitment to journalistic integrity. Deciding to confront the issue directly, Sam writes a letter to Jamie. This letter is an earnest attempt to understand the truth, express feelings of betrayal and disappointment, and perhaps find a way to salvage their friendship and professional respect.

Discovery Journal - 1 minute [Set Timer]

_____
_____
_____
_____
_____

WORKOUT COMPLETED [ ]

Every champion was once a contender
that refused to give up.
Rocky Balboa, Rocky

VOCAL WORK - 3 minutes [Set timer]
Lip Trills: Close your lips together lightly, like you're going to blow a raspberry. Then, blow air through your closed lips while making sounds. You should feel a tickling sensation. Pick a song and Lip Trill along with it. **Tip**: Stretch your range as much as you can and pick a song you've never listened to.

VERBAL IMPROV - 10 Minutes [Set Timer]

Find a space where you are comfortable and free to express yourself. Take a moment to **let this situation, character and prompt, sink in**. Then let your imagination run wild: **Picture who you are talking to** then **begin with *the prompt*** and **continue to verbalize everything** this character would say. **Tip**: This is exploration! There is no "getting it right". BE BRAVE to explore and discover.

Character: Riley, an avid amateur astronomer and member of a local stargazing club. Riley has been preparing for months to lead an important observation night, only to discover that their rival club member, who's always been competitive, has deliberately sabotaged their telescope equipment on the eve of the event.

Prompt: "You deliberately sabotaged my telescope, didn't you? What were you thinking?"

Who are you talking to:

Describe them in two specific words:

Discovery Journal - 2 minutes [Set Timer]

_____
_____
_____
_____
_____
_____
_____
_____

WORKOUT COMPLETED [ ]

Don't expect a pat on the back for merely
doing your job, but know that you'll get
one for doing it exceptionally well.
Lea Salonga

SELF AWARENESS

The more you understand yourself, the more you are able to understand and develop your characters. Like you, your characters have thoughts, beliefs, traumas, passions etc. When you become aware of your own and start to see how those experiences and beliefs have shaped your life, how you operate and view the world, then you can develop your characters that are much more rich and vivid.

PHYSICAL WARMUP - 2 minutes [Set Timer]

Freeform Dance: Put on some music and engage in freeform dancing. Allow your body to move spontaneously and without inhibition. This can help you tap into your creative instincts and develop physical expressiveness. **Tip**: Try music you've never listened to.

CURRENT EMOTIONAL INVENTORY - 3 Minutes [Set Timer]

Write down and **record your current emotions**. Identify what you're feeling at this moment and why. **Tip**: Be as specific as you can, **don't disregard anything.** You can also **scan your body** to see how and where your current emotion is affecting you. Your posture, the way you walk, bouncing foot, sore neck etc

CURRENT EMOTIONAL STATE:

SELF DISCOVERY QUESTIONS - 10 Minutes [Set Timer]

I suggest a journal or writing it in your phone's notes so you don't run out of space here.

What situations make me feel most confident? (Extra: Describe the feeling it gives you and how it affects your body)

What fears hold me back in my personal or professional life? (Extra: Where does that come from, how do they make me feel and affect my body)

WORKOUT COMPLETED [ ]

Don't let anyone ever make you feel like you don't deserve what you want.
Heath Ledger - 10 Things I Hate About You

IMAGINATION

We have a lot of tools in our arsenal as actors but I believe imagination is the most powerful. "If you hook into the character's belief system and you believe it 100%, there is no way the audience won't." - Meryl Streep. Everyone has an Imagination but it must be worked out to get stronger. Think of your imagination as a limitless playground. In this space, you can be anyone, go anywhere, and do anything. **Have the courage to allow yourself to play!**

VOCAL WORK - 2 Minutes - [Set timer]

Lip Trills: Close your lips together lightly, like you're going to blow a raspberry. Then, blow air through your closed lips while making sounds. You should feel a tickling sensation. Pick a song and Lip Trill along with it. **Tip**: Stretch your range as much as you can and pick a song you've never listened to.

IMPROVISED STORYTELLING - 5 Minutes [Set Timer]

Speak out the scenario provided and continue the story! Focus on vivid details, character development and how the main character overcomes the main obstacle. **Tip**: Try not to stop speaking so you don't have time to "think". Allow your imagination to keep moving forward without interruption. **Tip:** Record these stories on your device, in case it's great but more importantly to see your progress as you go on.

STARTING POINT: You are Morgan, an amateur botanist living in a small, seemingly mundane town. One day, while exploring the local forest, you stumble upon a rare, luminescent flower that only blooms at midnight. Intrigued, you take a sample home for study and soon realize that the flower has extraordinary properties: You find that each secret unravels more about the town's forgotten history and your own family's mysterious connection to the forest.

IMAGINARY WORLD EXPLORATION - 6 Minutes [Set Timer]

Find a quiet space to relax and focus. **Close your eyes** and let your imagination run wild. **Tip:** Engage all your senses to explore this environment. Touch, taste, smell etc and allow your emotions to guide you. **Extra:** After you explore this world with your senses, you could introduce characters and have a dialogue with them. Are they friends or foes?

IMAGINARY WORLD: THE CRYSTAL CAVERNS - A subterranean realm filled with glistening crystals of every colour, reflecting a kaleidoscope of light. In this magical world, you can explore the mesmerizing Crystal Caverns, each crystal holding a different emotion. As you move through this enchanting landscape, you can experience the depths of human emotions.

JOURNAL YOUR EXPERIENCE - 2 Minutes [Set Timer]

_____
_____
_____
_____
_____
_____

WORKOUT COMPLETED [ ]

After many years of self-flagellation, I've realized that beating myself up doesn't get me anywhere.
Chris Pine

ANCHORING INTO YOUR CHARACTER COLOUR & MUSIC

Anchoring yourself into your character is vital. It's one of the most freeing feelings when you understand their *essence* because everything they do, how they do it and what their purpose is, becomes so clear to you and the audience. Every choice you make after you find your *anchor*, feels easy, because you're acting from who and what your character is at the core. You can call it an essence, an aura, vibe, energy etc. We all have it and feel it from everyone around us. There are many ways into your character but music and colour are my favourite. Music can inform the script, your character, even each scene. Colours, I think you will find, can work incredibly because we as humans respond to colours like frequencies. Colours evoke many feelings and if you pay attention closely, you can see everyone has their own 'colour' that defines their core. An essence that informs how they operate and move through the world.

THEIR COLOUR - 2 Minutes [Set Timer]
Think of **someone you know**, and **define them with a colour**. **Tip**: Trust yourself. Your initial colour is usually close. **Tip**: Start with basic colours then eventually become much more specific. **Example**: Corinna is an earthy green with rays of sunlight flowing through the green. **Extra**: Ask someone who knows *that person* as well, what they think this person's colour is and why. See how close your answers are or not.

YOUR CHARACTERS COLOUR
Read the given character description just as you would an audition, **assign a colour to that character.** Now take that colour you chose and **allow it to infuse into your entire body**, affecting your every move, your speaking, the way you see the world etc. **Take any book** you have, flip to a random page and **read the text as this Colour/Character**. **Tip**: Be specific, choose a colour that excites you and don't be afraid to get creative.

CHARACTER DESCRIPTION: [KAI] Kai is a reclusive cryptozoologist, dedicated to the study of creatures considered mythical or unverified by mainstream science. Their home is akin to a natural history museum, filled with maps, old books, and cryptic sketches. Kai's obsession with the unknown is driven by a childhood encounter they can't fully explain. They are often seen in a weathered field jacket, ready for impromptu expeditions. Although regarded as eccentric by peers, Kai's unwavering belief and moments of childlike wonder reveal a deeper longing for discovery and understanding of the world's mysteries. Their character is an intriguing mix of scientific fervour, whimsical hope, and the pursuit of truth.

CHOOSE THEIR COLOUR - 4 Minutes [Set Timer]
THEIR COLOUR:

CHOOSE THEIR SONG - 4 Minutes [Set Timer]
THEIR SONG:

READ PASSAGE FROM BOOK - 2 Minutes [Set Timer]

FREEFORM DANCE - 2 minutes - [Set Timer]
Put on the selected music and **engage in freeform dancing, anchored in your colour/character,** Allow your body to move spontaneously and without inhibition. This can help you tap into your creative instincts and develop physical expressiveness *while staying in character.* **Tip**: Journal about the differences as opposed to how you normally dance.

JOURNAL YOUR EXPERIENCE - 1 Minute [Set Timer]

WORKOUT COMPLETED [ ]

An actor has to burn inside with an outer ease.
Michael Chekhov

HISTORICAL RESEARCH

We are in the information era and have access to the world and its rich history at our fingertips. This exploration is not about 'learning facts'; it's a journey to the heart of human experience. The empathy and the understanding, especially on the things you disagree with, are incredibly valuable. If you look closely, you'll find the way people think, at different times in history, their attitudes, choices, and the way they move their bodies can teach you so much about us, right now. Fill your toolbox so it's overflowing with information and ideas to pull from so your imagination has so much to play with.

PHYSICAL WARMUP - 2 minutes - [Set Timer]
Freeform Dance: Put on some music and engage in freeform dancing. Allow your body to move spontaneously and without inhibition. This can help you tap into your creative instincts and develop physical expressiveness. **Tip**: Try music you've never listened to.

RESEARCH - 13 Minutes [Set Timer]
YouTube, streaming platforms, the internet or books, **research the given era/person/moment in time,** journal or make notes on your device, so when you want to find this information, it's organized and readily accessible. As you go, **write anything and everything _you_ find fascinating. Tip:** If the topic doesn't interest you, choose your own, or take a chance and still research it, but from a different perspective. Physicalities, voice, ideals, etc. Trust your body that when you see something interesting, you'll know. **Extra**: Speak it out and copy their movements. Our memory recall is massively affected by our bodies. Be specific and when you re-read your notes, you'll be amazed by how much your mind and body remember.

TOPIC:
The 1904 Olympic Marathon: One of the most bizarre events in Olympic history, the men's marathon at the 1904 St. Louis Olympics was a chaotic affair. The winner, Fred Lorz, was initially disqualified for completing part of the race in a car. The actual winner, Thomas Hicks, was assisted by his trainers and given strychnine and brandy as stimulants during the race. Moreover, one of the participants, Andarín Carvajal, ran in street clothes and took a detour to eat during the race. This marathon is remembered for its oddities and extreme conditions, showcasing the early and unregulated days of modern Olympics.

WORKOUT COMPLETED [ ]

You've got the makings of greatness in you, but you got to take the helm and chart your own course. Stick to it, no matter the squalls. And when the time comes you get the chance to really test the cut of your sails, and show what you're made of... Well, I hope I'm there, catching some of the light coming off you that day.
John Silver - Treasure planet

BELIEF

Beliefs are the convictions that something exists or is true, especially without proof. That is also the definition of what we do as actors. We play make-believe. Our beliefs shape our world, especially our beliefs about ourselves and it works for the characters you play. Understand your beliefs and how they influence your mind, body and spirit, then you will be able to better understand others, so you can embody them. Allow the beliefs of your character to colour your perception of your world and your interaction with everything in it. "Acting is the best magic trick in the world. We applaud performances not because it's real, but because you made us believe."

VOCAL WORK - 2 Minutes - [Set timer]

Lip Trills: Close your lips together lightly, like you're going to blow a raspberry. Then, blow air through your closed lips while making sounds. You should feel a tickling sensation. Pick a song and Lip Trill along with it. **Tip**: Stretch your range as much as you can and pick a song you've never listened to.

BELIEF WORKOUT

Get your journal or write in here. **Define your personal belief/view** on the given subject. **Grab any book you own,** flip to a random page and **read it out loud,** colouring the words and intention with your belief system. **Tip:** Write trigger words you can hook into in the future: **Optimism-** Always smiling, grateful, opportunity, sunshine yellow.

YOUR PERSONAL BELIEF

Love & Romance - 7 Minutes [Set Timer]

_____
_____
_____
_____
_____

READ WITH BELIEF - 2 Minutes [Set Timer]

CHARACTERS BELIEF

Love & Romance

It's not even a choice in my life it's just built into who I am. Can't live without it. I haven't found my person yet but I know she's out there and I am so excited to meet her. That unexplainable feeling you get when romantic love is win your heart... I live my life that way.

READ WITH CHARACTERS BELIEF - 2 Minutes [Set Timer]

Forget your personal view and **fully embrace the character's belief. Read out loud again.**

JOURNAL YOUR EXPERIENCE - 2 Minutes [Set Timer]

_____
_____
_____
_____

WORKOUT COMPLETED [ ]

PERFORMANCE STRATEGY
FINAL REVIEW

TAKE A MOMENT OF REFLECTION AND BREAKDOWN WHERE YOU ARE RIGHT NOW IN YOUR CAREER AND AS AN ACTOR.
THE MORE SPECIFIC YOU ARE THE MORE CLEAR YOU CAN SEE WHERE YOU ARE NOW SO YOU CAN GET TO WHERE YOU WANT TO GO FASTER

★ ★ ★ ★ ★

" Your story here"

DATE:

MY WHY
WHY ARE YOU DOING WHAT YOU ARE DOING
BE SPECIFIC

FROM THE LAST 350 DAYS
5 STAR RATING

☆☆☆☆☆ ☆

YOUR KEY POINTS AND TAKEAWAYS - TAKE A LOOK AT WHERE YOU STARTED AND WHERE YOU ARE NOW. WHAT WAS YOUR JOURNEY and HOW HAVE YOU CHANGE

STRENGTHS:

WEAKNESSES:

IMPROVEMENT STRATEGY
HOW CAN YOU IMPROVE ON THESE AREAS FOR THE NEXT 14 DAYS:

GOAL FROM LAST :
DID YOU ACHIEVE IT?

WHY OR WHY NOT?

GOAL FOR THE NEXT STEPS OF YOUR CAREER
THE MORE SPECIFIC YOU ARE THE GREATER THE RESULT

Action Step(s):

GOING FORWARD

I hope you're incredibly proud of the work you've put in. It doesn't matter how long it took, one year of workouts isn't a small feat. That's 91 more hours you've come closer to perfecting your craft.

My hope for you is you've come closer to knowing yourself as an artist. What works for you, what doesn't. That you've taken pieces from this book or even just an idea and completely changed it to work for you. Whatever it is, just know, I hope your dreams come true.

Never forget **YOUR WHY**.
That fire inside you that makes you, you... That's the magic this world needs.

Love in your heart. Fire in your soul.

Victor Zinck Jr

STORIES & FEEDBACK

I WOULD LOVE ANY AND ALL FEEDBACK FROM YOUR EXPERIENCE! HOW IT HELPED, WHAT WORKED AND WHAT DIDN'T. EVEN JUST A HELLO! THIS BOOK IS THE FIRST I'VE EVER WRITTEN LIKE THIS SO IT WILL BE EVOLVING AS IT GOES AND I WOULD APPRECIATE ALL OF YOUR HELP MAKING IT EVEN BETTER.

VICZINCK@GMAIL.COM

RECOMMENDED BOOKS & RESOURCES

The Intent to Live - Larry Moss - Amazing and inspiring insight and a dictionary of great questions to ask for your characters and their backstory.
The Practical Handbook for the Actor - Melissa Bruder, Lee Michael Cohn, Madeleine Olnek - A very powerful and simple explanation of what we do as actors and how to do it. Great reminder to bring you back to the basics for your best performances.
The power of the Actor - Ivana Chubbuck - My favourite for imagination and creative ways to discover your characters and their world.

Surrender Experiment - Michael A Singer > Letting go of the reigns and trusting yourself in every choice you make.
Magic of Thinking Big - David J. Schwartz - The incredible power of our thoughts and our reality.
The Go Giver - Bob Burg and John David Mann - Your Belief system and the unbelievable affect when you always give more than you receive in payment, has on your life.
Think Big and Grow Rich - Napoleon Hill - One of my favourites for the power of who we surround ourselves with and our thoughts and imaginations to succeed.
The Power of NOW - Eckhart Tolle - Living in the present moment and the effect it has on every aspect of your life.
The Compound Effect - Darren Hardy - My favourite for understanding habits and how to apply his strategy to your day to day life.
PEAK - Anders Ericsson - How the best of the best train "purposefully" and how that specific focus can change your career and life.
Moonwalking with Einstein - For memory techniques - Incredible techniques for those of you like me who struggle with memory!
What Every Body Knows - Joe Navarro - FBI interrogator on instincts that drive body language
The Power of your Subconscious Mind - Jospeh Murphy - Understanding and changing the way we think.

The Alchemist - Paulo Coelho & The Prophet - Kahlil Gibran - My two favourite novels for a beautifully poetic way to look at the world and experience life simply and profoundly.

THANK YOU MOM, DAD, DANIEL, PHAN PHAN, MITTITA, BRITTANY, BILL, LUCAS, VALENTINA

www.ingramcontent.com/pod-product-compliance
Lightning Source LLC
Chambersburg PA
CBHW071330080526
44587CB00017B/2788